THE EUCHARIST
SACRAMENT OF THE KINGDOM

The Eucharist
Sacrament of the Kingdom

Alexander Schmemann

translated from the Russian by
Paul Kachur

ST. VLADIMIR'S SEMINARY PRESS
CRESTWOOD, NEW YORK 10707
1988

Library of Congress Cataloging-in-Publication Data

Schmemann, Alexander, 1921-1983
The Eucharist—sacrament of the Kingdom.

Translation of: Evkharistiia—tainstvo tsarstva.
1. Lord's Supper (Liturgy)   2. Lord's Supper—
Orthodox Eastern Church.   3. Orthodox Eastern Church—
Doctrines.   4. Orthodox Eastern Church—Liturgy.
I. Title.
BX355.S3613   1987   264'.019036   87-26380
ISBN 0-88141-052-7
ISBN 0-88141-018-7 (pbk.)

Typeset in Garamond No. 3 at
TGA Communications, New York
Printed in the United States of America at
Athens Printing Company, New York

Contents

FOREWORD 7

PREFACE 9

1 THE SACRAMENT OF THE ASSEMBLY 11

2 THE SACRAMENT OF THE KINGDOM 27

3 THE SACRAMENT OF ENTRANCE 49

4 THE SACRAMENT OF THE WORD 65

5 THE SACRAMENT OF THE FAITHFUL 81

6 THE SACRAMENT OF OFFERING 101

7 THE SACRAMENT OF UNITY..............................133

8 THE SACRAMENT OF ANAPHORA 159

9 THE SACRAMENT OF THANKSGIVING 171

10 THE SACRAMENT OF REMEMBRANCE 191

11 THE SACRAMENT OF THE HOLY SPIRIT 213

12 THE SACRAMENT OF COMMUNION 229

Foreword

THE LITERARY HISTORY OF A POSTHUMOUS WORK INEVITABLY IS complex. This is certainly true of the present book. Before his death on December 13, 1983, Fr Schmemann had completed its Russian version, since published by YMCA Press under the title *Evkharistiia* (Paris, 1984). He was also able to supervise the translation into English of the first two chapters. Beyond this, he himself had already prepared a few sections in English. Unfortunately he was not able to write the projected excursi to chapters 5 and 9 or to complete the footnotes or to devote his customary attention to polishing the entire text. The translator and editors of the present edition felt that major additions or modifications would not substantially improve the work but might rather distort its intended sense. For this reason, only a few notes have been supplied. In this, we have been aided by the excellent French translation prepared by Prof. Constantine Andronikof and published by O.E.I.L./YMCA Press under the title *L'Eucharistie: Sacrement du Royaume* (Paris, 1985). While the present text may lack Fr Alexander's remarkable sense of style, we hope that it does faithfully convey his thoughts on a subject perhaps closer to his heart than any other, the eucharist.

ST VLADIMIR'S SEMINARY PRESS
June 1987

Preface

THIS BOOK IS NEITHER A MANUAL OF LITURGICS NOR A SCHOL-
arly investigation. I wrote it during rare moments of leisure, in
the midst of many interruptions. Now, putting together these
chapters into one book, I do not pretend that they provide a complete or systematic study of the divine liturgy. Rather, this book
represents a series of reflections on the eucharist. These reflections, however, do not come from scientific analysis but from my
own experience, limited though it may be.

For more than thirty years I have served the Church as a priest
and a theologian, as a pastor and a teacher. Never in those thirty
years have I ceased to feel called to think about the eucharist and
its place in the life of the Church. Thoughts and questions on this
subject, which go back to early adolescence, have filled my whole
life with joy—but, alas, not only with joy. For the more real became my experience of the eucharistic liturgy, the sacrament of
Christ's victory and of his glory, the stronger became my feeling
that there is a eucharistic crisis in the Church. In the tradition of
the Church, nothing has changed. What has changed is the perception of the eucharist, the perception of its very essence. Essentially, this crisis consists in a lack of connection and cohesion
between what is accomplished in the eucharist and how it is perceived, understood and lived. To a certain degree this crisis has
always existed in the Church. The life of the Church, or rather of
the people in the Church, has never been perfect, ideal. With
time, however, this crisis has become chronic. That schizophrenia
that poisons the life of the Church and undermines its very foundations has come to be seen as a normal state.

Meanwhile, it can be said without exaggeration that we live
in a frightening and spiritually dangerous age. It is frightening
not just because of its hatred, division and bloodshed. It is fright-

ening above all because it is characterized by a mounting rebellion against God and his kingdom. Not God, but man has become the measure of all things. Not faith, but ideology and utopian escapism are determining the spiritual state of the world. At a certain point, western Christianity accepted this point of view: almost at once one or another "theology of liberation" was born. Issues relating to economics, politics and psychology have replaced a Christian vision of the world at the service of God. Theologians, clergy and other professional "religious" run busily around the world defending—from God?—this or that "right," however perverse, and all this in the name of peace, unity and brotherhood. Yet in fact, the peace, unity and brotherhood that they invoke are not the peace, unity and brotherhood that has been brought to us by our Lord Jesus Christ.

Perhaps many people will be astonished that, in response to this crisis, I propose that we turn our attention not to its various aspects but rather to the sacrament of the eucharist and to the Church, whose very life flows from that sacrament. Yes, I *do* believe that precisely here, in this holy of holies of the Church, in this ascent to the table of the Lord in his kingdom, is the source of that renewal for which we hope. And I do believe, as the Church has always believed, that this upward journey begins with the "laying aside of all earthly cares," with leaving this adulterous and sinful world. No ideological fuss and bother, but a gift from heaven—such is the vocation of the Church in the world, the source of her service.

I also believe that, by God's mercy, Orthodoxy throughout all ages has kept and guarded this vision, this consciousness of the Church, this knowledge that "where the Church is, there is the Holy Spirit and the fulness of grace" (Irenaeus of Lyons, *Against the Heresies* 3:24:1). But precisely because this is so, we the Orthodox faithful must find the inner strength to plunge into this eucharistic renewal of the Church. It is not reform, adjustments and modernization that are needed so much as a return to that vision and experience that from the beginning constituted the very life of the Church. To remind us of this is the goal of this book.

PROTOPRESBYTER ALEXANDER SCHMEMANN
November 1983

CHAPTER ONE

The Sacrament of the Assembly

"When you assemble as a church..."
I CORINTHIANS 11:18

I

"W̶HEN YOU ASSEMBLE AS A CHURCH..." WRITES THE
apostle Paul to the Corinthians. For him, as for all of
early Christianity, these words refer not to a temple but to the
nature and purpose of the gathering. As is well known, the very
word "church"—ἐκκλησία—means "a gathering" or "an assembly," and to "assemble as a church" meant, in the minds of the
early Christians, to constitute a gathering whose purpose is to reveal, to realize, the Church.[1]

This gathering is *eucharistic*—its end and fulfilment lies in its
being the setting wherein the "Lord's supper" is accomplished,
wherein the eucharistic "breaking of bread" takes place. In the
same epistle St Paul reproaches the Corinthians for partaking of a
meal other than the Lord's supper in their gathering, or assembling for a purpose other than the eucharistic breaking of bread
(11:20-22ff). Thus, from the very beginning we can see an obvious, undoubted triunity of the *assembly*, the *eucharist* and the
Church, to which the whole early tradition of the Church, following St Paul, unanimously testifies. The fundamental task of litur-

[1]Dom Gregory Dix, *The Shape of the Liturgy* (Westminster: Dacre Press, 1945); H. Chirat,
L'assemblée chrétienne à l'âge apostolique (Paris, 1949).

11

gical theology consists therefore in uncovering the meaning and essence of this unity.

This task is all the more urgent in that, while this triunity was self-evident to the early Church, it has ceased to be self-evident to the consciousness of contemporary Christianity. What we customarily call "school" theology—which arose after the break with patristic tradition, and chiefly from a western understanding of both the method and the very nature of theology—generally ignores the bond between the assembly, the eucharist and the Church. The eucharist is regarded and defined as one of the sacraments, but not as the "sacrament of the assembly"—as it was defined by the fifth-century author of the *Areopagitica*.[2] It would be no exaggeration to say that this "scholastic" dogmatics is simply unaware of the ecclesiological meaning of the eucharist, and at the same time it has forgotten the eucharistic dimension of ecclesiology, i.e., the doctrine of the Church.

We shall speak in greater detail of this divorce between theology and the eucharist and its tragic consequences for church consciousness. For now, we should note that the idea of the eucharist as the "sacrament of the assembly" gradually disappeared from *piety* as well. The liturgics textbooks do categorize the eucharist under "public worship" and state that the liturgy is normally served in the presence of a "congregation of worshipers." But this "congregation of worshipers"—i.e., the assembly—has ceased to be apprehended as the primary *form* of the eucharist, and liturgics has ceased to look to the eucharist to both see and feel the primary form of the Church. Liturgical piety has become thoroughly individualistic, and the most eloquent testimony to this is the contemporary practice of receiving communion, which is completely subordinated to the "spiritual needs" of the individual believer. No one—neither among the clergy nor the laity—apprehends it in the spirit of the eucharistic prayer itself: "And unite all of us to one another who become partakers of the one Bread and Cup in the communion of the Holy Spirit."

Thus, we have witnessed in both piety and "churchliness" (*tserkovnost'*) a gradual and distinct "reduction" of the eucharist, a narrowing of its primary and original meaning and place in the

2*Ecclesiastical Hierarchy* 3.

life of the Church. Consequently, any explanation of the eucharist in liturgical theology must begin by surmounting this reduction, by returning to the original understanding of the eucharist as the "sacrament of the assembly" and, hence, the "sacrament of the Church."

At this point we need to indicate that both reductions of the eucharist—in piety and in theology—openly contradict the very *ordo* of the eucharist, as it was preserved by the Church from the very beginning. By "ordo" we mean here not the various details of the rites and sacraments, which obviously underwent development and change and grew in complexity, but rather the fundamental structure of the eucharist, its *shape*, to use the expression of Dom Gregory Dix, which can be traced back to the fundamental, apostolic principle of Christian worship.

As I have already pointed out elsewhere,[3] the basic defect of school theology consists in that, in its treatment of the sacraments, it proceeds not from the living experience of the Church, not from the concrete liturgical tradition that has been preserved by the Church, but from its own a priori and abstract categories and definitions, which hardly conform to the reality of church life. In early times the Church knew full well that the *lex credendi* (rule of faith) and the *lex orandi* (rule of prayer) were inseparable and that they mutually substantiated each other—that, in the words of St Irenaeus, "our teaching is in harmony with the eucharist, and the eucharist confirms our teaching."[4] But theology constructed on western scholastic models is completely uninterested in worship as it is performed by the Church and in the logic and "order" proper to it. Proceeding from its own abstract presuppositions, this theology decides a priori what is "important" and what is "secondary." And it turns out, in the final analysis, that what is deemed "secondary," as having no theological interest, is precisely worship itself, the very activity by which the Church actually lives, in all its complexity and diversity. The theologian directs his entire attention to the important "moments" that he artificially singles out: in the eucharist, the "moment" of the

[3]*Introduction to Liturgical Theology*, 3d ed. (Crestwood, N.Y.: SVS Press, 1986) 16-32, and the chapter on "Theology and Liturgy" in *Church, World, Mission* (Crestwood, N.Y.: SVS Press, 1979) 129-46.

[4]*Against Heresies* 4:18:5.

change of the holy gifts and then the partaking of communion; in baptism, the "triple immersion"; in marriage, the "consecratory formula"—"crown them with glory and honor. . ." etc. It has never occurred to the theologian who thinks in these categories that the "importance" of these moments cannot be isolated from their liturgical context.

This is the root of the striking poverty and onesidedness of the explanations of and the very approach to the sacraments that we find in our school dogmatics. It is also the root of the narrowness and onesidedness in our liturgical piety. For, not being nourished and directed, as in the time of the fathers, by a "liturgical cate-chesis"—a genuine theological explanation—it falls prey to all manner of symbolic and allegorical interpretations of the services, a peculiar liturgical "folklore."

And therefore, as we have already stated, the first principle of liturgical theology is that, in explaining the liturgical tradition of the Church, one must proceed not from abstract, purely intellectual schemata cast randomly over the services, but from the services themselves—and this means, first of all, from their *ordo*.

2

ANY SERIOUS STUDY OF THE EUCHARISTIC ORDO CANNOT BUT convince us that this ordo is entirely, from beginning to end, con-structed on the principle of correlation—the mutual dependence of the celebrant of the service and the people. One may even more precisely define this bond as a *co-serving* or *concelebration*, as it was articulated by the late Professor Nicholas Afanasiev in his splen-did though not yet fully appreciated work *The Lord's Supper.*[5]

This idea, however, plays no role whatsoever in school theol-ogy and the liturgical piety engendered by it, and is for all practi-cal purposes denied. The word "concelebration" is applied only to the clergy taking part in the service, while the participation of the laity is conceived of as entirely passive. For a good example of this we need only consider the "prayers during the Divine Liturgy," which are included in several prayerbooks intended expressly for

[5]*Trapeza Gospodnia* (Paris, 1952).

the laity. Their compilers apparently considered it self-evident that the eucharistic prayers themselves exist solely for the benefit of the clergy. What is even sadder, the ecclesiastical censors who for decades approved these special prayers obviously held the same opinion. When enumerating the necessary conditions for celebrating the liturgy, even the most literate and trustworthy liturgics textbooks (such as Archimandrite Kiprian Kern's *The Eucharist*[6]) usually mention everything—from a canonically ordained priest right down to the quality of the wine—except the "assembly as the Church," which is evidently not considered a "condition" of the liturgy.

Meanwhile, all early evidence we possess points to the fact that the *gathering* or *assembly* (σύναξις) was always considered the first and basic act of the eucharist. This is also attested to by the ancient liturgical designation of the person who performs the eucharist: the "presider" (προϊστάμενος), whose primary function was to stand at the head of the assembly as the "president of the brethren." Thus, the assembly is the first liturgical act of the eucharist, its foundation and beginning.

In the early Christian period, in contrast to the current practice, the gathering of the people *preceded* the entrance of the celebrant. "The church," writes St John Chrysostom, "is a house common to us all, and you are awaiting us when we enter ... That is why immediately afterward we greet you by giving the peace."[7] Further on, when we discuss the so-called "Little Entrance," we shall speak in greater detail about the place and meaning of the *entrance* in the eucharistic ordo. A few words, however, are in order here about our present practice, in which the entire beginning of the liturgy—the entrance of the celebrants, the vesting, the washing of hands and, finally, the preparation of the gifts—not only has become "private," concerning only the clergy, but also isolated, transferred into a special "office" of the liturgy, with its own dismissal.

Although this practice has been formally legitimized in our service books, it should be examined in the light of another practice, which is more ancient, though still preserved to this day.

---

[6]*Evkharistia* (Paris, 1947).

[7]*Homily on Matthew* 32 (33), 6, PG 57:384. Cf J. Mateos, "Évolution historique de la Liturgie de S. Jean Chrysostome," part 1, *Proche-Orient Chrétien* 15 (1965) 333-51.

This is the pontifical celebration of the eucharist. When the liturgy is performed by a bishop, the people gather in the church first
and are already there to greet him when he enters, the vesting
takes place amidst the congregation, the bishop does not proceed
to the altar until the Little Entrance and, finally, the prothesis is,
as it were, repeated just before the offertory—i.e., what we now
term the "Great Entrance."

It would be wrong to suppose that all this arose as the result of
a special "solemnity" being attached to the pontifical service,
which we sometimes hear in the protests of proponents of a
"primitive Christian simplicity." On the contrary, not in all details of course, but on the whole, the pontifical service goes much
further in preserving the form and spirit of the early eucharistic
practice, because in the early Church it was precisely the bishop
who customarily presided over the eucharistic assembly.[8] Only
much later, with the gradual transformation of the local church
community into an administrative district ("diocese") broken up
into a multitude of "parishes," was the position of the priest converted from that of an extraordinary celebrant of the eucharist, as
the deputy of the bishop, into that of the "ordinary" celebrant.
From the point of view of liturgical theology, it is precisely the
pontifical order of the entrance into the assembly that must be
considered "normative." The "priestly" order, which arose "out
of expediency," was perhaps practical and inevitable, but to no
extent does it do away with the significance of the *assembly as the
Church* as, in actuality, the principle, the first and basic act of the
eucharist.

3

THE CORRELATION BETWEEN THE CELEBRANT AND THE PEOPLE
—their concelebration—finds further expression in the eucharistic
prayers, which are all, without exception, structured as dialogues. Every prayer is "sealed" by the gathering with one of the
key words of Christian worship, "amen,"[9] thus binding the cele-

[8]Mateos, "Evolution historique," 333.

[9]Dix, *op. cit.*; H. Schlier, "Amen," in Kittel, *Theologisches Wörterbuch zum Neuen Testament*
1:341; A. Baumstark, *Liturgie comparée*, 3d ed. (Chevetogne, 1953) 52, 85.

brant and the people of God at whose head he stands into one organic whole. Every prayer (with the exception of the "prayer of the priest for himself," read during the Cherubic Hymn, which we shall discuss in due time) is spoken on behalf of *us*. All of the constituent parts of the solemn eucharistic ceremony—the reading of the word of God, the anaphora, the partaking of communion—begin with the exchange of *peace*: "Peace be to all... And to your spirit." Finally, all of these prayers have as their content *our* praise, *our* repentance, *our* thanksgiving, *our* communion—"unite all of us to one another who become partakers... in the communion of the Holy Spirit."

The same may be said of the individual rites of the eucharist: all express to some degree not only the unity of the celebrant and the people but also their "synergy"—collaboration, concelebration in the literal sense of these terms. Thus, the reading of the word of God and its elaboration in the sermon—which according to the unanimous testimony of all early evidence comprises the first part of the eucharistic celebration—self-evidently presupposes listeners, people who receive the preaching. The transferral of the proskomidē to the sanctuary and the appearance of a special "table of oblation" for it did not erase the original practice of offering the gifts in the assembly, from the people—which is accomplished nowadays in the "Great Entrance." Finally, the "kiss of peace," though now performed only among the clergy, is accompanied by the exclamation "Let us love one another," and thus relates to the entire gathering—as does the concluding exclamation, "Let us depart in peace."

What has been said thus far merits attention all the more in that the Byzantine rite of the liturgy gradually and systematically developed in the direction of an ever greater separation of the "laity" from the "clergy," those who "pray" from those who "serve." As we endeavored to show elsewhere, and as was brilliantly elaborated by Professor Afanasiev,[10] Byzantine liturgical piety gradually fell under the grip of a *mysteriological* perception of worship, which was constructed on the contraposition of the "initiated" and the "uninitiated." But this influence proved to be too

[10]*Trapeza Gospodnia.* Cf Schmemann, *Introduction to Liturgical Theology*, 103-13, and also the essay on "Sacrament and Symbol," in *For the Life of the World*, rev. ed. (Crestwood, N.Y.: SVS Press, 1973) 135-51.

feeble at its very root to alter the original *order* of the eucharist, for each word and each act continues to express the concelebration of all with each other, with everyone in his proper place and proper ministry in the single *leitourgia* of the Church.

It is quite another matter that the primary, direct and immediate meaning of these words and acts ceased to penetrate the consciousness of both clergy and laity and that in their minds there arose instead a peculiar dichotomy between the "data" of theology and its interpretation. As a result of this dichotomy, all manner of "symbolic" explanations for the most simple words and acts appeared and spread like weeds, while their direct, literal meaning was often hardly considered. We have already spoken and will speak again about the causes and consequences of this new "nominalistic" liturgical piety, which, unfortunately, reigns almost unchallenged in the Church. For now, it is important only to emphasize that this new piety succeeded neither in eclipsing nor distorting beyond recognition the actual *communal* character of the eucharist, which could never be torn away from the Church and, consequently, from the *assembly*.[11]

Even the most obvious and in all likelihood the saddest result of this new "piety"—the excommunication, for all practical purposes, of the laity, for whom the partaking of communion, having ceased to have its source in their participation in the liturgy, became something exceptional—amounts to nothing before the direct testimony of the eucharistic ordo itself: "all of *us* . . . who become partakers of the one bread and cup"; "In the fear of God and with faith draw near," etc. All these texts, appeals and words undoubtedly concern the entire assembly and not certain separate or isolated participants in it.

As Professor Afanasiev so aptly put it: "If we discarded everything that was brought into our liturgical life, especially in the last few centuries, we would find no particularly significant divergence between what would be left and the early practice of the Church. The basic defect of our liturgical life consists in that we impart greater significance to the particularities, fortuitous or

---

[11]"Now when thou teachest, command and warn the people to be constant in assembling in the Church, and not withdraw themselves, but always to assemble, lest any man diminish the Church by not assembling." Quoted in *Antenicene Christian Liturgy*, Antenicene Christian Library, ed. A Roberts and J. Donaldson, II:59, p. 124.

not, of our liturgical offices than to their essence. The fundamental principles of doctrine concerning the eucharist are perfectly clear in the services. In them the nature of the eucharist is preserved unsullied.... Our task, therefore, consists not so much in making various changes in our liturgical life, but rather in coming to realize the genuine nature of the eucharist."[12]

4

FINALLY, THIS SAME IDEA OF ASSEMBLY AND CONCELEBRATION is expressed and embodied in the very physical setting in which the eucharist is accomplished: the temple. The liturgics textbooks deal at great length with the church building, its layout or plan and the "symbolic" meaning of its various details. Their definitions and descriptions, however, contain virtually no mention of the self-evident link between the Christian temple and the assembly, the conciliar or *sobornal* character of the eucharist.

There is no need to repeat here what we have already said elsewhere about the complex development of the church building and "temple piety" in the Orthodox East. It is enough to recall that the original Christian temple was above all the *domus ecclesiae*, the site of the gathering of the Church together and the eucharistic breaking of bread. And in this subordination to the idea of the assembly lies both the newness of the Christian temple and the principle of its development. Whatever were the complexities of this development, whatever was the impact of what we have earlier termed "mysteriological" piety, it is precisely the idea of the eucharistic assembly that proved to be its unifying and guiding factor. Just as in the earliest Christian era, so also today, in its best Byzantine or Russian incarnation, the temple is experienced and perceived as *sobor*,[13] as the gathering together of heaven and earth and all creation in Christ—which constitutes the essence and purpose of the Church.

[12]*Trapeza Gospodnia*, 90.
[13]See Schmemann, *Introduction to Liturgical Theology*, 105ff. See also *Martyrium*, Recherches sur le culte des reliques et l'art chrétien antique, I: Architecture, and II: Iconographie (Paris: Collège de France, 1946); L. Ouspensky, *The Theology of the Icon in the Orthodox Church* (Crestwood, N.Y.: SVS Press, 1978); Y. Congar, *Le mystère du temple* (Paris, 1958). The Russian word *sobor* means both "assembly," or "council," and "cathedral."

The *form* of the church building and its iconography also at-
test to this. The form—the temple as "organization of space"—
essentially expresses that same correlation, that same "dialogic
structure" that, as we have seen, is the determining factor in the
order of the eucharistic assembly. Here it is a correlation between
the altar and the sanctuary, on the one hand, and the "ark" or
nave—the place of the assembly—on the other. The nave is directed toward the altar, in which we find its end and purpose; but the
"altar" necessarily entails the nave and exists only in relation to it.

While it is true that contemporary liturgical piety perceives
the sanctuary as something self-contained, accessible only to the
"initiated"—a particularly "holy" place with its own brand of
"sanctity," as if to emphasize the "profane" category to which the
laity standing outside it belong—it is also not difficult to show
that this perception is relatively recent, false and, most im-
portantly, profoundly harmful for the Church. It serves only to
continually nourish that "clericalism"—so utterly alien to Orthodoxy—that reduces the laity to the status of second-class citizens,
defined primarily in negative terms as those who "do not have the
right" to enter certain places, to touch certain things or to take
part in certain activities. And because of this there has, alas,
arisen among us the type of priest who sees virtually the essence of
his priesthood in the unyielding "defense" of the holy things from
contact with the laity, and who finds a peculiar, almost volumptu-
ous gratification in this "defense."

But let us repeat once more: such a perception of the altar is
not the original one and is false. It owes much, of course, to the
corresponding understanding of the iconostasis as primarily a *wall*
that separates the altar from the laity and places an impassable
barrier between them. Yet, as strange as it may seem to the majority of Orthodox today, the iconostasis originated from a completely opposite purpose: not to separate but to unite. The icon is
a witness, or, better still, a consequence of the unification of the
divine and the human, of heaven and earth, that has been accomplished in Jesus Christ. All icons are in essence icons of the incarnation. Thus, the iconostasis originated from the experience of
the temple as "heaven on earth," as testimony to the fact that "the
kingdom of heaven has drawn near." Like all the rest of the iconography in the church building, it is an incarnation of the vision

of the Church as *sobor*, as the union of the visible and invisible worlds, as the manifestation and presence of the new and transfigured creation.

What is tragic is that the authentic tradition of Orthodox iconography experienced a prolonged process of alienation, in which the perception of the correlation between the icons and the temple disappeared almost entirely from church consciousness. Our churches today are no longer painted over with icons: either we hang a large number of icons that often have no relation whatsoever to the temple as a whole, or we "decorate" the church with all sorts of "ornaments," and not only do the details invariably predominate over the whole, but the icon itself becomes a "detail" in some decorative ensemble. Another aspect of this same tragedy is the gradual degeneration first of the form and then of the meaning of the iconostasis. From an ordo, a "framework" or harmonic system of icons, which naturally required a standing support (στάσις), it was transformed into a wall adorned with icons—in other words, the opposite of its original function. At first the icons demanded a wall form, but now the wall demands the icons, and in this manner inherently subordinates them to itself.

One can only hope that the interest that is awakening everywhere in iconography—which embraces both the understanding of icons and the iconographic art itself—will bring about a rebirth of the genuine significance of the iconostasis to the church building, as well as a return to the experience that we sense in a number of ancient churches: the icons seem to take part in the assembly of the Church, they express its meaning, they provide its eternal movement and rhythm. The entire Church, the entire assembly, with all the "ranks"—prophets, apostles, martyrs and saints—seems to ascend to heaven, elevated and lifted up by Christ to his table in his kingdom.

We must point out here that this new attitude toward the sanctuary and toward the iconostasis as entailing a division is also false in that it obviously contradicts the Church's liturgical tradition itself. This tradition knows only the consecration of a temple and an altar table, and does not know any consecration of a sanctuary separate from the nave. Like the altar table, the entire temple is anointed with the holy chrism; the *whole* church is thus

"sealed" as a sanctuary, a holy place. We see this clearly in the
complex, truly "Byzantine" office of the consecration of a temple,
when the relics are about to be brought in and placed inside the
altar table. It is not at the royal doors of the sanctuary but at the
outside doors of the church that the celebrant exclaims: "Receive
your princes, O ye gates...Who is this king of glory?...The
Lord of Hosts, he is the King of Glory!" In expounding on this
rite, Symeon of Thessalonica—himself one of the most eminent
representatives of the "symbolical" and "mysteriological" interpretation of the services—writes: "The martyrs, in the form of the
holy relics, and the hierarch himself represent Christ, and the
church represents heaven.... The bishop reads the *prayer of the entrance*, summoning the concelebrants and the accompanying angels. Then, pointing to the doors of the temple and opening
them, the celebrants enter the temple as in heaven, the witnesses
of Jesus Christ through the majestic Father, at the time of the
opening for us of the heavenly abode."[14]

It is quite clear, as a great number of other documents confirm, that this rite developed in a period when the "royal doors"
referred not to the doors of the sanctuary but to the doors of the
church itself, when the temple itself was experienced and perceived as heaven on earth, as the place in which, through the eucharistic assembly of the Church, the Lord enters "the doors being
shut," and with him and in him enters his kingdom.

We shall speak more fully about the meaning of the altar in
the eucharist in connection with the so-called "Little Entrance."
For now, it is sufficient to stress not only the fundamental connection between the temple and the assembly, but also the meaning of the temple itself as precisely *sobor*, as the "assembly as the
Church," incarnate in architectural forms, colors and images.

5

THE LITURGY IS THE "SACRAMENT OF THE ASSEMBLY." CHRIST
came to "gather into one the children of God who were scattered
abroad" (Jn 11:52), and from the very beginning the eucharist

---

[14]*On the Holy Temple*, PG 155:321D.

was a manifestation and realization of the unity of the new people of God, gathered by Christ and in Christ. We need to be thoroughly aware that we come to the temple not for individual prayer but to *assemble together as the Church*, and the visible temple itself signifies and is but an image of the temple not made by hands. Therefore, the "assembly as the Church" is in reality the first liturgical act, the foundation of the entire liturgy; and unless one understands this, one cannot understand the rest of the celebration. When I say that I am going to church, it means I am going into the assembly of the faithful in order, together with them, to *constitute the Church*, in order to be what I became on the day of my baptism—a *member*, in the fullest, absolute meaning of the term, of the body of Christ. "You are the body of Christ and individually members of it," says the apostle (1 Co 12:27). I go to manifest and realize my membership, to manifest and witness before God and the world the mystery of the kingdom of God, which already "has come in power."

It has come and is coming in power—in the Church. This is the mystery of the Church, the mystery of the body of Christ: "where two or three are gathered in my name, there am I in the midst of them" (Mt 18:20). The miracle of the church assembly lies in that it is not the "sum" of the sinful and unworthy people who comprise it, but the body of Christ. How often do we say we are going to church to obtain help, strength or consolation? We forget, meanwhile, that we are the Church, we make it up, that Christ abides in his members and that the Church does not exist outside us or above us, but *we are in Christ and Christ is in us.* Christianity consists not in bestowing on each the possibility of "personal perfection" but first of all in calling and commanding Christians to be the Church—"a holy nation, a royal priesthood, a chosen race" (1 Pt 2:9)—to manifest and confess the presence of Christ and his kingdom in the world.

And the holiness of the Church is not our holiness, but Christ's, who loved the Church and gave himself for her "that he might sanctify her... that she might be holy and without blemish" (Eph 5:25-27). Likewise, the holiness of the saints as well is but the revelation and realization of that sanctification, that holiness that each of us received on the day of baptism and in which we are all called to increase. But we could not grow in it if we did not already possess it as a gift of God, as his presence in us through the Holy Spirit. This is why in early times all Christians were called *saints*; this is why "assembling as the Church" is our task, our chief trust and duty. We have been consecrated to this task, and it will remain with us until such time as we cut ourselves off from it.

In antiquity, those who did not take part in the eucharistic assembly without due cause excommunicated themselves from the Church, since they had severed themselves from the organic unity of the body of Christ, which is manifested in the liturgy. The eucharist, we repeat, is not "one of the sacraments" or one of the services, but the very manifestation and *fulfilment* of the Church in all her power, sanctity and fulness. Only by taking part in it can we increase in holiness and fulfil all that we have been commanded to be and do. The Church, gathered in the eucharist, even when limited to "two or three," is the image and realization of the body of Christ, and only those who are gathered will be able to *partake*, i.e., be communicants of the body and blood of Christ, because they manifest him by their very assembly. No one could ever partake, no one could ever be of proper and "sufficient" holiness for this, unless it were given and commanded in the Church, in the assembly, in that mystical unity in which we, who constitute the body of Christ, are able to blamelessly call God Father and be partakers and communicants of the divine life.

It should now be obvious to what degree our contemporary "individual" entries into the temple, at any moment during the service, violate the essence of the eucharist. One who maintains his "individuality" and "freedom" in such manner does not know, has not discovered the mystery of the Church; he does not take part in the sacrament of the assembly, in this miracle of the reunification of the splintered and sinful human nature in the divine-human unity of Jesus Christ.

6

FINALLY, IF THE "ASSEMBLY AS THE CHURCH" IS THE IMAGE of the body of Christ, then the image of the head of the body is the *priest*. He presides over, he heads the gathering, and his standing at their head is precisely what makes a group of Christians the gathering of the Church in the fulness of her gifts. If according to his humanity the priest is only one—and perhaps the most sinful and unworthy—of those assembled, then by the gift of the Holy Spirit, which has been preserved by the Church since Pentecost and handed down without interruption through the laying on of hands of the bishop, he manifests the power of the priesthood of Christ, who consecrated himself for us and who is the one priest of the New Testament: "and he holds his priesthood permanently, because he continues for ever" (Heb 7:24). Just as the holiness of the assembly is not that of the people who constitute it but Christ's, so the priesthood of the priest is not his but Christ's, bestowed on the Church because she is his body. Christ is not *outside* the Church, and neither his power nor his authority is delegated to anyone. He himself abides in the Church and, through the Holy Spirit, he fulfils her entire life. The priest is neither a "representative" nor a "deputy" of Christ: in the sacrament he is Christ himself, just as the assembly is his body. Standing at the head of the body, he manifests in himself the unity of the Church, the oneness of the unity of all her members with himself. Thus, in this unity of the celebrant and the assembled is manifested the divine-human unity of the Church—in Christ and with Christ.

The vesting of the priest, even if it is done today before the liturgy, likewise is linked with the assembly, for it is an image, an *icon*, of the unity of Christ and the Church, of the indissoluble union of the many who constitute the one. The white garment— the *podriznik* or *stikharion* (alb)—is first of all the same white baptismal robe that each of us received at baptism. It is the garment of all the baptized, the garment of the Church herself, and in putting it on the priest manifests the oneness of the assembly, uniting all of us with himself. The *epitrakhilion* (stole) is the image of the Savior's taking on of our nature for its salvation and theosis, a sign of the priesthood of Christ himself. Such is also the case with the *epimanikia* (cuffs): the priest's hands, with which he blesses and performs the service, are no longer his own but the hands of Christ. The belt or girdle has always been a sign of obedience, preparedness, brotherhood and service. The priest does not take himself to the "high places" on his own authority; he "is not greater than his master." Rather, he is sent to this ministry by his master, whom he follows and by whose grace he serves. Finally, the *phelonion* or *riza* (chasuble) represents the glory of the Church as the new creation, the joy, truth and beauty of the new life, the prefiguration of the kingdom of God and the King who forever "reigns; he is robed in majesty" (Ps 93:1).

The vesting concludes with the washing of the celebrant's hands. The eucharist is for those whose sins have been forgiven, who have abandoned lawlessness, who have been reconciled with God. It is the service of the new humanity, "who once had not received mercy but now have received mercy" (1 Pt 2:10). We go to the temple, we "assemble as the Church," we are clothed in the garments of the new creation—these are the first rites of the "sacrament of sacraments," the most holy eucharist.

CHAPTER TWO

The Sacrament of the Kingdom

*"...as my Father appointed a king-
dom for me, so do I appoint one for you
that you may eat and drink at my
table in my kingdom."*

LUKE 22:29-30

I

*I*F ASSEMBLING AS THE CHURCH IS, IN THE MOST PROFOUND
sense of the term, the *beginning* of the eucharistic celebration,
its first and fundamental condition, then its *end* and completion is
the Church's entrance into heaven, her fulfilment at the table of
Christ, in his kingdom. It is imperative to indicate and to confess
this as the sacrament's end, purpose and fulfilment immediately
after confessing the "assembly as the Church" as its beginning
because this "end" also reveals the unity of the eucharist, its order
and essence as movement and ascent—as, above all and before all,
the sacrament of the kingdom of God. And it is no accident, of
course, that in its present form the liturgy begins with the solemn
blessing of the kingdom.

Today we particularly need to remind ourselves of this "end"
because our school teaching on the sacraments—which took hold
in the Orthodox East in the "dark ages" of the Church's western
"captivity"—makes no mention either of the "assembly as the
Church" as the beginning and condition of the sacrament or of her
ascent to the heavenly sanctuary, to the "table of Christ." The

27

sacrament was reduced to two "acts," two "moments": the change of the eucharistic gifts into the body and blood of Christ and the communion itself. Its definitions consisted in answering the questions of *how*, i.e., on account of what "causality," and *when*, i.e., at what moment, did the change occur. In other words, our school theology determined for each sacrament a *consecratory formula*, inherent to the given sacrament and at the same time both necessary and sufficient for its accomplishment.

Thus, as an example, in the authoritative *Longer Catechism* of Metropolitan Filaret (Drozdov) of Moscow, which was accepted by the entire Orthodox East, this "formula" is defined as "the pronouncing of the words that Christ spoke at the institution of the sacrament: take, eat, this is my body...drink of it all of you, this is my blood...and then the invocation of the Holy Spirit and the blessing of the gifts, the bread and wine that had been offered. ...When this takes place, the bread and wine are changed into the very body and very blood of Christ."[1]

The influence of the scholastic theology of the sacraments that underlies the "consecratory formula" is unfortunately evident in our own liturgical practice. It is expressed in the patent desire to *single out* that part of the eucharistic prayer that can be identified with the "consecratory formula," to make it, so to speak, independent and self-contained. With this end in view, the reading of the eucharistic prayer is as it were "interrupted" by the threefold reading of the Troparion of the Third Hour: "O Lord, who didst send down Thy Most Holy Spirit upon Thine apostles at the third hour: Take Him not from us, O Good One, but renew Him in us who pray to Thee"—a supplication related neither grammatically nor semantically to the anaphora.[2] With this same intention we ritually and verbally single out from the eucharistic prayer a dialogue between the deacon and the priest whose essence lies in separate consecrations first of the bread and then of the cup, and

[1](Paris, 1926; repr. Jordanville, N.Y., 1961) 86-7. See A. Katansky, *Dogmaticheskoe uchenie o semi tserkovnykh tainstvakh* (Dogmatic teaching concerning the seven sacraments of the Church in the works of the Fathers and Doctors of the Church, St. Petersburg, 1877); V.J. Malachov, "Presushchestvlenie Sviatikh Darov v Tainstve Evkharistii" (The transformation of the Holy Gifts in the sacrament of the Eucharist), *Bogoslovskii Vestnik* (1898) 113-40. Cf Thomas Aquinas' treatise *De sacramentis* and, more recently, Dom A. Vonier, *The Key to the Doctrine of the Eucharist* (New York, 1925).

[2]Fr Kiprian (Kern), *Evkharistia*, 277ff.

finally of the gifts together. Further testimony to the fact that we are dealing with a "consecratory formula" is the completely illiterate transferral of the last words of the benediction, "Making the change by Thy Holy Spirit," from the anaphora of St John Chrysostom to that of St Basil the Great.

As far as the other rites of the liturgy are concerned, they are either generally ignored—since they are unnecessary for the accomplishment of the sacrament and are thus not a subject for theological comprehension—or, as in the above-cited catechism, they are construed as symbolic "illustrations" of one or another event in Christ's ministry, whose recollection is "edifying" for the faithful in attendance.

We will have to return later to this doctrine of a "consecratory formula." For now, in this initial stage of our work, the important thing to note is that it isolates the eucharist from the liturgy, and thus *separates* the eucharist from the Church, from its ecclesiological essence and meaning.

This separation is, of course, external, for the spirit of tradition is too strong in the Orthodox Church to allow a change in or betrayal of the ancient forms of worship. Nevertheless, the separation is a real one, for, in this approach, the Church ceases to perceive herself not only as the "dispenser" of the sacraments but as their very *object*: they represent her fulfilment of herself in "this world" as the sacrament of the kingdom of God, which "has come in power." The very fact that the eucharist's beginning, the "assembly as the Church," and its end and fulfilment, its realization as "that which it is," the manifestation and presence of the kingdom of God, simply dropped out of the experience as well as the explanations and definitions of the eucharist amply demonstrates the truly tragic *damage* of this approach and of the reduction it contains.

2

BUT WHAT IS THE CAUSE OF THIS REDUCTION, AND HOW DID IT penetrate church consciousness? This question is of immeasurable importance not only for an interpretation of the sacraments and the eucharist but above all for an understanding of the Church herself, her place and ministry in "this world."

We can best begin our analysis of this reduction with a concept that, although occupying an enormous position in all "discussions" of church worship, remains vague and obscure. This is the idea of the *symbol*.[3] It has long been normal to speak of the "symbolism" of Orthodox worship. Indeed, even apart from these "discussions," one can hardly doubt that it is in fact *symbolic*. But what is understood by this term, what is its concrete content?

The most prevalent, "current" answer to this question consists in an identification of the symbol with a *representation* or *illustration*. When someone says that the "Little Entrance" "symbolizes" the Savior's coming out to preach the gospel, he understands by this that the rite of entrance represents a certain event of the past. And this "illustrative symbolism" has come to be applied to worship in general, whether taken as a whole or in each of its separate rites. And since this interpretation of "symbolism" (the flowering of which had begun already during the Byzantine period) is undoubtedly rooted in the most pious of feelings, it would occur to very few that not only does it not correspond to the basic and original Christian conception of worship, but actually distorts it and provides one of the reasons for its present decline.

The reasons for this lie in the fact that "symbol" here designates something not only *distinct* from reality but in essence even *contrary* to it. Further on we shall see that the specifically western, Roman Catholic emphasis on the "real presence" of Christ in the eucharistic gifts grew primarily out of a fear that this presence would be degraded into the category of the "symbolic." But this could only happen when the word "symbol" ceased to designate something *real* and became in fact the antithesis of reality. In other words, where one is concerned with "reality" there is no need for a symbol, and, conversely, where there is a symbol there is no reality. This led to the understanding of the liturgical symbol as an "illustration," necessary only to the extent that what is represented is not "real." Thus, two thousand years ago the Savior came forth to preach the gospel in *reality*, and now we illustrate this act *symbolically* in order to recall for ourselves the

[3]On liturgical symbolism see R. Bornet, *Les commentaires byzantins de la divine liturgie du VIIe au XVe siècle* (Paris, 1966); Dom Odo Casel, *Le mystère du culte dans le christianisme* (Paris, 1946); B. Neunheuser, *L'Eucharistie, II: Au Moyen Age et à l'époque moderne* (Paris, 1966).

meaning of the event, its significance for us, etc.

I repeat, these are pious and legitimate intentions in and of themselves. However, this type of symbolism is not only quite frequently utilized arbitrarily and artificially (thus, the *entrance* at the liturgy is turned into a symbol of Christ *going out*), but in fact reduces ninety percent of our rites to the level of didactic dramatization—not unlike acting out a "procession on a donkey" on Palm Sunday or the mystery play of the "youths in the furnace of Babylon." Such reduction deprives the rites of their inner necessity, their relation to the *reality* of worship. They become "symbolical" settings, mere decorations for the two or three acts or "moments" that alone provide, so to speak, "reality" to the liturgy—and which alone are necessary and therefore "sufficient." This is demonstrated by our school theology, which long ago in fact dismissed the entire *ordo* of the eucharist from its field of interest and attention and concentrated entirely upon a single moment: the isolated consecratory formula. On the other hand, it is also demonstrated—however strange it may seem—in our very piety. It is no accident, of course, that an increasing number of people in the Church find this piling up of symbolical representations and explanations disturbing to their prayer and to their genuine participation in the liturgy, distracting them from that spiritual reality the direct contact with which is the very essence of prayer. The same "illustrative" symbolism that is unnecessary for the theologian is also unnecessary for the serious believer.

3

THIS SEPARATION, THIS CONTRAPOSITION OF SYMBOL AND reality is the foundation of that perception and subsequent definition of the sacraments—and above all of the eucharist—whose focus is the *consecratory formula*. This approach came to us from the West, where, in contrast to the East, the sacraments quite early became a subject of special teaching and definition. Particular attention should be given to the scholastic treatise *De sacramentis*, in its progressive development, for the peculiar *estrangement* of the sacraments from the Church. This estrangement, of course, is not to be understood in the sense that the sacraments were established and function outside or independently of the Church. Rather, they are given to the Church, they are performed within her and only through the power given her to perform them and, finally, they are performed on her behalf. Yet while being accomplished in and through the Church, they constitute—even in the Church herself—a special reality, distinct unto itself. They are special in their being established directly by Christ himself, special in their essence as the "visible signs of invisible grace," special in their "efficacy" and, finally, special as the "causes of grace" (*causae gratiae*).

One result of the setting apart of the sacraments as a new, sui generis reality was the scholastic definition of the sacraments as being established only in view of man's fall and his salvation by Christ. In the state of "original innocence" man had no need of them; they are necessary only because man sinned and requires *medicine* for the wounds of sin. The sacraments are precisely this medicine: "quaedam spirituales medicamenta quae adhibentur contra vulnera peccati." Finally, the sole source of these medicines is the *passio Christi*, the suffering and sacrifice of the cross, through which Christ redeemed and saved mankind. The sacraments are accomplished by the power of the passion of Christ (*in virtute passionis Christi*) which they apply to mankind (*passio Christi quaedam applicata hominibus*).

Summing up the results of the development of western sacramental theology, the Catholic theologian Dom Vonier, in his well-known book *The Key to the Doctrine of the Eucharist*, writes: "The world of the sacraments is a new world, created by God entirely apart from the natural and even from the spiritual world. . . . Neither in heaven nor on earth is there anything like the sacraments. . . . They have their own form of existence, their own psychology, their own grace. . . . We must understand that the idea of the sacraments is something entirely sui generis."[4]

⁴Vonier, 41-3. Cf n. 1.

4

THERE IS NO NEED FOR US TO ENTER INTO A DETAILED examination of this system, well constructed and internally consistent though it may be. Enough has been said, I believe, to realize how *alien* this doctrine is to the Orthodox experience of the sacraments, how incompatible it is with the age-old liturgical tradition of the Orthodox Church. But I say alien to experience, not to doctrine, because the teaching on the sacraments, and above all on the eucharist, that we find in our dogmatics textbooks, patterned as they are on western models and constructed in western categories, not only does not correspond to this experience but openly contradicts it.

But when we speak of *experience*, what has been preserved from the beginning by the Church in her *lex orandi*, then the most profound alienation of western sacramental scholasticism from this experience cannot but become obvious. The chief source of this estrangement is the Latin doctrine's denial and rejection of *symbolism*, which is inherent to the Christian perception of the world, man and all creation, and which forms the ontological basis of the sacraments. In this perspective, the Latin doctrine is the beginning of the disintegration and decomposition of the symbol. On the one hand, being "reduced" to "illustrative symbolism," the symbol loses touch with reality; and, on the other, it ceases to be understood as a fundamental *revelation* about the world and creation. When Dom Vonier writes that "Neither in heaven nor on earth is there anything like the sacraments," does he not indicate above all that, although the sacraments in any event depend on creation and its nature for their accomplishment, of this nature they do not reveal, witness or manifest anything?

This doctrine of the sacraments is alien to the Orthodox because in the Orthodox ecclesial experience and tradition a sacrament is understood primarily as a revelation of the genuine *nature* of creation, of the world, which, however much it has fallen as "this world," will remain God's world, awaiting salvation, redemption, healing and transfiguration in a new earth and a new heaven. In other words, in the Orthodox experience a sacrament is primarily a revelation of the *sacramentality* of creation itself, for

the world was created and given to man for conversion of creaturely life into participation in divine life. If in baptism water can
become a "laver of regeneration," if our earthly food—bread and
wine—can be transformed into partaking of the body and blood of
Christ, if with oil we are granted the anointment of the Holy
Spirit, if, to put it briefly, everything in the world can be identified, manifested and understood as a gift of God and participation
in the new life, it is because all of creation was originally summoned and destined for the fulfilment of the divine economy—
"then God will be all in all."

Precisely in this *sacramental* understanding of the world is the
essence and gift of that *light of the world* that permeates the entire
life of the Church, the entire liturgical and spiritual tradition of
Orthodoxy. Sin is itself perceived here as a *falling away* of man,
and in him of all creation, from this sacramentality, from the
"paradise of delight," and into "this world," which lives no longer according to God, but according to itself and in itself and is
therefore corrupt and mortal. And if this is so, then Christ accomplishes the salvation of the world by renewing the world and life
itself as sacrament.[5]

5

A SACRAMENT IS BOTH COSMIC AND ESCHATOLOGICAL. IT
refers at the same time to God's world as he first created it and to
its fulfilment in the kingdom of God. It is cosmic in that it embraces all of creation, it returns it to God as God's own—"Thine
own of Thine own . . . on behalf of all and for all"—and in and by
itself it manifests the victory of Christ. But it is to the same degree eschatological, oriented toward the *kingdom which is to come*.
For, having rejected and killed Christ—its Creator, Savior and
Lord—"this world" sentenced itself to death, as it does not have
"life in itself" and rejected him of whom it was said, "In him was
life and this life was the light of men" (Jn 1:4). As "this world" it

---

[5]On the sacramental nature of creation see Schmemann, *For the Life of the World*. The nature
of "the world as sacrament" appears particularly clearly (unfortunately without having been care-
fully studied) in the Church's prayer and hymnody (the psalms, the Lenten Triodion, the Pentecos-
tarion, the Octoechos and other liturgical texts). "The heavens were seized with astonishment, the
earth with trembling": in texts like this we behold the cosmic dimension of the Church.

comes to an end—"heaven and earth will pass away"—and thus those who believe in Christ and accept him as the "Way, the Truth and the Life" live in hope of the age to come. They no longer have here a "lasting city, but...seek the city which is to come" (Heb 13:14). But this is precisely the joy of Christianity, the paschal essence of its faith: this "age which is to come," though future in relation to "this world," is already "in our midst." And our faith itself is already "the substance [ὑπό-στασις, reality] of things hoped for, the evidence [ἔλεγχος, proof] of things not seen" (Heb 11:1). It is, it manifests and it grants that to which it is directed: the presence among us of the approaching kingdom of God and its unfading light.

This in turn means that in the Orthodox experience and tradition the *Church* is herself a sacrament. Historians of theology have many times noted that in the early patristic tradition we find no *definition* of the Church. The reason for this, however, lies not in the "lack of development" of the theology of that time—as several learned theologians suppose—but in the fact that in her early tradition the Church was not an object of "definition" but the living experience of the new life. This experience—in which we find also the *institutional* structure of the Church, her hiearchy, canons, liturgy, etc.—was *sacramental, symbolical* by its very nature, for the Church exists in order to be always changing into that same reality that she manifests, the fulfilment of the invisible in the visible, the heavenly in the earthly, the spiritual in the material.

Hence, the Church is a sacrament in both of the higher dimensions we have indicated, the cosmic and the eschatological. She is a sacrament in the cosmic sense because she manifests in "this world" the genuine world of God, as he first created it, as the *beginning*, and only in the light of and in reference to this beginning can we know the full heights of our lofty calling—and also the depths of our falling away from God. She is a sacrament in the eschatological dimension because the original world of God's creation, revealed by the Church, has already been saved by Christ. And in liturgical experience and the life of prayer it is never severed from that *end* for the sake of which it was created and saved, that "God may be all in all" (1 Co 15:28).

6

BEING A SACRAMENT IN THE MOST PROFOUND AND COM-
prehensive sense of the term, the Church creates, manifests and
fulfils herself in and through the sacraments, and above all
through the "sacrament of sacraments," the most holy eucharist.
For if, as we have just said, the eucharist is the sacrament of the
beginning and the end, of the world and its fulfilment as the
kingdom of God, then it is completed by the Church's ascent to
heaven, to the "homeland of the heart's desire," the *status pa-
triae*—the messianic banquet of Christ, in his kingdom.

This means that all this—the "assembly as the Church," the
ascent to the throne of God and the partaking of the banquet of
the kingdom—is accomplished *in and through the Holy Spirit*.
"Where the Church is, there is the Holy Spirit and the fulness of
grace."[6] In these words of St Irenaeus of Lyons is engraved the
experience of the Church as the sacrament of the Holy Spirit. For
if where the Church is the Holy Spirit is also, then where the
Holy Spirit is there is the renewal of creation, there we find the
"beginning of another life, new and eternal," the dawn of the
mysterious, unfading day of the kingdom of God. For the Holy
Spirit is "the Spirit of truth, the gift of sonship, the pledge of
future inheritance, the first fruits of eternal blessing, the life-cre-
ating power, the fountain of sanctification, through whom every
creature of reason and understanding worships Thee and always
sings to Thee a hymn of glory" (from the anaphora of the Liturgy
of St Basil the Great). In other words, where the Holy Spirit is,
there is the kingdom of God. Through his coming on the "last
and great day of Pentecost" the Holy Spirit transforms this *last*
day into the first day of the new creation and manifests the
Church as the gift and presence of this first and "eighth" day.

Thus, everything in the Church is by the Holy Spirit, everything is in the Holy Spirit and everything is partaking of the Holy
Spirit. It is by the Holy Spirit because with the descent of the
Spirit the Church is revealed as the transformation of the end into
the beginning, of the old life into the new. "The Holy Spirit

6*Against Heresies* 3:24:1.

grants all things; he is the source of prophecy, he fulfils the priesthood, he gathers the entire church assembly" (hymn of Pentecost). Everything in the Church is in the Holy Spirit, who raises
us up to the heavenly sanctuary, to the throne of God. "We have
seen the true light, we have received the heavenly Spirit" (another
hymn of Pentecost). Finally, the Church is entirely oriented toward the Holy Spirit, "the treasury of blessings and giver of life."
The entire life of the Church is a thirst for acquisition of the Holy
Spirit and for participation in him, and in him of the fulness of
grace. Just as the life and spiritual struggle of each believer consists, in the words of St Serafim of Sarov, in the acquisition of the
Holy Spirit, so also the life of the Church is that same acquisition,
that same eternally satisfied but never completely quenched thirst
for the Holy Spirit. "Come to us, O Holy Spirit, and make us
partakers of your holiness, and of the light that knows no eve-
ning, and of the divine life, and of the most fragrant dispensation..." (compline canon of the feast of the Holy Spirit).

7

HAVING SAID ALL THIS, WE CAN NOW RETURN TO WHAT WE
began this chapter with: the definition of the eucharist as the sacrament of the kingdom, the Church's ascent to the "table of the
Lord, in his kingdom."

   We know now that this definition "slipped out" of our scholarly, theological explanations of the liturgy, which were adopted
by Orthodox theology from the West. The main reason for this
was the disintegration, in Christian consciousness, of the key concept of the *symbol*, its contraposition to the concept of *reality* and
thus its reduction to the category of "illustrative symbolism." Inasmuch as the Christian faith from the very beginning confessed
precisely the *reality* of the change of the gifts of bread and wine
into the body and blood of Christ—"this is indeed the *very* body,
and this is indeed the *very* blood of Christ"—any "confusion" of
this reality with "symbolism" came to be seen as a threat to eucharistic "realism" and hence also to the *real presence* of the body
and blood of Christ on the altar. This led to the reduction of the
sacrament to the "consecratory formula"—which by its very nar-

rowness "guarantees" in time and space the reality of the change—
and this "fear" also led to the more and more detailed definition
of the "modus" and "moment" of the change, as well as its "efficacy." Hence the persistent reminders that *before* the consecration
of the gifts the paten holds only bread and the chalice contains
only wine; but *after* the consecration we find only body and blood.
Hence the attempts to explain the "reality" of the change by us-
ing Aristotelian categories of "essence" and "accidents" and to describe the change as "transubstantiation." Finally, we find here
the source of the denial of the real relation of the liturgy—both in
its many details as well as taken as a whole—to the change of the
holy gifts and the practical exclusion of the liturgy from explanations of the sacrament.

Here and now, we must ask whether this understanding of
the symbol and symbolism, their contraposition to "reality," corresponds to the original meaning of the idea of the "symbol," and
whether it applies to the Christian *lex orandi*, the liturgical tradition of the Church. To this fundamental question I answer in the
negative. And this is precisely the heart of the matter: the primary meaning of "symbol" is in no way equivalent to "illustration."
In fact, it is possible for the symbol *not* to illustrate, i.e., it can be
devoid of any external similarity with that which it symbolizes.

The history of religions shows us that the more ancient, the
deeper, the more "organic" a symbol, the less it will be composed
of such "illustrative" qualities. This is because the purpose and
function of the symbol is *not* to illustrate (this would presume the
absence of what is illustrated) but rather to *manifest* and to *communicate* what is manifested. We might say that the symbol does not so
much "resemble" the reality that it symbolizes as it *participates* in
it, and therefore it is capable of communicating it in reality. In
other words, the difference (and it is a radical one) between our
contemporary understanding of the symbol and the original one
consists in the fact that while today we understand the symbol as
the representation or sign of an *absent* reality, something that is
not really in the sign itself (just as there is no real, actual water in
the chemical symbol H_2O), in the original understanding it is the
manifestation and presence of the *other* reality—but precisely as
other, which, under given circumstances, cannot be manifested
and made present in any other way than as a symbol.

This means that in the final analysis the true and original symbol is inseparable from faith, for faith is "the evidence of things unseen" (Heb 11:1), the knowledge that there is another reality different from the "empirical" one, and that this reality can be entered, can be communicated, can in truth become "the most real of realities." Therefore, if the symbol presupposes faith, faith of necessity requires the symbol. For, unlike "convictions," philosophical "points of view," etc., faith certainly is contact and a thirst for contact, embodiment and a thirst for embodiment: it is the manifestation, the presence, the operation of one reality within the other. All of this *is* the symbol (from συμβάλλω, "unite," "hold together"). In it—unlike in a simple "illustration," simple sign, and even in the sacrament in its scholastic-rationalistic "reduction"—the empirical (or "visible") and the spiritual (or "invisible") are united not *logically* (this "stands for" that), nor *analogically* (this "illustrates" that), nor yet by *cause and effect* (this is the "means" or "generator" of that), but *epiphanically*. One reality *manifests* (ἐπιφαίνω) and *communicates* the other, but—and this is immensely important—only to the degree to which the symbol itself is a participant in the spiritual reality and is able or called upon to embody it. In other words, in the symbol *everything* manifests the spiritual reality, but *not* everything pertaining to the spiritual reality appears embodied in the symbol. The symbol is always partial, always imperfect: "for our knowledge is imperfect and our prophecy is imperfect" (1 Co 13:9). By its very nature the symbol unites disparate realities, the relation of the one to the other always remaining "absolutely other." However *real* a symbol may be, however successfully it may communicate to us that other reality, its function is not to quench our thirst but to intensify it: "Grant us that we may more perfectly partake of Thee in the never ending day of Thy Kingdom." It is not that this or that part of "this world"—space, time, or matter—be made *sacred*, but rather that everything in it be seen and comprehended as expectation and thirst for its complete spiritualization: "that God may be all in all."

Must we then demonstrate that only this ontological and "epiphanic" meaning of the word "symbol" is applicable to Christian worship? And not only is it applicable—it is inseparable. For the essence of the symbol lies in the fact that in it the dichotomy between reality and symbolism (as *unreality*) is overcome: reality is experienced above all as the *fulfilment* of the symbol, and the symbol is comprehended as the fulfilment of reality. Christian worship is symbolic not because it contains various "symbolical" depictions. It may indeed include them, but chiefly in the imagination of various "commentators" and not in its own ordo and rites. Christian worship is symbolic because, first of all, the world itself, God's own creation, is symbolic, is *sacramental*; and second of all, because it is the Church's nature, her task in "this world," to fulfil this symbol, to realize it as the "most real of realities." We can therefore say that the symbol reveals the world, mankind and all creation as the "matter" of a single, all-embracing sacrament.

Now we can raise the basic question: What does the eucharist symbolize? What symbolism unites into a single whole the entire ordo and all of its rites? Or, to put it differently, what *spiritual reality* is manifested and given to us in this "sacrament of all sacraments"? And this leads us back to what we began this chapter with—the identification and confession of the eucharist as the *sacrament of the kingdom*.

8

THE DIVINE LITURGY BEGINS WITH THE SOLEMN DOXOLOGY: "Blessed is the Kingdom of the Father, and of the Son, and of the Holy Spirit, now and ever and unto ages of ages." The Savior likewise began his ministry with the proclamation of the kingdom, the ringing announcement that it has *come*: "Jesus came into Galilee, preaching the gospel of God, and saying: 'The time is fulfilled and the kingdom of God is at hand; repent, and believe in the gospel'" (Mk 1:14-15). And it is with desire for the kingdom that the first and foremost of all Christian prayers begins: "Thy kingdom come..."

Thus, the kingdom of God is the content of the Christian faith—the goal, the meaning and the content of the Christian life. According to the unanimous witness of all scripture and tradition, it is the knowledge of God, love for him, unity with him and life in him. The kingdom of God is unity with God, the source of all life, indeed life itself. It is life eternal: "And this is eternal life, that they know thee" (Jn 17:3). It is for this true and eternal life in the fulness of love, unity and knowledge that man was created. But man lost this in the fall, and by man's sin, evil, suffering and death triumphed in the world. The "prince of this world" began his reign; the world rejected its God and King. Yet God did not reject the world: as we pray in the anaphora of St John Chrysostom, "and when we had fallen away [Thou] didst not cease to do all things until Thou hadst brought us up to heaven, and hadst endowed us with Thy kingdom which is to come." The prophets of the Old Testament hungered for this kingdom, prayed for it, foretold it. It was the very goal and fulfilment of the entire sacred history of the Old Testament, a history holy not with human sanctity (for it was utterly filled with falls, betrayals and sins) but with the holiness of its being God's preparation for the coming of his kingdom.

And now, "the time is fulfilled and the kingdom of God is at hand" (Mk 1:15). The only-begotten Son of God became the Son of man, in order to proclaim and to give to man forgiveness of sins, reconciliation with God and new life. By his death on the cross and his resurrection from the dead he has come into his kingdom: God "made him sit at his right hand in the heavenly places, far above all rule and authority and power and dominion, and above every name that is named...and he has put all things under his feet and has made him the head over all things" (Eph 1:20-22). Christ reigns, and everyone who believes in him and is born again of water and the Spirit belongs to his kingdom and has him within himself. "Christ is the Lord"—this is the most ancient Christian confession of faith, and for three centuries the world, in the form of the Roman empire, persecuted those who spoke these words for their refusal to recognize *anyone* on earth as lord except the one Lord and one King.

The kingdom of Christ is accepted by faith and is hidden "within us." The King himself came in the form of a servant and reigned only through the cross. There are no external signs of this kingdom on earth. It is the kingdom of "the world to come," and thus only in the glory of his second coming will all people recognize the true king of the world. But for those who have believed in it and accepted it, the kingdom is already here and now, more obvious than any of the "realities" surrounding us. "The Lord has come, the Lord is coming, the Lord will come again." This triune meaning of the Aramaic expression *maranatha!* contains the whole of Christianity's victorious faith, against which all persecutions have proven impotent.

At first glance all of this might sound like some sort of pious platitudes. But reread what has just been said and compare it with the faith and "experience" of the vast majority of contemporary Christians, and you cannot but be convinced that there is a deep abyss between what we have said and the modern "experience." One can say without any exaggeration that the *kingdom of God*—the central concept in evangelical preaching—has ceased to be the central content and inner motivation of the Christian faith. Unlike the early Christians, those of later ages came, little by little, to lose the perception of the kingdom of God as being "at hand." They came to understand it only as the kingom *to come*—at the end and *after* the end, referring only to the "personal" death of individual believers. "This world" and "the kingdom," which in the gospels are set side by side and in tension and struggle with one another, have come to be thought of in terms of a chronological sequence: now—only the world; then—only the kingdom. For the first Christians the all-encompassing joy, the truly startling novelty of their faith lay in the fact that the kingdom was *at hand*. It *had appeared*, and although it remained hidden and unseen for "this world," it was already present, its light had already shone, it was already at work in the world. Then, as the kingdom was "removed" to the end of the world, to the mysterious and unfathomable reaches of time, Christians gradually lost their awareness of it as something hoped for, as the desired and joyous fulfilment of all hopes, of all desires, of life itself, of all that the early Church implied in the words "Thy kingdom come."

It is characteristic that our scholarly tomes of dogmatic theology (which cannot, of course, pass over the early doctrine in silence) speak of the kingdom in quite sparing, dull and even boring terms. Here, *eschatology*—the doctrine of the "final destiny of the world and man"—is virtually reduced to the doctrine of "God as the Judge and Avenger." As to piety, i.e., the personal experience of individual believers, the interest is narrowed to the question of one's personal fate "after death." At the same time, "this world," about which St Paul wrote that its form is "passing away," and which for the early Christians was transparent to the kingdom, reacquired its own value and existence independent of the kingdom of God.

9

THIS GRADUAL NARROWING, IF NOT RADICAL METAMORPHOSIS of Christian eschatology, its peculiar break with the theme and experience of the kingdom, has had tremendous significance in the development of liturgical consciousness in the Church. Returning to what we said above about the symbolism of Christian worship, we can now affirm that the Church's worship was born and, in its external structure, "took shape" primarily as a *symbol of the kingdom*, of the Church's ascent to it and, in this ascent, of her fulfilment as the body of Christ and the temple of the Holy Spirit. The whole newness, the uniqueness of the Christian *leitourgia* was in its eschatological nature as the presence here and now of the future *parousia*, as the epiphany of that which is to come, as communion with the "world to come." As I wrote in my *Introduction to Liturgical Theology*, it is precisely out of this eschatological experience that the "Lord's day" was born as a *symbol*, i.e., the manifestation, now, of the kingdom. It is this experience that determined the Christian "reception" of the Jewish feasts of Passover and Pentecost, as feasts precisely of a "pass-over" from the present "aeon" to the one which is to come, and thus—symbols of the kingdom of God.

But, of course, the symbol of the kingdom par excellence, the one that fulfils all other symbols—the Lord's day, baptism, Pascha, etc.—as well as all of Christian life "hid with Christ in God" (Col 3:3), is the *eucharist*, the sacrament of the coming of the risen Lord, of our meeting and communion with him "at his table in his kingdom." Secretly, unseen by the world, "the doors being shut," the Church—that "little flock" to whom it was the Father's good pleasure to give the kingdom (Lk 12:32)—fulfils in the eucharist her ascension and entrance into the light and joy and triumph of the kingdom. And we can say without any exaggeration that it was from this totally unique and incomparable experience, from this fully *realized* symbol, that the whole of the Christian *lex orandi* was born and developed.

It should now be clear why it was that with the weakening and the eclipse of the original eschatology the liturgical symbolism of the kingdom became overgrown little by little with the wild grass of secondary explanations and allegorical commentaries, i.e., with the "illustrative symbolism" that—as I have tried to show above—in fact means the collapse of the symbol. The more time went on, the more the symbolism of the kingdom, so fundamental for the Church, was forgotten. Inasmuch, however, as the liturgy, the *lex orandi* of the Church, with all its forms and its entire *ordo*, already existed and was perceived as an untouchable part of tradition, it naturally came to demand a new explanation—in the same "key" in which Christian consciousness was beginning to apprehend the place and ministry of the Church in "this world." This was the beginning of an ever-deeper infiltration of "illustrative symbolism" into the explanation of worship. And, paradoxical as it may seem, in this process the otherworldly, heavenly *reality* of the eucharist came to be "included" in "this world," in its causality, its time, the categories of its thought and experience, while the symbolism of the kingdom of God, so inherent to and inseparable from creation—the true key for the Church and her life—was reduced to the category of this *unnecessary* illustrative symbolism.

10

THIS PROCESS, TO BE SURE, WAS LONG AND COMPLICATED AND not some kind of instant "metamorphosis." And we must decidedly affirm that, whatever its external triumph, "illustrative" symbolism has never completely succeeded in supplanting the original, eschatological symbolism of the liturgy, which is rooted in the faith itself. No matter how much development took place, for instance, in Byzantine worship in the direction of what, in my *Introduction to Liturgical Theology*, I termed "external solemnity," no matter how overgrown it became with decorative and allegorical details, with the pomp borrowed from the imperial cult and with terminology adopted from mysteriological "sacredness," worship as a whole, as well as its deep intuition in the minds of the faithful, continued to be determined by the *symbolism of the kingdom of God*. And there is no better witness to this than the fundamental Orthodox *experience* of the temple and of iconography, an experience that crystalized precisely during the Byzantine period and in which the "holy of holies" of Orthodoxy is expressed better than in the redundant rhetoric of the "symbolic" liturgical interpretations.

"Standing in the temple we stand in heaven." I have spoken of the origins of the Christian temple in the experience of the "assembly as the Church." We can now add that insofar as this assembly is undoubtedly conceived of as *heavenly*, the temple is that "heaven on earth" that realizes the "assembly as the Church." It is the symbol that unites these two realities, these two dimensions of the Church—"heaven" and "earth," one manifested in the other, one made a reality in the other. And this experience of the temple, I repeat, has survived almost unchanged and unweakened throughout the entire history of the Church, despite the numerous declines and breakdowns in the authentic traditions of church architecture and iconography. This experience constitutes that "whole" that unites and coordinates all the elements of the temple: space, form, shape, icons, all that can be termed the *rhythm* and *order* of the temple. As to the icon, it is in its very essence a symbol of the kingdom, the "epiphany" of the new and transfigured creation, of heaven and earth full of God's glory, and it is for this reason that the canons forbid the introduction into iconography of any allegorical or illustrative "symbolism." For the icon does not "illustrate"—it *manifests*, and does so only to the degree that it is itself a *participant* in what it manifests, inasmuch as it is both presence and communion. It is enough to have stood, be it only once, in the "temple of all temples," Hagia Sophia in Constantinople—even in its present devastated and kenotic state—to *know* with one's whole being that the temple and the icon were born and nurtured in the living *experience of heaven*, in communion with the "peace and joy of the Holy Spirit" (Rm 14:17).

This experience was frequently darkened. Historians of Christian art often speak of the decline of church architecture and the icon. And it is important to note that this decline usually came about by the *whole*—of the temple, of the icon—being weakened and lost beneath the thickening growth of details. Thus, the temple almost disappears under a thick layer of self-contained decorations, and in the icon, Byzantine as well as Russian, the original wholeness is replaced by an ever-growing attention to cleverly drawn details. Is this not the same movement—from the "whole" to the "particular," from the experience of the whole to a discursive "explanation," and, in short, from symbol to "symbolism"? And yet, as long as the "Christian world," be it imperfectly and sometimes nominally, "refers" itself to the kingdom of God, the "homeland of the heart's desire," this centrifugal movement cannot fully overpower the centripetal force.

One might say that, at first and for a long period of time, the "illustrative" symbolism—be it in worship, in the icon or in the temple—developed *inside* the initial and ontological symbolism of the kingdom. The deeper and truly tragic rupture between the two of them, the initial replacement of the one by the other, began with the break from the patristic tradition and the coming of the long (and in many ways continuing) "western captivity" of the Orthodox mind. It is not accidental that the luxuriant and unchecked flowering of "illustrative" symbolism corresponded in time with the triumph of western juridicism and rationalism in Orthodox theology, of pietism and sentimentality in iconography, of embellished "pretty" baroque in church architecture, of "lyricism" and emotionalism in church music. All of these manifest one and the same "pseudomorphosis" of the Orthodox consciousness.

Yet even this deep and truly tragic decline cannot be considered final. In its depths, the Church's consciousness ultimately remains untouched by all this. Thus, everyday experience shows us that "illustrative symbolism" is foreign to the living, authentic faith and life of the Church, just as "scholastic" theology remains foreign, in the last analysis, to such faith. "Illustrative symbolism" is at home in that superficial, "showy" and routine religiosity in which a widespread but shallow curiosity toward anything "holy" is lightly taken as religious feeling and "interest in the Church." But where there is a living, authentic and, in the best sense of the word, *simple* faith, it becomes *unnecessary*, for genuine faith lives not by curiosity but by thirst.

Just as he did a thousand years ago, so today the "simple"

believer goes to Church in order primarily to "touch other worlds" (Dostoevsky). "And almost free, the soul breathes heaven unhindered" (Vladislav Khodasevich). In a sense, he is not "interested" in worship, in the way in which "experts" and connoisseurs of all liturgical details are interested in it. And he is not interested because "standing in the temple" he receives all that for which he thirsts and seeks: the light, the joy, and the comfort of the kingdom of God, the *radiance* that, in the words of the agnostic Chekhov, beams from the faces of the "old people who have just returned from the church." What use could such a believer have for complex and refined explanations of what this or that rite "represents," of what the opening and closing of the royal doors is supposed to mean? He cannot keep up with all these "symbolisms," and they are unnecessary for his faith. All he knows is that he has left his everyday life and has come to a place where everything is *different* and yet so essential, so desirable, so vital that it illumines and gives meaning to his entire life. Likewise he knows, even if he cannot express it in words, that this *other* reality makes life itself worth living, for everything proceeds to it, everything is referred to it, everything is to be judged by it—by the kingdom of God it manifests. And, finally, he knows that even if individual words or rites are unclear to him, the kingdom of God has been given to him in the *Church*: in that common action, common standing before God, in the "assembly," in the "ascent," in unity and love.

II

THUS WE RETURN TO WHERE WE BEGAN, INDEED TO WHERE the eucharist itself begins: to the blessing of the kingdom of God. What does it mean to *bless* the kingdom? It means that we acknowledge and confess it to be our highest and ultimate value, the object of our desire, our love and our hope. It means that we proclaim it to be the goal of the sacrament—of pilgrimage, ascension, entrance—that now begins. It means that we must focus our attention, our mind, heart and soul, i.e., our whole life, upon that which is truly the "one thing needful." Finally, it means that now, already in "this world," we confirm the possibility of communion with the kingdom, of entrance into its radiance, truth and joy. Each time that Christians "assemble as the Church" they witness before the whole world that Christ is King and Lord, that his kingdom has already been revealed and given to man and that a new and immortal life has begun. This is why the liturgy begins with this solemn confession and doxology of the King who comes *now* but abides forever and shall reign unto ages of ages.

"It is time [καιρός] to begin the service to the Lord," the deacon announces to the celebrant. This is not simply a reminder that it is now "opportune" or "convenient" for the performance of the sacrament. It is an affirmation and confession that the *new time*, the time of the kingdom of God and its fulfilment in the Church, now enters into the fallen time of "this world" in order that we, the Church, might be lifted up to heaven, and the Church transfigured into "that which she is"—the body of Christ and the temple of the Holy Spirit.

"Blessed is the Kingdom of the Father, and of the Son, and of the Holy Spirit..." *Amen*, answer the people. This word is usually translated as "so be it," but its meaning is really stronger than this. It signifies not only agreement, but also active acceptance. "Yes, this is so, and *let* it be so." With this word the ecclesial assembly concludes and, as it were, *seals* each prayer uttered by the celebrant, thereby expressing its own organic, responsible and conscious participation in each and every sacred action of the Church. "To that which you are—say Amen," writes St Augustine, "and thus seal it with your answer. For you hear 'the body of Christ' and answer 'Amen.' *Be* a member of the body of Christ, which is realized by your Amen...Fulfil that which you are."[7]

CHAPTER THREE

The Sacrament of Entrance

*"O Master, Lord our God, who hast
appointed in heaven orders and hosts
of angels and archangels for the service
of Thy glory: Grant that with our entrance there may be an entrance of holy
angels, serving with us and glorifying
Thy goodness..."*

PRAYER OF ENTRANCE

I

*I*N EARLY TIMES, THE FIRST ACT OF THE LITURGY AFTER
the assembly of the faithful was the *entrance of the celebrant.*[1]
"When the president of the assembly enters," writes St John
Chrysostom, "he says 'peace be with all of you.'"[2] It is precisely
with and through the entrance that the solemn ceremony begins
—as is evident to this very day in our order of the pontifical reception. Later on, for various reasons, this initial entrance was
supplanted in its own turn by another "beginning," so that now
what we call the "Little Entrance" is no longer understood as precisely the first, fundamental rite of the liturgy. And from here,

[1]On the entrance and its evolution, the three antiphons, etc., see J. Mateos, "Evolution
historique de la Liturgie de S. Jean Chrysostome," part 2, *Proche-Orient Chrétien* 16 (1966) 133-61,
and *La célébration de la Parole dans la liturgie byzantine*, Orientalia Christiana Analecta 191 (Rome,
1971), chapters 2-3, pp. 46-90. See also R. Taft, *The Great Entrance*, Orientalia Christiana Analecta 200 (Rome, 1978).

[2]*Homily on Colossians* 3:4, PG 62:322-3.

49

incidentally, also comes its popular interpretation in the category of "illustrative symbolism" as Christ's going out to preach, etc. It is appropriate here, however, to remind ourselves of the original practice not because of some kind of archeological pedantry but because the idea of *entrance* has a truly decisive significance for the understanding of the eucharist. And in the end, the purpose of our investigation is to show that the meaning of the eucharist is contained in the *entry* of the Church into the kingdom of God; that in a sense the eucharist is entirely *entrance*; and that the lifting up, the ἀναφορά, is related not only to the holy gifts ("that we may offer the Holy Oblation in peace...") but to the Church herself, to the very assembly. For—and I shall repeat this again and again—the eucharist is the *sacrament of the kingdom*, accomplished by the ascent and entry of the Church into the heavenly sanctuary.

Today, however, the *entrance* is preceded by a certain introductory part consisting of the *Great Litany*, three *antiphons* and three *prayers*, and thus we must explain, however briefly, how and why this "pre-entry section" arose and became, as a general rule, the beginning of the liturgy. Let us begin with the *Great Litany* —i.e., the series of supplicatory petitions that, in our present-day order of worship, begins all the "liturgical" services of the Church without exception. We find it in the beginning of vespers, matins, the marriage services, the funeral rite, the blessing of the waters, etc. In all probability of Antiochian origin, the Great Litany appeared comparatively early in the Byzantine order of services as precisely the initial, general prayer of the assembled Church. However, right up to the twelfth-thirteenth century this litany was said not as it is today—at the beginning of the liturgy—but *after* the entrance and the singing of the *Trisagion*, the hymn of the entrance, which is a confession of the holiness of God: "Holy God, Holy Mighty, Holy Immortal, have mercy on us." In certain manuscripts the Great Litany is called the "Trisagion litany" or the "Trisagion petitions." This once again demonstrates that the genuine beginning of the eucharistic celebration was precisely the *entrance*, and hence it also follows that the Great Litany was transferred to its present place—before the *antiphons*—at the time when these antiphons were added to the liturgy as its beginning.

We must note above all that the "service of the three antiphons"—i.e., the unification in a single unit or sequence of the

antiphonal (i.e., alternating between two singers or choirs) singing of the three psalms (or three groups of psalms), separated from
each other by prayers—is quite widespread in the Byzantine type
of worship. We find such antiphons in the so-called "sung office," i.e., the Sunday vigil of the Constantinopolitan order, and
in the services of the daily cycle: matins, vespers, nocturn, etc.
We must consider it beyond doubt that they were joined to the
eucharistic celebration precisely as a "whole," as a liturgical unit
that already existed apart from the liturgy.

Usually, they stood as part of a service in commemoration of a
certain saint or event and were performed during the procession to
the church where the festal eucharist celebrating this "memory"
was to be performed. We must remember that, in contrast to our
present organization, in which each parish is liturgically "independent" and celebrates the entire liturgical cycle on its own, in
the Byzantine Church the *city*—especially, of course, Constantinople—was considered as one ecclesiastical *whole*, so that the liturgical *Typikon of the Great Church* embraced all the individual
churches, each of which was dedicated to a certain "memory."

On appointed days the church procession began at Hagia
Sophia and made its way to the church dedicated to the saint
or event of the feastday, in which the entire Church—and not a
separate "parish"—would celebrate the commemoration. Thus,
for example, on January 16, on the feastday of "the chains of the
apostle Peter," the procession, according to the instructions of the
Typikon of the Great Church, "goes out from the Great Church
[i.e., Hagia Sophia] and makes its way to the Church of St Peter,
where the festal eucharist is celebrated." The singing of the
antiphons took place during this procession and was completed at
the doors of the church with the reading of the "prayer of entrance," and only then did the clergy and the people of God
actually enter the church for the performance of the eucharist.
From here stems the diversity of the antiphons, their "variabil-
ity," depending on the event celebrated by the feast; from here
stems the existence to this day of special antiphons prescribed for
the major Lord's feasts, etc. Sometimes, however, special troparia
to the saint are sung in place of the antiphons; in that case the
Typikon, noting these troparia, prescribes: "...and with the entrance into the Church of St Peter is to be sung the 'Glory' with

this same troparion. *There are no antiphons*, but immediately the *Trisagion...*"[3]

Even from this brief analysis—though it would be possible to extend it a hundredfold—it is evident that the "antiphons" originally constituted a separate service, which took place before the eucharist and, at first, outside of the church building. It belonged to the type of *litē* (procession around the city), which was extraordinarily popular in Byzantium and which in our contemporary worship is preserved as the *litē* in the all-night vigil and the processions around the church on certain feasts. Later on, following that logic of liturgical development in which a kind of law functions according to which the "peculiarities" become the "general rule," this service came to be seen as an inseparable part of the eucharist, as a liturgical expression of the "assembly as the Church." However, even here it was still understood as a separate, introductory section: the patriarch, for example, entered the church only after the singing of the antiphons. This is also evident to the present day in our pontifical liturgy, in which the hierarch does not in fact take part until the "Little Entrance," so that the initial "blessing of the kingdom" and all the exclamations are done by the priests. From all that has been said, it is clearly apparent, as a Catholic specialist on the history of Byzantine worship has written, that at first the three antiphons were sung not in the church, but outside of it and only on the occasion of a solemn procession. What is now called the "Little Entrance" was none other than the entrance of the people and clergy into the church—either at the conclusion of the procession, or without any preliminary procession.[4]

2

ALL THIS WOULD BE OF MERELY HISTORICAL AND ARCHEOlogical interest if it did not serve to emphasize not only that the *entrance* actually comprises the *beginning* of the eucharistic ceremony, but also the *entering*, dynamic character of this ceremony, the

[3]J. Mateos, *Le Typikon de la Grande Eglise*, I, Orientalia Christiana Analecta 165 (Rome, 1962) 198-9.
[4]Mateos, "Evolution historique," part 1, 344.

eucharist as *movement*. We no longer live in a Christian or, to put it better, "Christianized" world, in which the liturgical symbols—the litē, processions, etc.—can reveal its *relation* to the Church as the way to the kingdom, and therefore its own orientation toward the kingdom of God. Our churches are surrounded by, if not an openly hostile, then in any case a "religiously neutral," "secularized" and indifferent world. But this is why it is so important that we realize and sense that fundamental, original and immutable *correlation* of the Church and the world, which in another time, in entirely different conditions, found its liturgical expression in these processions of the people to the church. If "assembling as the Church" presupposes separation from the world (Christ appears "the doors being shut"), this exodus from the world is accomplished *in the name of the world*, for the sake of its salvation. For we are flesh of the flesh and blood of the blood of this world. We are a part of it, and only by us and through us does it ascend to its Creator, Savior and Lord, to its goal and fulfilment. We separate ourselves from the world in order to bring it, in order to lift it up to the kingdom, to make it once again the way to God and participation in his eternal kingdom. In this is the task of the Church; for this she was left in the world, as part of it, as a symbol of its salvation. And this symbol we fulfil, we "make real" in the eucharist.

As we follow the order of the eucharist this purpose will be more clearly and deeply revealed. But already, from the very beginning, in these "common supplications" made "with one accord," in these joyous and triumphal antiphons, which proclaim and glorify the kingdom of God, we signify that the "assembly as the Church" is above all the joy of the regenerated and renewed creation, *the gathering of the world*, in contrast to its fall into sin and death. The sacrament of the Church—the eucharist—is likewise the sacrament of the world, which "God so loved...that he gave his only Son" (Jn 3:16).

3

LET US RETURN NOW TO THE GREAT LITANY.[5] "IN PEACE LET US
pray to the Lord," the deacon exclaims. After the confession and
glorification of the kingdom, we offer "common supplications"
made "with one accord." Do we understand the entire significance and, chiefly, the entire *newness* of these prayers—prayers of
the Church herself? Do we understand that this is not "simply"
the prayer of a man or a group of people, but the prayer of Christ
himself to his Father, which has been granted to us, and that this
gift of Christ's prayer, of his mediation, of his intercession is the
first and greatest gift of the Church? We pray in Christ, and he,
through his Holy Spirit, prays in us, who are gathered in his
name. "And because you are sons, God has sent the Spirit of his
Son into our hearts, crying, 'Abba! Father!'" (Ga 4:6). We can
add nothing to his prayer, but according to his will, according to
his love, we have become members of his body, we are one with
him and have participation in his protection and intercession
for the world. The apostle Paul, urging the faithful "First of
all...that supplications, prayers, intercessions, and thanksgiv-
ings be made for all men," adds: "For there is one God, and there
is one mediator between God and men, *the man* Jesus Christ"
(1 Tm 2:1, 5). And that is why the prayer of the Church is a
divine-human prayer, for the Church is Christ's humanity, with
him standing at its head: "I in them and thou in me, that they
may become perfectly one, so that the world may know that thou
hast sent me" (Jn 17:23).

"For the peace from above and for the salvation of our
souls..." In the Church we are given the peace of Christ, just as
we are *given* the anointment of the Holy Spirit. Everything is giv-
en to us, and for everything we unceasingly pray: come and save
us, thy kingdom come. For what is given must be accepted, and
we are called to grow unceasingly in this gift. Sin and grace, the
old and the new man carry on in us an incessant struggle, and
what is given by God is all the time being contested by the enemy
of God. And the Church—the assembly of the saints—is also an

[5]*Ibid.*

assembly of sinners, who receive but do not accept, who are forgiven but reject grace and unceasingly fall away from her. We above all pray for what in the gospels is called the "one thing needful." But the "peace from above" is the kingdom of God, the "righteousness and peace and joy in the Holy Spirit" (Rm 14:17). It is that for the sake of which we must be prepared to give up everything, to refuse everything, to sacrifice all: "seek first his kingdom...and all these things shall be yours as well." The acquisition of this kingdom, this "peace from above," is also salvation of the soul. For, in the language of holy scripture, the *soul* signifies the man himself, in his genuine nature and calling. This is the divine particle that makes man the image and likeness of God, and because of which the foremost sinner is, in the eyes of God, a priceless treasure, for whose salvation the shepherd left the ninety-nine righteous ones. The soul is the gift of God to man, and therefore "what will it profit a man, if he gains the whole world and loses his soul? Or what shall a man give in return for his soul?" (Mt 16:26). The first petition of the Great Litany indicates to us the ultimate, highest purpose of our life, that for which we have been created, to which we must strive and what must become for us the "one thing needful."

"For the peace of the whole world...," that this peace of Christ may be spread over all, that the leaven, sown in the world, might leaven the whole lump (1 Co 5:6), that everyone, far and near, might become participants in the kingdom of God.

"For the welfare of the holy churches of God..." "You are the salt of the earth," Christ said to his disciples, and this means that the Church is left in the world to witness to Christ and his kingdom and that his work is bequeathed to her. "But if salt has lost its taste, how shall its saltness be restored?" (Mt 5:13). If Christians neglect their *ministry*, to which all, from first to last, are appointed, then who will ring out the good news of the kingdom of God and introduce people to the new life? The prayer for *welfare* is a prayer for the fidelity and steadfastness of Christians, that the Church, diffused over the whole earth, may in each place be faithful to herself, to her essence, to her purpose—that she may be the "salt of the earth and the light of the world."

"For the union of all..." The unity of all in God constitutes the ultimate aim of creation and salvation. Christ came in order to "gather into one the children of God who are scattered abroad" (Jn 11:52). The Church prays for this unity, for the overcoming of all divisions, for the fulfilment of the prayer of Christ: "that they may become perfectly one" (Jn 17:23).

"For this holy house and for those who enter with faith, reverence, and the fear of God..." Here we find the condition for our genuine participation in the prayer and the sacrament, and everyone who enters the temple must examine himself: does he have in his heart a living faith and reverence for the presence of God—that saving "fear of God" that we so often lose, being "accustomed" or "used to" the Church and the worship services?

"For the episcopate, for all the clergy and the people...," for the Church, to which we belong and which, in the unity of all her servants—bishops, priests, deacons and the people of God—manifests and fulfils herself, here and now, as the body of Christ.

"For the country, for the city, for the authorities, for all people, for seasonable weather, for the abundance of the fruits of the earth, for travelers by land or by sea, for the sick and the suffering, for captives..." The prayer extends to and embraces the entire world, all nature, all mankind, all life. The Church is given power and authority to lift up this universal prayer, interceding before God for his entire creation. Whenever we narrow our faith and our religious life to ourselves, to our own concerns and wants, we forget that the calling of the Church is always and everywhere "to offer prayers, petitions and thanksgiving for all mankind." And, as we come to the liturgy, we need again and again to learn to live according to the rhythm of the Church's prayer, to expand ourselves and our consciousness to the fulness of the Church.

And, finally, "commemorating all the saints," i.e., the whole Church with the Mother of God at her head, "let us commend ourselves and each other, and all our life unto Christ our God" —and not only for protection, help and success. "Set your minds on things that are above, not on things that are on earth. For you have died, and your life is hid with Christ in God. When Christ who is our life appears, then you also will appear with him in glory" (Col 3:2-4). We return our life to Christ because he is our life, because in the baptismal font we died to the simple "natural life," and our true life is hid in the mysterious heights of the kingdom of God.

4

AFTER THE GREAT LITANY COME THE THREE ANTIPHONS AND the three prayers, which are inscribed in the service books as the "prayer of the first antiphon," "of the second," etc. We have already spoken of the antiphons, of their origin and insertion into the order of the liturgy, and inasmuch as they obviously relate to the changeable part of the service we shall not discuss them right now. Regarding the three prayers, however, with which the celebrant in a certain sense "elevates" these songs of praise and thanksgiving, we must say a few words.

We all know that in the contemporary practice, whose origin we shall come to speak of separately, almost all the prayers offered by the celebrant are read *silently*, "to himself," so that the assembly hears only the concluding doxology, usually in the form of a subordinate clause—"...for Thou art..."—which is usually called the exclamation. This practice is relatively recent. Originally the prayers of the liturgy were read aloud, for in their direct meaning and content they are prayers of the entire assembly or, to put it better, of the Church herself. But, once fixed in the services, this practice led to the multiplication of the so-called *little litanies*, which consist of the first and last two petitions of the Great Litany. And now these little litanies are chanted by the deacon while the celebrant reads the prayers in secret. When the service is performed without a deacon, the priest must both pronounce the litany and read the prayer. But this led to the prayers being read *at the same time* as the singing of the antiphons. And so, this practice—besides the fact that it resulted in the frequent and monotonous repetition of the little litanies—disturbed the unity of the "assembly as the Church," it separated it precisely from those "common supplications made with one accord" in which this unity is expressed.

In the "prayer of the first antiphon" the celebrant confesses the Church's faith that God's power is *incomparable*, that his glory is *incomprehensible*, that his mercy is *immeasurable* and that his love for man is *inexpressible*. All these terms, which in the Greek text begin with negative particles (the so-called *alpha privative*), express the Christian experience of the absolute transcendence of

God—his incommensurability with our words, concepts and definitions, the *apophatic* foundations of the Christian faith, of Christian knowledge of God. This incommensurability was always felt
with special strength by the saints.

Yet God himself desired to *reveal* himself, and, at the same
time as we confess his incommensurability, the Church invites
him to "look down on us and on this holy house with pity...and
impart the riches of Thy mercy and Thy compassion to us." And
God not only revealed himself to people, but he also united them
with himself, he made them *his own*. This belonging of the
Church to God is confessed in the "prayer of the second antiphon": "save *Thy* people and bless *Thine* inheritance. Preserve the
fullness of *Thy* Church. Sanctify those who love the beauty of *Thy*
house"—for in the Church is revealed his power, his kingdom, his
strength and glory.

And, finally, according to the witness of the "prayer of the
third antiphon," to this new humanity, united with God, is giv-
en the knowledge of the truth in this age, and the truth bestows
eternal life: "granting us in this world the knowledge of Thy
truth, and in the world to come, life everlasting."

5

WE MEET THE EXPRESSION "LITTLE ENTRANCE" (AS DISTINCT
from the *Great Entrance* at the beginning of the liturgy of the
faithful) for the first time in manuscripts of the fourteenth century. This was the time of the final and definitive consolidation of
the eucharistic ordo into its contemporary state. We know already
that for a long time this entrance was the *beginning* of the liturgy,
its first rite. But when it lost this significance and the succession
of "antiphons" (or "typical psalms") became the first part of the
service, the chief stress—in its perception at least—was transferred
to the *carrying out of the gospels*. In contemporary practice this entrance is above all the entrance with the gospels, i.e., the solemn
carrying of the book out from and then back into the altar
through the royal doors. In several manuscripts it is even called
the "entrance of the gospels." And it is precisely this, as already
mentioned, that served as the starting point in the development

of that "illustrative symbolism" that, when applied to the Little Entrance, interprets it as a "representation" of Christ's going out to preach the gospel. We shall speak of the real significance of this bringing out of the gospels in the following chapter, dedicated to the liturgy as the sacrament of the word. Within the limits of this chapter, our chief emphasis is only that our current Little Entrance can obviously be traced to two diverse rites, two themes, which it unites: the entrance as such, and the ceremonies connected with the reading of the word of God. In the present chapter it is appropriate to include a brief analysis of the first of these.

We will stress once more that, in spite of all its complexity, the Little Entrance preserves the character precisely of an entrance, a beginning, a drawing near. Witnesses to this are, in the first place, our repeated references to the peculiarities of the hierarchical order of the liturgy and, in the second, the *prayer of the entrance*, which, as we also mentioned, was formerly read during the entrance of the celebrant and people into the temple and even today—in the order of consecration of a new temple—is read at the outer doors, and not before the royal doors of the iconostasis. In this prayer there is not even the slightest indication of any kind of "illustration," but instead we see the *heavenly* character of the entrance: in it the heavenly powers and hosts, i.e., the angels, are "serving with us."

A new element that cropped up out of the development of the Byzantine temple and the complication of the idea of the entrance was the transferal of the idea of the *sanctuary* from the temple as a whole to the *altar*, i.e., to that part of the temple that contains the altar table and is separated from the nave by the iconostasis. Under the influence of "mysteriological" theology, about which I wrote in my *Introduction to Liturgical Theology* and at whose center stands the contraposition of the "initiated" and the "uninitiated" —meaning the clergy and the laity—there arose inside the temple an inner *sanctuary*: the *altar*, access to which was open only to the "initiated." All "entrances" came to be performed here, in the altar. And this development certainly weakened the perception and experience of the "assembly as the Church" itself as the entrance and ascent of the Church, the people of God, to the heavenly sanctuary. For "Christ has entered, not into a sanctuary made with hands, a copy of the true one, but into *heaven itself*, now to appear in the presence of God on our behalf" (Heb 9:24).

6

THIS TYPICALLY "BYZANTINE" COMPLICATION, HOWEVER, DID not affect the main thing: precisely that in essence the *entrance* consists in drawing near to the *altar,* which from the beginning was the focus of the temple, its holy place. The word "altar" itself refers primarily to the altar table and only gradually came to be applied to the space surrounding it and separated from the temple by the iconostasis. We shall dwell in greater detail on the significance of the altar when we speak of the offering of the holy gifts. For now it is enough to say that, according to the witness of all tradition, the altar is a symbol of Christ and Christ's kingdom. It is the table at which Christ gathers us, and it is the sacrificial table that unites the high priest and the sacrifice. It is the throne of the King and Lord. It is heaven, that kingdom in which "God is all in all." And it is precisely from this experience of the altar as the focus of the eucharistic mystery of the Church that all the "mystique" of the altar developed—as heaven, as the eschatological pole of the liturgy, as that sacramental *presence* that converts the entire temple into "heaven on earth." And therefore the entrance, the drawing near to the altar, is always an *ascent.* In it the Church ascends to the place where her genuine "life is hid with Christ in God." She ascends to heaven, where the eucharist is celebrated.

It is important to remember all this because, under the influence of the western understanding of the eucharist, we usually perceive the liturgy not in the key of *ascent* but of *descent.* The entire western eucharistic mystique is thoroughly imbued with the image of Christ *descending* onto our altars. Meanwhile, the original eucharistic experience, to which the very order of the eucharist witnesses, speaks of our *ascent* to that place where Christ ascended, of the heavenly nature of the eucharistic celebration.

The eucharist is always a going out from "this world" and an ascent to heaven, and the altar is a symbol of the reality of this ascent, of its very "possibility." For Christ has ascended to heaven, and his altar is "sacred and spiritual." In "this world" there *is not and cannot be* an altar, for the kingdom of God is "not of this world." And that is why it is so important to understand that we regard the altar with reverence—we kiss it, we bow before it, etc. —not because it is "sanctified" and has become, so to speak, a "sacred object," but because its very sanctification consists in its *referral* to the reality of the kingdom, in its conversion into a symbol of the kingdom. Our reverence, our veneration is never related to "matter," but always to that which it reveals, of which it is an *epiphany*, i.e., a manifestation and presence. Any *consecration* in the Church is not a creation of "sacred objects," by their sanctity contraposed to the "profane," i.e., the unconsecrated, but their *referral* to their original and at the same time ultimate meaning —God's conception of them. For the entire world was created as an "altar of God," as a temple, as a symbol of the kingdom. According to its conception, it is all *sacred*, and not "profane," for its essence lies in the divine "very good" of Genesis. The sin of man consists in the fact that he has darkened the "very good" in his very being and as such has torn the world away from God, made it an "end in itself," and therefore a fall and death.

But God has saved the world. He saved it in that he again revealed its *goal*: the kingdom of God; its *life*: to be the path to this kingdom; its *meaning*: to be in communion with God, and in him with all creation. And therefore, in contrast to the pagan "sanctification," which consists in the *sacralization* of separate parts and objects of the world, the Christian sanctification consists in the restoration to everything in the world of its symbolic nature, its "sacramentality," in referring everything to the ultimate aim of being. All our worship services therefore are an ascent to the altar and a return back to "this world" for witness to "What no eye has seen, nor ear heard, nor the heart of man conceived, what God has prepared for those who love him" (1 Co 2:9).

7

THIS ESCHATOLOGICAL MEANING OF THE ENTRANCE, AS DRAW-ing near to the altar and ascent to the kingdom, is best of all expressed in the prayer and singing of the *Trisagion*, with which the entrance is concluded. Having entered into the sanctuary and standing before the altar, the celebrant intones the "Trisagion prayer": "Thou hast vouchsafed to us, Thy humble and unworthy servants, even in this hour to stand before the glory of Thy holy altar, and to offer worship and praise which are due unto Thee...accept even from the mouths of us sinners the thrice-holy hymn, and visit us in Thy goodness. Forgive us every transgression...Sanctify our souls and bodies..."

This prayer begins with the salutation "O holy God," with confession of the holiness of God and with supplication for our own sanctification, i.e., for participation in this holiness. But what does the word *holy*—which in the words of the prophet Isaiah comprises the eternal content of the angelic glorification, in which we in "this hour" are preparing ourselves to take part—mean and express as a word for God? No discursive thought, no logic is capable of explaining this, yet meanwhile it is precisely this sensation of the holiness of God, this feeling for the holy that is the foundation and source of religion. And here, arriving at this moment, we perhaps more powerfully than ever comprehend that the services, while not explaining to us what the holiness of God is, *reveal* it to us, and that in this manifestation is the age-old essence of *cult*—those rites that are as fundamental and ancient as man himself and whose meaning is almost indistinguishable from the gestures, the blessings, lifting up of the hands, prostrations, to which it gave rise. For the cult also was born from necessity, from the thirst of man for partaking of *the holy*, which he sensed before he could "think" about it.

"It is as though the liturgy alone," writes Louis Bouyer, "knows the full meaning of this notion impenetrable to reason. In any event, the liturgy alone is able to transmit it and teach it....That religious trembling, that interior vertigo before the Pure, the Inaccessible, the wholly Other, and at the same time that sense of an invisible presence, the attraction of a love so infinite and yet so personal that, having tasted it, we know only that it surpasses all that we still call love: only the liturgy can communicate the unique and incommunicable experience of all this. ...In it, this experience somehow flows from every element—the words, the gestures, the lights, the perfume that fills the temple, as in the vision of Isaiah—coming from what is behind all this and yet not simply all this, but which communicates this, in the same way that the striking expression of a face permits us in an instant to discover a soul, without our knowing how."[6]

Thus *we have entered* and stand now before the holy. We are sanctified by his presence, we are illumined by his light. And the trembling and the sweet feeling of the presence of God, the joy and peace, which has no equal on earth, is all expressed in the threefold, slow singing of the Trisagion: "Holy God, Holy Mighty, Holy Immortal"—the heavenly hymn, which is sung on earth but testifies to the accomplished reconciliation of earth and heaven, to the fact that God revealed himself to men and that it is given to us to "share his holiness" (Heb 12:10).

With this singing the celebrant ascends still higher, to the very heart of the temple, to the "high place," to the holy of holies. And in this rhythm of ascent—from "this world" to the gates of the temple, from the gates of the temple to the altar, from the altar to the high place—he witnesses to the accomplished unification, to the heights to which the Son of God has lifted us. And, after ascending to the "high place"—from there, but turning his face to the gathering, as one of the gathered but also as the image of the Lord, vested in his power and authority—the celebrant grants us *peace* for listening to the word of God.

[6]Neither the English nor the French translators have been able to locate the source of this passage, attributed by the author to Fr Louis Bouyer, even after consultation with the latter.

CHAPTER FOUR

The Sacrament of the Word

*"Illumine our hearts, O Master who
lovest mankind, with the pure light of
Thy divine knowledge. Open the eyes
of our mind to the understanding of
Thy gospel teachings. Implant also in
us the fear of Thy blessed commandments, that trampling down all car-
nal desires, we may enter upon a
spiritual manner of living, both
thinking and doing such things as are
well-pleasing unto Thee . . ."*
PRAYER BEFORE THE GOSPEL

I

*A*CCORDING TO THE UNANIMOUS TESTIMONY OF ALL EARLY
evidence, the reading of holy scripture from the very beginning constituted an inseparable part of the "assembly as the
Church" and, specifically, the eucharistic gathering. In one of the
first descriptions of the eucharist that we have, we read: "on the
day called Sunday there is a meeting in one place of those who live
in the cities or the country, and the memoirs of the apostles or the
writings of the prophets are read as long as time permits. When
the reader has finished, the president in a discourse urges and invites [us] to the imitation of these noble things. Then we all stand
up together and offer prayers . . . and when we have finished the

prayer, bread is brought, and wine and water..."[1] Here the link between the reading of scripture and the homily, on the one hand, and the offering of the eucharistic gifts, on the other, is obvious. And we find further witness to this in the contemporary order of the eucharist, in which there is an inseparable link between the so-called liturgy of the catechumens, dedicated primarily to the word of God, and the liturgy of the faithful, consisting of the offering, consecration and distribution of the holy gifts.

Meanwhile, our official textbooks, our theological explanations and definitions of the eucharist practically ignore this unanimous testimony. In the life and practice of the Church the eucharist consists of two inseparably linked parts. But in theological reflection it is reduced to only one—the second—part, i.e., to what is accomplished over the bread and wine, as if this second part were self-contained and unrelated, whether spiritually or theologically, to the first.

This "reduction" is explained, of course, by the influence on our school theology of western ideas, in which *word* and *sacrament* long ago lost touch with each other and became subjects of independent study and definition. However, this rift constitutes one of the chief deficiencies in the western doctrine on the sacraments. After being adopted de facto by our school systems, it sooner or later led to an erroneous, onesided and distorted understanding both of *word*—i.e., holy scripture and its place in the life of the Church—and *sacrament*. I daresay that the gradual "decomposition" of scripture, its dissolution in more and more specialized and negative criticism, is a result of its alienation from the eucharist—and practically from the Church herself—as an experience of a spiritual reality. And in its own turn, this same alienation deprived the sacrament of its evangelical content, converting it into a self-contained and self-sufficient "means of sanctification." The scriptures and the Church are reduced here to the category of two formal *authorities*, two "sources of the faith"—as they are called in the scholastic treatises, for which the only question is which authority is the higher: which "interprets" which.

As a matter of fact, by its own logic, this approach demands a further contraction, a further "reduction." For if we proclaim

[1]Justin Martyr, *First Apology*, 67:3-5, tr. C.C. Richardson, *Early Christian Fathers*, Library of Christian Classics 1 (New York, 1970) 287.

holy scripture to be the supreme authority for teaching the faith in the Church, then what is the "criterion" of scripture? Sooner or later it becomes "biblical science"—i.e., in the final analysis, naked reason. But if, on the other hand, we proclaim the Church to be the definitive, highest and inspired interpreter of scripture, then through whom, where and how is this interpretation brought about? And however we answer this question, this "organ" or "authority" in fact proves to be standing *over* the scriptures, as an *outside* authority. If in the first instance the meaning of scripture is dissolved in a multiplicity of private—and therefore devoid of ecclesial authority—"scientific theories," then in the second case the scriptures are considered the "raw material" for theological definition and formulation, "biblical matter" available to be "interpreted" by theological reason. And it would be incorrect to think that this position is characteristic only of the West. The very same thing, though possibly in a different manner, happens also in the Orthodox Church. For, if Orthodox theologians firmly hold to the formal principle that the authoritative interpretation of scripture belongs to the Church and is accomplished in the light of tradition, then the vital content and "practical" application of this principle remain unclear and in fact lead to a certain paralysis of the "understanding of scripture" in the life of the Church. Insofar as it exists, our biblical scholarship finds itself entirely in the grasp of western presuppositions and timidly repeats outmoded western positions, clinging as much as possible to the "moderate," i.e., in fact the penultimate, western theories. And as far as church preaching and piety are concerned, they too have long since ceased to be "fed" by, to find their true source in the scriptures.

This "rupture" between word and sacrament has pernicious consequences also for the doctrine on the sacraments. In it, the sacrament ceases to be biblical and, in the deepest sense of the word, *evangelical*. It was no accident, of course, that the chief focus of interest in the sacraments for western theology was not their essence and content but rather the conditions and "modi" of their accomplishment and "efficacy." Thus, the interpretation of the eucharist revolves around the question of the method and moment of the transformation of the gifts, their conversion into the body and blood of Christ, but with almost no mention of the meaning of this transformation for the Church, for the world, for each of us. As much as it may seem paradoxical, "interest" in the *real presence* of the body and blood of Christ replaces "interest" in Christ. Partaking of the gifts is perceived as one of the means for "receiving grace," as an act of personal sanctification, but it ceases to be perceived as our *participation* in Christ's cup: "Are you able to drink the cup that I drink, or to be baptized with the baptism with which I am baptized?" (Mk 10:38). Alienated from the word, which is always the word of Christ ("You search the scriptures...and it is they that bear witness to me"—Jn 5:39), the sacrament is in a certain sense torn away from Christ. Both in theology and in piety he remains, of course, their "founder," but he ceases to be their *content*—the gift to the Church and to the faithful of his very self and of his divine-human life. Thus, the sacrament of confession is experienced not as "reconciliation and reunification with the Church in Christ Jesus" but as the *authority* to "forgive" sins; thus, the sacrament of marriage has "forgotten" its foundation in "the great mystery of Christ and the Church," etc.

Yet in the liturgical and spiritual tradition of the Church, the Church's essence as the incarnation of the Word, as the fulfilment in time and space of the divine incarnation, is realized precisely in the unbreakable link between the word and the sacrament. Thus the book of Acts can say of the *Church*: "the word...grew and multiplied" (12:24). In the sacrament we partake of him who comes and abides with us in the word, and the mission of the Church consists precisely in announcing this good news. The word presupposes the sacrament as its fulfilment, for in the sacrament Christ the Word becomes our life. The Word assembles the Church for his incarnation in her. In separation from the word the sacrament is in danger of being perceived as magic, and without the sacrament the word is in danger of being "reduced" to "doctrine." And, finally, it is precisely through the sacrament that the word is interpreted, for the interpretation of the word is always witness to the fact that the Word has become our life. "And the Word became flesh and dwelt among us, full of grace and truth" (Jn 1:14). The sacrament is his witness, and therefore in it lies the source, the beginning and the foundation of the exposition and comprehension of the word, the source and criterion of theology.

Only in this unbreakable unity of word and sacrament can we truly understand the meaning of the affirmation that the Church alone preserves the true meaning of scripture. That is why the necessary *beginning* of the eucharistic ceremony is the first part of the liturgy—the *sacrament of the word*, which finds its fulfilment and completion in the offering, consecration and distribution to the faithful of the eucharistic gifts.

2

IN SEVERAL EARLY MANUSCRIPTS OF THE SERVICE BOOKS THE Little Entrance is called the *entrance with the gospels*. And in its contemporary form its central focus is in actuality the gospel book: it is triumphally carried out of the northern door of the iconostasis by the deacon and then brought through the royal doors and placed on the altar. Taking into consideration what was said above about the original meaning of the Little Entrance as the entrance of the celebrant and the people into the temple, it is obvious that the "entrance with the gospels" is, as it were, its second "form." In antiquity, after the entrance into the temple the celebrant and the concelebrating clergy assumed "their places" to listen to the scriptures. Today, the original Little Entrance having ceased to be the real beginning of the liturgy, it is precisely the "entrance with the gospels" that has taken over the meaning of this procession. In order to understand this meaning, it is necessary to say a few words about the original "topography" of the church building.

In contemporary practice, the altar is the natural and self-evident "place" of the celebrant and the clergy. But in ancient times this was not so. *Approach* to the altar and serving at it was restricted exclusively to the liturgy of the faithful, i.e., the offering and consecration of the holy gifts—the eucharist in the strict sense of the term. The celebrant would go up to the altar only at the moment of the offering of the gifts. The rest of the time—just as in the services of the daily and yearly cycle—the place of the celebrant and the clergy was on the "bema," i.e., among the people. This is indicated to this very day by the location of the bishop's throne—in the middle of the church among the Russians, on the right side of the ambo among the Greeks. And in fact even now, the most important parts of the noneucharistic services—the *polye-leion*, for example—are performed in the middle of the church and not in the altar. Thus, the altar table was exclusively the *table* of the Lord's supper, the sacrificial table on which the bloodless sacrifice was offered. The service had, as it were, two centers: one in the gathering itself and another at the altar. Therefore the first part of the liturgy—the "assembly as the Church," the listening to the scriptures and the homily—took place not in the altar but in the temple, with the celebrant and the clergy having assumed their special places on the bema. The *entrance* into the temple (the first meaning of the Little Entrance) was followed by the ascent of the celebrant and the clergy to "their place" for the celebration of the liturgy of the word (the second meaning of the Little Entrance), and after this, their ascent into the sanctuary and to the altar table for the offering and consecration of the gifts (the current Great Entrance). Through these three "entrances" (processions) the fundamental symbolism of the gathering of the Church as her ascent to the kingdom of God was expressed.

What caused the disruption and alteration of this original order was, in the first place, the disappearance of the first entrance —the entrance into the temple—and, secondly, the gradual disappearance of the bema as the place of the celebrant and the clergy during virtually all services *except the eucharist itself*. This disappearance was furthered when the gospel book began to be kept on the altar. During the persecution of Christianity, the gospels were not kept in the temple, as one form of persecution of the Church was confiscation of the holy books. Therefore, at each liturgy the gospel book was brought into the church from outside. But with the cessation of persecution and the appearance of majestic Christian basilicas, the place for the keeping of the gospels naturally became the temple, and in it, its "holy of holies"—the altar. The altar became the focus of both parts of the liturgy, although in different ways. Thus, in the so-called liturgy of the catechumens, as well as in all noneucharistic services, the gospels are *brought out* from the altar and to this day are read in the middle of the church, on the ambo or from the cathedra, while the eucharist is always performed at the altar.

All these "technical" details are necessary for us only in order to show that the Little Entrance gradually united three fundamental dimensions: the beginning of the eucharist as *entrance* into the assembly; then, the fulfilment of this first entrance in the ascent, in the entrance of the Church into the heavenly sanctuary (the prayer and singing of the Trisagion, the approach to the altar); and, finally, the fulfilment of this beginning of the liturgy in the "sacrament of the word."

Returning now to the "entrance with the gospels," we can say that it is no less important for an understanding of the liturgy of the word and its connection with the eucharist than is the basic act of the reading of the holy scriptures. Here we find a parallelism with the eucharist, in which the consecration of the gifts is preceded by the *offering*. It is appropriate here to recall that the gospels are part of the Orthodox liturgical tradition not only in their reading, but precisely as a *book*. This book is rendered the same reverence as an icon or the altar. We are called to kiss it and to cense it, and the people of God are blessed with it. Finally, in several rites—the *cheirotonia* of a bishop, the sacraments of confession and holy unction, etc.—the gospels take part as a *book*, and not as one or another text contained in it. This is because, for the Church, the gospel book is a verbal icon of Christ's manifestation to and presence among us. Above all, it is an icon of his resurrection. The entrance with the gospels is therefore not a "representation," a sacred dramatization of events of the past—e.g., Christ's going out to preach (in which case it would be not the deacon, but the celebrant, as the image of Christ in the ecclesial assembly, who should carry the gospel book). It is the image of the appearance of the risen Lord in fulfilment of his promise: "where two or three are gathered in my name, there am I in the midst of them" (Mt 18:20). As the consecration of the eucharistic gifts is preceded by their offering at the sacrificial table, so the reading and proclamation of the word is preceded by its *appearance*. The "entrance with the gospels" is a meeting, a joyous meeting with Christ, and this meeting is accomplished by means of the bringing out to us of this book of books, the book that is always transformed into power, life and sanctification.

3

"PEACE BE UNTO ALL!" THE CELEBRANT PROCLAIMS TO THE
assembly, and the people answer him: "And to your spirit." We
have already pointed out that *Peace* is the name of Christ himself.
The western form of this greeting is *Dominus vobiscum*, "the Lord
be with you." And this greeting, with which the celebrant ad-
dresses the Church before each new part of the eucharistic ceremony—before the reading of the word of God, before the kiss of
peace, before the distribution of communion—is each time a reminder that Christ himself is "in our midst," that he himself
heads our eucharist, for he himself is "the Offerer and the Offered, the Receiver and the Received."

Then the *prokeimenon* is intoned. This word, which in Greek
means "what is set forth"—i.e., what *precedes*—is now used to refer
to two or three verses of the psalms, sung antiphonally—by the
reader and the people, or the choir. In antiquity the prokeimenon
usually consisted of the entire psalm, the singing of which "preceded" the reading of holy scripture. And since the prokeimenon
to this day occupies a special and undoubtedly important place in
Orthodox worship, it is necessary to say a few words about it.

In order to understand the prokeimenon, we must first recall
the special place the psalms held in the early Church. Without
exaggeration it could be said that in the early Church the psalms
were not only one of the prophetic or liturgical "high points" of
the Old Testament, but a kind of special "revelation inside the
revelation." If all scripture prophesies about Christ, the exceptional significance of the psalms lies in the fact that in them
Christ is revealed as though from "within." These are *his* words,
his prayer: ". . . ipse Dominus Jesus Christus locutus," "the Lord
Jesus Christ himself speaks in them" (Augustine).[2] And because
they are his words, they are also the prayer and words of his body,
the Church. "In this book speak, pray and weep only Jesus Christ
and his Church," writes Augustine. "These many members, united in the bonds of love and peace under one head—our Savior
—constitute, as you know . . . one man. And in the better part of

[2]*Enarratio in Ps.* XXX, 11, PL 36:237.

the psalms, their voice sounds as the voice of one man. He implores for all, because all are one in unity."[3] This understanding, this *experience* of the psalms also lies at the heart of their liturgical usage. Thus, for example, it is impossible to understand the pre-eminent place of Psalm 119 ("Blessed are those whose way is blameless") in matins of Holy Saturday unless we know that in this lengthy confession of love for the "law of God," for his will, for his design for the world and mankind, the Church in a way hears the voice of the Lord himself, as he lies in the tomb and reveals to us the meaning of his lifegiving death. In this way, the psalms are not only a divinely inspired "exegesis," an explanation of scripture and the events of sacred history. In them is expressed and incarnated and handed down to us that spiritual *reality* that allows us to comprehend the true meaning both of the sacred texts and of the rites.

The *prokeimenon*—"the psalm that precedes"—*introduces* us to the sacrament of the word. For the word of God is addressed not to the reason alone, but to the whole man—to his depths or, in the language of the holy fathers, to his *heart*, which is also an organ of religious knowledge, in contrast to the imperfect, discursive and rational knowledge of "this world." The "opening of the mind" precedes the hearing and understanding of the word: "Then he opened their minds to understand the scriptures" (Lk 24:45). We can say that the joyous, repeated exclamation of the prokeimenon, its "communication" to the assembly and its acceptance by the gathering also express that moment in worship of the "opening of the mind," its union with the *heart*, when we listen to the word of the scriptures, the word of the Lord.

4

AFTER THE PROKEIMENON COMES THE READING OF THE *epistle*, i.e., a passage from the second—the "apostolic"—part of the New Testament. We have every reason to think that in antiquity the reading of holy scripture included passages from the Old Testament. A detailed study of the "lectionary," i.e., the princi-

---

[3]*Enarratio in Ps.* LXIX, 1, PL 36:866.

ples on which the liturgical distribution of the reading of holy
scripture was based, belongs to that part of liturgical theology
that I call the *liturgy of time*,[4] and therefore we may put aside its
explanation for now. It is enough to say that the *lectionary* experienced a long and complex evolution, and that one of the vital
tasks of our time consists in reviewing it in the light of our contemporary liturgical "situation." In order to grasp the seriousness
of this issue, it is enough to recall that the current lectionary excludes the greater part of the Old Testament from liturgical
reading. As for the New Testament, since the lectionary is constructed on the presupposition of a daily liturgy, only a comparatively small part of the New Testament texts actually reaches the
ears and consciousness of the faithful. Hence the striking ignorance of the holy scriptures among the overwhelming majority of
Orthodox and, stemming from this ignorance, the absence of interest in them. They are not perceived as the chief, incomparable
and truly *saving* source of faith and life. In our Church the "akath-
ist" is immeasurably more popular than the scriptures. Inasmuch
as all our worship is structured in a "biblical" key, this ultimately
leads to incomprehension of the services, to a rupture between
liturgical piety and the genuine meaning of the *lex orandi*, the
rule of prayer.

    After the epistle the gospel is read. The reading is preceded
by the singing of the *alleluia* and the *censing*. In contemporary
practice the alleluia verses take up no more than two or three minutes, allowing the deacon time only to take the gospel book from
the priest and proceed toward the ambo. As a result, the censing
is not done as prescribed—during the singing of the alleluia—but
rather during the reading of the epistle. Finally, the celebrant's
prayer before the reading of the gospel, in which the Church asks
God to "open the eyes of our mind to the understanding of Thy
gospel teachings," is now read silently, depriving the faithful of
the opportunity of hearing it. All this, taken together, obscures
the original meaning of the *rite* of the liturgy of the word. Nevertheless, this rite is important for understanding the link betweeen
the liturgy of the word and the sacrament of the eucharist, and
therefore it is necessary to say a few words about it.

---

[4]See Schmemann, *Introduction to Liturgical Theology*, 49-57.

Our first consideration here must be the singing of the alleluia verses, which in antiquity comprised an important part of all Christian worship. Inherited by Christianity from Hebrew worship, the alleluia belongs to the type of the so-called *melismatic* singing. In the history of church music, melismatic, as opposed to *psalmodic*, refers to a form in which the melody takes precedence over the word. One may suppose that before the appearance of more "learned" hymnology—troparia, kontakia, stichera, in which the music and the text mutually define each other—the Church knew only two types of singing, corresponding to two fundamental aspects of the Christian perception of worship. *Psalmodic* singing, i.e., the melodic, rhythmic and musical reading of the psalms, scriptures and prayers, expressed the *verbal* nature of Christian worship, its inner subordination to the word: the holy scriptures, the apostolic witness, the tradition of faith. *Melismatic* singing, however, expressed the experience of worship as a real contact with the *transcendent*, an entry into the supernatural reality of the kingdom. Whatever was the source of melismatic singing—and there are several scholarly theories about its origin—there is no doubt that in early Christian worship it occupied a significant place and that one of its chief expressions was precisely the singing of the *alleluia*. For this term itself is not simply a word, but a certain melodic exclamation. Its logical content can of course be translated with the words "praise God," but by this content it is not exhausted and not in fact translated, for the word itself *is* a transport of joy and praise before the appearance of the Lord, a "reaction" to his coming. The historian of religion G. Van der Leeuw writes that, "when moved by the presence of God, man cries out." He "lifts up" his voice. "But the most important type of profoundly emotional utterance is *praise*: the *song of praise*."[5] The alleluia is a *greeting* in the most profound sense of the term. And a genuine greeting, in the words of the same Van der Leeuw, is "always a confirmation of a fact." It presupposes a *manifestation*, and it is a reaction to this manifestation. The alleluia verses precede the reading of the gospel because, as we have already said above, the appearance of the Lord in the "assembly as the Church" and his opening of the minds of the faith-

[5]*Religion in Essence and Manifestation* (London, 1938) 430.

ful precedes the *hearing*. The ancient melody of the alleluia has come down to us as a sound, a melody expressing the joy and praise and experience of a presence that is more real than any words, than any explanations.

At the same time as the singing of the alleluia—and not during the reading of the epistle, as is usually the case today—the *censing* of the gospel book and of the assembly takes place. This ancient religious rite, common to a multitude of religions, was not immediately accepted by the Church because of its ties with pagan cults: in the era of persecution, Christians were ordered to burn incense before images of the emperor, thus rendering him divine worship. But it subsequently entered into church worship precisely as a "natural" religious rite, in which everything—the burning charcoal and incense transformed into fragrance and ascending to heaven as smoke—"expresses" the creatures' adoration of the Creator and his holiness, present among the people.

The celebrant reads the *prayer before the gospel*, in which he asks God to send down the "pure light of Thy divine knowledge. Open the eyes of our mind to the understanding of Thy gospel teachings." This prayer, which is now read silently, occupies the same place in the sacrament of the word that the *epiklesis*, the supplication for the Father to send down his Holy Spirit, occupies in the eucharistic prayer. Like the consecration of the gifts, *understanding* and *acceptance* of the word depend not on us, not only on our desire, but above all on the sacramental transformation of the "eyes of our mind," on the coming to us of the Holy Spirit. The blessing that the priest bestows on the deacon as he is about to read the gospel testifies to this: "May God...enable you to proclaim the glad tidings with *great power, to the fulfillment of the gospel...*"

5

THE HOMILY IS A WITNESS TO THE HEARING OF THE WORD OF God, its reception and understanding. Therefore it is organically connected to the reading of scripture and, in the early Church, constituted a necessary part of the "synaxis," an essential liturgical act of the Church. This act is the eternal self-witness of the

Holy Spirit, who lives in the Church and guides her into all the truth (Jn 16:13), the Spirit of truth, "whom the world cannot receive, because it neither sees him nor knows him"—but "you know him, for he dwells with you, and will be in you" (Jn 14:17). In these "texts" the Church hears and recognizes, and will forever continue to recognize, hear and proclaim the word of God. Only in this way can she genuinely proclaim to "this world" the good news about Christ, can she witness to him—and not just expound her "doctrine"—because she herself always listens to the word of God, she lives by it, so that her very life is to *increase in the word*: "And the word of God increased; and the number of the disciples multiplied greatly" (Ac 6:7); "So the word of the Lord grew and prevailed mightily" (Ac 19:20).

One can observe an undoubted decline or even crisis in preaching in contemporary church life. The essence of this crisis lies not in the inability to speak, in a loss of "style" or in any intellectual deficiency on the part of the preacher, but in something far deeper: in an oblivion to *what* preaching in the church assembly is supposed to be. The homily can be, and often is even today, intelligent, interesting, instructive and comforting, but these are not the criteria by which we can distinguish a "good" homily from a "bad" one—these are not its real essence. Its essence lies in its living link to the gospel that was read in the church assembly. For the genuine sermon is neither simply an explanation of what was read by knowledgeable and competent persons, nor a transmission to the listeners of the theological knowledge of the preacher, nor a meditation "a propos" of the gospel text. In general, it is not a sermon *about the gospel* ("on a gospel theme"), but the preaching of the gospel itself. The crisis of preaching consists chiefly in that it has become a sort of "personal" matter of the preacher. We say, for example, that a given preacher has or does not have a gift for speaking. Yet the genuine gift for speaking, for proclaiming the good news, is not an "immanent" gift of the preacher, but a charism of the Holy Spirit, given in the Church and to the Church. Genuine proclamation of the good news does not exist without faith that the "assembly as the Church" is really an assembly in the Holy Spirit, where the same one Spirit opens the preacher's lips to proclamation and the hearers' minds to acceptance of what is proclaimed.

The condition for true preaching therefore must be precisely
the complete self-denial of the preacher, the repudiation of everything that is *only his own*, even his *own* gifts and talents. The mystery of church preaching, in contrast to any purely human "gift
for speaking," is accomplished, according to the words of the
apostle Paul, "not [by] proclaiming [it] to you... in lofty words
or wisdom. For I decided to know nothing among you except Jesus Christ and him crucified.... and my speech and my message
were not in plausible words of wisdom, but in demonstration of
the Spirit and power, that your faith might not rest in the wisdom
of men but in the power of God" (1 Co 2:1-5). Witness to Jesus
Christ by the Holy Spirit is the content of the word of God, and
this alone constitutes the essence of preaching: "And the Spirit is
the witness, because the Spirit is the truth" (1 Jn 5:7). The ambo
is the place where the sacrament of the word takes place, and
therefore it must never be turned into a tribune for the proclamation of even the most elevated, most positive, but only human
truth, only human wisdom. "Yet among the mature we do impart wisdom, although it is not the wisdom of this age or of the
rulers of this age, who are doomed to pass away. But we impart a
secret and hidden wisdom of God, which God decreed before the
ages for our glorification" (1 Co 2:6-7).

Here we see why all church theology, all *tradition*, grows precisely out of the "assembly as the Church," out of this sacrament
of proclamation of the good news. Here we see why in it is comprehended the living, and not abstract, meaning of the classic
Orthodox affirmation that only the Church is given custody of the
scriptures and their interpretation. For tradition is not *another*
source of the faith, "complementary" to the scriptures. It is the
very same source: the living word of God, always heard and received by the Church. Tradition is the interpretation of the word
of God as the source of life itself, and not of any "constructions"
or "deductions." When St Athanasius the Great said that "the
holy and God-inspired scriptures are sufficient for the exposition
of truth,"[6] he was not rejecting tradition, and still less preaching
any specifically "biblical" method of theology—as a formal, terminological faithfulness to the scriptural "text"—for, as everyone

---

[6]*Against the Pagans*, 1, PG 25:4A.

knows, in expounding the faith of the Church he himself daringly introduced the nonbiblical term *homoousios*. He was affirming precisely the living, and not formal or terminological, link between scripture and tradition, tradition as the reading and hearing of scripture in the Holy Spirit. The Church alone knows and keeps the meaning of scripture, because in the sacrament of the word, accomplished in the church assembly, the Holy Spirit eternally gives life to the "flesh" of scripture, transforming it into "spirit and life." Any genuine theology is rooted in this sacrament of the word, in the church assembly, in which the Spirit of God exhorts the Church herself—and not simply her individual members —into all truth. Thus, any "private" reading of scripture must be rooted in the Church: outside of the mind of the Church, outside of the divine-human life of the Church it can neither be heard nor truly interpreted. So, the sacrament of the word, accomplished in the church gathering in a twofold act—reading and proclamation—is the source of the growth of each and all together into the fulness of the mind of truth.

Finally, in the sacrament of the word is revealed the collaboration of the hierarchy and the laity in the preservation of truth, which, in accordance with the famous Epistle of the Eastern Patriarchs (1869), is "entrusted to the whole people of the Church."[7] On the one hand, in preaching the gift of *teaching* is realized: it is a charism given to the celebrant as his service in the church assembly. On the other hand, and precisely because preaching is not a "personal gift" but a charism given by the Church and realized in her gathering, the teaching service of the hierarchy is not separate from the gathering but finds in it its grace-filled source. The Holy Spirit rests on the entire Church. The ministry of the celebrant is preaching and teaching. The ministry of the people of God is in accepting this teaching. But both these ministries are of the Holy Spirit, both are accomplished by him and in him. One can neither accept nor proclaim the truth without the gift of the Holy Spirit, and this gift is given to the entire assembly. For the entire Church—and not one "sector" in it—have "received not the

[7]*Encyclical Letter of the One, Holy, Catholic and Apostolic Church to the Orthodox Christians of All Lands* (the response of the patriarchs of Constantinople, Alexandria, Antioch and Jerusalem and the synods of Constantinople, Antioch and Jerusalem to Pius IX's encyclical of January 6, 1848 to the Christians of the East).

spirit of the world, but the Spirit which is from God, that we
might understand the gifts bestowed on us by God." "No one
comprehends the thoughts of God except the Spirit of God," and
therefore those who are teaching do so "in words not taught by
human wisdom but taught by the Spirit, interpreting spiritual
truths to those who possess the Spirit," and those who accept the
teaching accept it by the Holy Spirit. "For the unspiritual man
does not receive the gifts of the Spirit of God, for they are folly to
him, and he is not able to understand them" (1 Co 2:11-14). In
the Church, the bishop and priests are given the gift of teaching,
but they are given it because they are witnesses to the faith of the
Church, because the teaching is not theirs but the Church's, her
unity of faith and love. Only the entire Church, manifested and
actualized in the "assembly as the Church," has the mind of
Christ. Only in the church gathering are all gifts, all ministries
revealed in their unity and indivisibility, as manifestations of the
one Spirit, who fills the whole body. And therefore, finally, each
member of the Church, whatever his "rank" in the Church, must
be a witness before this world of the entire fulness of the Church,
and not just his *own* understanding of it.

In antiquity, the assembly responded to the celebrant's sermon with a triumphal *amen*, testifying by this to the acceptance of
the word, sealing their unity in the Spirit with the celebrant.
Here, in this *amen* of the people of God, is the source and principle of that "reception" of teaching by church consciousness, of
which Orthodox theologians speak so often, contraposing it to the
Roman division of the Church into the *learning* Church and the
teaching Church, and also to Protestant individualism. But if it is
so difficult to explain in what this "reception" consists and in
what manner it is realized, perhaps this is because in our own
consciousness we have almost entirely forgotten that this act is
rooted in the church assembly and in the sacrament of the word
accomplished in it.

CHAPTER FIVE

The Sacrament of the Faithful

"Let us, the faithful..."

I

*T*HE FIRST PART OF THE LITURGY, WHICH, AS WE HAVE seen, consists of the assembly as the Church, the entrance and the sacrament of the word, is completed with the so-called "Litany of Fervent Supplication" or "Augmented Litany," special petitions and prayers for the catechumens, i.e., those who are preparing for baptism, and their dismissal from the church assembly. Like the Great Litany, the "Augmented" Litany is an inalienable part not only of the eucharistic liturgy but of every church service. But while we find the Great Litany at the beginning of each service, the Augmented Litany as a rule comes at its conclusion. Today the distinction between the two—the opening and closing litanies—has almost entirely vanished. The Augmented Litany consists of the same petitions in the same order as the Great Litany, and thus, in the Greek practice, for instance, it is simply omitted as being redundant, and the service proceeds directly to the next part of the eucharistic ceremony. But in its original design, the Augmented Litany was not only not "repetitious"—i.e., a repetition, with minor changes, of the Great Litany—but fulfilled a function in the service the opposite of that which the Great Litany embodies. What was this function?

In order to answer this question, one must recall that all of Christianity, the entire life of the Church, is constructed on the

conjoining of what at first glance appear to be two mutually contradictory affirmations. On the one hand the Church, like Christ,
and because she is Christ's, is directed to the whole world, to all
of creation, to all humanity. Christ sacrificed himself "on behalf
of all and for all," and he sent his disciples, and therefore the
Church, "into all the world [to] preach the gospel to the whole
creation" (Mk 16:15). He is the *Savior of the world*. On the other
hand, the Church affirms that through his saving love Christ is
turned to each human being, for each human being, unique and
unrepeatable, is not only an object of this love of Christ's but is
also linked with Christ by the uniqueness of God's design for each
human being. From here stems the antinomy that lies at the foundation of Christian life. The Christian is called to deny himself, to
"lay down his life for his friends"; and the same Christian is summoned to "despise the flesh, for it passes away, but to care instead
for the soul, for it is immortal." In order to save "one of the least
of these" the shepherd left the ninety-nine, but the same
Church—for the sake of her purity and fulness—cuts off sinners
from herself.

We find this same polarization in religious thought. There
are always those in the Church who experience the cosmic, universal calling of the Church with special force, but there are also
those who are, as it were, blind and deaf to all this and see in
Christianity above all a religion of "personal salvation." The same
holds true in piety, in the prayers and intercessions of the Church.
On the one hand they call man to the unity of love and faith, in
order to fulfil the Church as the body of Christ. On the other,
they are open to my needs, to my sorrows, to my joy. While not
rejecting the "liturgy," i.e., the Church as the *common task*, afterward the believer requests that *his* prayer service, *his* memorial
service, be served. And here, whatever possible distortions are
contained in both experiences of Christianity, one can hardly
doubt that they both are equally rooted in its very essence. For the
antinomy of Christianity consists in the fact that it is simultaneously directed to the whole—to the entire creation, the whole
world, all mankind—and to each unique and unrepeatable human
person. And if the fulfilment of the human personality lies in
"keeping council with all," then the fulfilment of the world lies
in its becoming life for everyone to whom God has given this

world as life. The Christian faith can say that the world was created for each individual, and it can say that each person was created for the world, to surrender himself for "the life of the world."

In practice, in everyday life, it proves to be very difficult to maintain a balance between these two "dimensions," inseparable from each other and equally essential for Christianity. But if it is inevitable and even legitimate that there be a certain variety in the experience of each separate person, in the mystery of his personal calling and participation in the "economy" of the Church, then in the Church's rule of faith, expressed in her rule of prayer, is disclosed to us the fulness of the Church's twofold calling.

In order to sense and identify this, let us compare the first—the "great"—litany, with the last and concluding—the "augmented"—litany. The Great Litany bestows on us, reveals the prayer of the Church, or, still better, *the Church as prayer*, as precisely the "common task," in its full cosmic and universal extent. In the church assembly man is called above all to give up, to "lay aside" his "cares" for everything that is only *his own*, personal, private, and as it were to "dissolve" himself and what is his own in the prayer of the Church. The Great Litany discloses the Christian "hierarchy of values"; and only to the extent that each participant accepts it as his own can he fulfil his "membership," overcoming that egoism that very often taints and perverts the Church and religious life itself. The personal and the concrete, however, are not excluded from the Church's prayer. And here is the essence of the concluding, Augmented Litany: in it the Church focuses her prayer on the "private," personal needs of men. If in the first case, in the Great Litany, everything private "dies" as it were in the *whole*, then here all the power of the Church's prayer, all her love, is concentrated on *this person*, on his *needs*. But it is only because we could first identify ourselves with the *general*, in the love of Christ, because we could liberate ourselves from our egocentrism, that we can now, through the love of Christ, abiding in the Church, turn to "every Christian soul that is afflicted and weary in well-doing, in need of God's mercy and help" (petition from the vesperal litē).

In its contemporary form the Augmented Litany does not quite fulfil this function, as it reflects the tendency, common to the services, of becoming *fixed*. Thus, for example, at every liturgy, in one of its petitions we pray "for the priests, hieromonks, and all our brotherhood in Christ." This petition originated and became established in the liturgy in Jerusalem; it is a "local" petition regarding the members of the Brotherhood of the Holy Sepulchre. Fully appropriate in Jerusalem, it is incomprehensible for the overwhelming majority of the faithful in other locales. Yet even with this "fixing" the Augmented Litany remains to a certain measure open: even now special petitions—for the sick, travelers, people celebrating some family event, etc.—are inserted. This practice needs to be explained in greater depth. For whenever private memorial and prayer services are detached from the liturgy, from the "common task," and become private "services of need" (treby), the correlation of the *common* and the *personal* in church consciousness itself is weakened, and we cease to perceive the liturgy as simultaneously the cosmic sacrament of the salvation of the world and the offering to God of "the afflictions of the people, the sighings of the captives, the sufferings of the poor, the needs of travelers, the afflictions of the infirm, the infirmities of the aged, the wailing of the infants, the promises of virgins, the prayers of widows, the tenderness of orphans..." (prayer of St Ambrose of Milan).

Regarding this separation of private "services of need" from the liturgy, Archimandrite Kiprian Kern writes: "...the serving of any *treby* after the liturgy so contradicts the spirit of our worship...The serving of prayer services after the liturgy is a liturgical contradiction."[1] The whole point, however, is that this essentially correct accusation remains fruitless as long as the balance between the common and the private is not restored within the liturgy itself, as long as, in other words, everything personal and private is not again embraced by and directed to the general, to the one and undivided love of Christ—the sacrament of which we accomplish in the eucharist.

2

AFTER THE "FERVENT SUPPLICATION" WE RECITE THE LITANY for the catechumens, read the prayer associated with it and then

[1]*Evkharistia*, 341-2.

"dismiss" the catechumens. In antiquity, *catechumens* referred to Christians who were preparing for baptism—which at that time was not performed as it is now, on any day whatsoever and, moreover, as a private "service of need," but on paschal eve. This preparation for baptism, as we already know, sometimes lasted for a rather long period of time—a year or two—and consisted of both the instruction of the new converts in the truths of the faith and their gradual introduction into the liturgical life of the Church. In time, the institution of the catechumenate gradually vanished, for baptism came to be primarily performed on infants, and the contemporary prayers for the catechumens sound somewhat like an anachronism and, even more serious, a case of nominalism. "It is not known whom the church community directs to pray," writes Fr Kiprian Kern, "when the deacon exclaims 'pray to the Lord, you catechumens'; it is not known whom the deacon is asking to leave the liturgical assembly when he says 'depart, catechumens...' There are no catechumens, and the prayer and the litany are pronounced for people whom the Church in general doesn't have among her members or in general doesn't intend to teach, enlighten and baptize."[2] Because of this, the Greek Orthodox Church long ago dispensed with this litany, proceeding directly from the "fervent supplication" to the Cherubic Hymn, i.e., the beginning of the offering. And among the Russians, even before the revolution, during the preparations for the Moscow church council, a part of the hierarchy came out in favor of omitting this part of the liturgy because it did not answer to any real needs of the Church. All these arguments, of course, are weighty enough and true, according to Archimandrite Kiprian, who observed that "the reasoning of the majority of the church conservatives, that we should humbly apply the words and petitions about the catechumens to ourselves and equate ourselves with them, is stretching it a bit."[3] Nominalism can have no place in church life. But at some point it is appropriate to ask how nominal these petitions are and what is the proper meaning of the "relevance of the services to real needs"?

One of the essential functions of liturgical tradition is to preserve the fulness of the Christian conception and doctrine of the

[2] *Ibid.*, 188-9.
[3] *Ibid.*, 189.

world, of the Church, of man—a fulness that neither one individual man, one epoch nor one generation by itself is capable of
either accommodating or preserving. Each of us as well as each
"culture" or society will, conscious of it or not, *choose* precisely
what it is in Christianity that answers to our "needs" or problems.
It is therefore extremely important that the *tradition* of the
Church, her order, dogmatic definitions and rule of prayer, not
allow any of these "choices," or opinions and adaptations, to be
identified with the fulness of Christian revelation. A process of
reevaluation of tradition from the point of view of its relevance to
the "needs of the time" and the "questions of contemporary man"
is occurring right now in western Christianity. And the criterion
for what is eternal and what is obsolete in Christianity is almost
without any argument declared to be precisely "contemporary
man" and "contemporary culture." In order to suit these, some
are ready to discard from the Church everything that appears to be
"irrelevant." This is the eternal temptation of modernism, which
periodically disturbs the church organism. And therefore, when
people talk about this or that obsolete custom or tradition, it is
always necessary to show the utmost care and to put the question
not in terms of its relevance or irrelevance to what is "contemporary," but in terms of whether it expresses something eternal and
essential in Christianity, even if it outwardly seems "obsolete."

Applying what has been said to the prayers for the catechumens, we must ask ourselves above all what they express, to what
they are relevant in the order of Christian worship. Is it accidental
that in the past the Church attached such significance to them
that the entire first part of the eucharistic gathering eventually
came to be called the "liturgy of the catechumens"? Does this not
mean that there was a profound direction to the whole first part,
its very essence, which one cannot simply do away with without
touching something very important to the basic meaning of the
liturgy? Or, by analogy, it could be asked: inasmuch as the liturgy is often served without communicants even on a Sunday, why
not serve it only when there are communicants? Certain Protestant communities do precisely that, thinking that in this way
they avoid "nominalism." In other words, what must we see in
the prayers for the catechumens—only a dried and withered limb
(not unlike the royal Many Years, which fell away when there no

longer was an Orthodox tsar), or an essential part of the very *order of Christian worship?*

I believe that the latter is closer to the truth. For the prayers for the catechumens are above all a liturgical expression of a fundamental calling of the Church—precisely *the Church as mission.* The Church came into the world as mission—"Go into all the world and preach the gospel to the whole creation" (Mk 16:15)—and cannot, without betraying her nature, cease to be mission. Historically, of course, the prayers for the catechumens were introduced at a time when the Church not only contained the institution of the catechumenate but in actuality considered herself directed toward the world with the aim of converting it to Christist, when she considered the world as an object of mission. Then the historical setting changed, and it seemed that the world had become Christian. But do we not live again today in a world that has either turned away from Christianity or has never even heard of Christ? Is not *mission* again in the center of church consciousness? And is it not a sin against this basic calling when the Church, the ecclesial community, locks herself in her "inner" life and considers herself called only "to attend to the spiritual needs" of her members and thus for all intents and purposes denies that mission is a basic ministry and task of the Church in "this world"?

Perhaps in our day it is important precisely to preserve the structure of worship that conjoins mission and the fruits of mission: the "liturgy of the catechumens" and the "liturgy of the faithful." For whom do we pray when we hear the petitions of the Litany of the Catechumens: "that the Lord may have mercy on them...that He may teach them the word of truth...reveal to them the gospel of righteousness...unite them to His Holy, Catholic, and Apostolic Church"? In the first place, of course, for all those who are indeed about to enter the Church: children, new converts, "seekers." But even more, for those whom *we* can draw to the "Sun of Righteousness," were it not for our laziness, our indifference, our habit of considering the Church "our" property, existing for us and not for the divine task, not for him who "desires *all* men to be saved and to come to the knowledge of the truth." Thus, while preserving its direct meaning, the prayers for the catechumens must become for us a constant reminder and judgment: what are you doing—what is your church doing—for

Christ's mission in the world? How are you fulfilling the basic command of the Head of the Church: "go into all the world and preach the gospel to all creation"?

3

THE FIRST PART OF THE LITURGY DRAWS TOWARD ITS CON-clusion with the dismissal of all who are not baptized but still only preparing for baptism. In antiquity, those doing *penance*, i.e., who were temporarily excommunicated from participation in the sacrament, also left immediately after the catechumens. "Let no catechumen, no one whose faith is not firm, no one under penance, no one impure draw near to the holy sacrament." The works of St Gregory the Great, referring to this exclamation by the deacon, admonish: "Whoever is not receiving communion, let him leave the assembly."[4] Only the *faithful*, i.e., baptized members of the Church, are left in the church assembly, and they are now summoned through a general prayer to prepare them-selves for the eucharistic offering.

"Let us, the faithful"—*only* the faithful. With these words we reach a turning point in the service, the deepest meaning of which is almost lost to contemporary church consciousness. In our day the doors of the temple are open throughout the entire liturgy, and anyone can enter or leave at any time. And this is because in contemporary understanding it is essentially only the priest who "serves" and the service takes place in the altar, *for* and *on behalf of* the laity, who are present and take part in it "individually"—through prayer, through paying attention, sometimes through receiving communion. Not only the laity but the clergy as well have simply forgotten that the eucharist, by its very nature, is a closed assembly of the Church, and that in this assembly all are *ordained* and all *serve*, each in his place, in the one liturgical action of the Church. Who is serving, in other words, is not the clergy, and not even the clergy with the laity, but the Church, which is constituted and made manifest in all fulness by everyone together.

4*Dialogues* 1:23, PL 77:233.

There is much talk today about the participation of the laity in church life, about their "royal priesthood," about the raising of their "church consciousness." But one fears that all these efforts to restore to the laity their rightful place in the Church lead nowhere as long as they proceed—as they do now—exclusively from the correlation of "clergy–laity" and not from the correlation, above all, of "Church–world," which alone can truly make clear the nature of the Church and, consequently, the place and correlation of her various members. The deficiency in contemporary church psychology lies in regarding the whole life of the Church in terms of the interrelation of clergy and laity. We have equated the Church with the clergy, and the "laity" with the world—witness the Russian and Greek terms for laity: *miriane* (from *mir*, world) and *kosmikoi*—and this in turn distorts both this interrelationship itself and the clergy's and laity's understanding of their place in the Church.

We find ourselves before a paradox. On the one hand, the purpose of the "clergy" seems to consist in "ministering to" the laity—which means to perform the services, govern and manage church affairs, teach, tend to the spiritual and moral condition of the flock. On the other hand, many consider it wrong that the laity themselves take no part in this ministry and that all direction and leadership of church life is concentrated in the hands of the clergy alone. Today when one speaks of the participation of the laity in church life, he usually has in mind their participation in church administration, in liturgical preaching, in councils —i.e., precisely all those things that, by essence and from time immemorial, were the express ministry of the hierarchy, for the sake of which they were established and still exist in the Church. A false dilemma arises: either the laity are a "passive" element and all activity in the Church belongs to the clergy, or else some share of the clergy's functions can, and therefore must, be transferred to the laity. This dilemma in fact results in a conflict between pure "clericalism," which divides the Church into "active" and "passive" parts and demands of the laity only blind submission to the clergy, and a peculiar form of church "democracy," according to which the only special sphere of activity of the clergy is the services (performing the sacraments and various minor offices), and everything else is to be shared with the laity. But if the first case results in everyone who wishes to be "active" almost inevitably joining the clergy, then in the second the problem becomes providing "representation" for the laity in all church affairs.

All this, however, is a false dilemma, a dead end. For the question of the interrelationship of the clergy and laity is in fact inseparable from the question of the *purpose of the Church herself*, and apart from this it has no meaning. Before we clear up the role of clergy and laity in the conduct of church "business," we must remind ourselves of the fundamental task to which the Church herself is called and how she is commanded to carry it out. The point is, being the new people of God, gathered, redeemed and sanctified by the Lord Jesus Christ, the Church is *consecrated* by him for witness about him *in the world and before the world*.

Christ is the savior of the world. And the salvation of the world was already accomplished in his incarnation, his sacrifice on the cross, death, resurrection and glorification. In him God became man, and man is deified, sin and death are conquered, life is made manifest and triumphant. And thus, first of all, the Church is his life, "which was with the Father and was made manifest to us" (1 Jn 1:2)—i.e., Christ himself, living in the people who have accepted him and who in him have unity with God and with each other. Inasmuch as this unity in Christ with God is also unity in Christ with all, inasmuch as this new and eternal life, eternal not only in duration but also in "quality," is the goal of creation and salvation, the Church in herself has no other "business" than the incessant acquisition of the Holy Spirit and growth into the fulness of Christ, who lives in her. In Christ everything is "done" and no one needs to add anything to his work. Therefore, "in herself" the Church always abides in "the last days," and her life, according to St Paul, is "hid with Christ in God." In every liturgy she meets the coming Lord and has the fulness of the kingdom, which is coming in power; in her everyone who hungers and thirsts is granted, here, on this earth, in this age, the contemplation of the imperishable light of Tabor, the possession of perfect joy and peace in the Holy Spirit. In this new life there is no difference between strong and weak, slave and free, male and female, but "if any one is in Christ, he is a new creation" (2 Co 5:17). God gives the Spirit without measure, all are consecrated by him, all are called to fulness and perfection, to "life abundant."

But that is why the hierarchical structure of the Church itself, the distinction between priests and laymen and all the multitude of her ministries has no other purpose than the growth of each and all together into the fulness of the body of Christ. The Church is not a religious society in which God rules *through* the priests *over* the people, but the very body of Christ, with no other source and content of her life than the divine-human life of Christ himself. This means that in the Church no one submits to another (as laity to clergy), but all together submit to each other in the unity of the divine-human life. In the Church the authority of the hierarchy is indeed "absolute"—but not because this authority is granted to them by Christ. Rather, it is because it is the authority of Christ himself, just as the obedience of the laity is itself the obedience of Christ. For Christ is not *outside* the Church, he is not *above* the Church, but he is in her and she is in him, as his body. "We should regard the bishop as the Lord himself," writes St Ignatius of Antioch concerning the authority of the hierarchy,[5] and regarding obedience he says: "follow the bishop as Jesus Christ did the Father."[6] There is a certain deep misunderstanding of the mystery of the Church in the various endeavors to "limit" the authority of the hierarchy, to lower their ministry solely to the "sacramental" or liturgical sphere, as if the ministry of administration or any other service could have any other source besides precisely the "sacramental," i.e., the Holy Spirit himself, as if "authority" and "obedience" did not cease, precisely in their "sacramentality," to be merely human and did not become Christ-like, as if, finally, both authority and obedience and all other ministries in the Church could have some other content besides the love of Christ, and some other goal besides the service of all for all, toward the fulfilment of the Church in all her fulness. "Let no one's position swell his head, for faith and love are everything—there is nothing preferable to them," writes St Ignatius.[7] And if, in their ministry, members of the Church betray the Christ-like nature of their service and regress from grace and love to the law, and from the law to lawlessness, then, of course, it will not be through the "law of this world," through constitutions and legislatures, that the

[5]*Ephesians* 6:1, tr. Richardson, *Early Christian Fathers*, 89.
[6]*Smyrneans* 8:1, tr. Richardson, 115.
[7]*Smyrneans* 6:1, tr. Richardson, 114.

spirit of Christ will return to church life, but through unceasing "rekindling of the gift of God" (2 Tm 1:6), which never abandons the Church.

But being made perfect in Christ, salvation is accomplished in the world even while the hour of the final triumph of Christ, when "God will be all in all" (1 Co 15:28), is still to come. The whole world still lies in evil, and the "prince of this world" still has dominion in it. And therefore the sacrifice, offered once and for all, is always offered and the Lord is crucified for the sins of the world. He remains the priest and intercessor for the world before the Father, and thus the Church, his body, a participant in his flesh and blood, takes part in his priesthood and intercedes by his intercession. She offers not a new sacrifice, for all the fulness of salvation has been given to the world "through the offering of the body of Jesus Christ once for all" (Heb 10:10), and "by a single offering he has perfected for all time those who are sanctified" (Heb 10:14), but, being his body, *she is herself priesthood, offering and sacrifice.* And if we live in the Church through the love of Christ, if love is the source and content and goal of her life, then this love exists in order that "as he is, so are we in this world" (1 Jn 4:17). He came to save the world and to give his life for it. By what is the world saved if not by Christ's sacrifice, and how can we further fulfil the ministry of Christ if we do not take part in his sacrifice? This is also the "universal priesthood" of the Church: the very priesthood of Christ, in which she is consecrated, being his body. This is her first service in relation to the world, for which she was left and abides in the world: "to proclaim the death of the Lord, to confess his resurrection, to await his coming." And to this ministry everyone who in baptism was joined with Christ and made a member of his body is ordained. We are ordained so that, together constituting the Church, we may offer his sacrifice for the sins of the world, and in offering it, witness to salvation.

The "royal" or "universal" priesthood in the Church does not consist in her being a society of priests—for there are both priests and "laymen" in her—but in the fact that she as a whole, as the body of Christ, has a priestly ministry in relation to the world, she fulfils the priesthood and intercession of the Lord himself. Again, the very distinction between clergy and "laity" inside the

Church is necessary in order that the Church may be in her fulness a sacred organism—for, if the priests are the ministers of the sacraments, then through the sacraments the entire Church is sanctified and consecrated for the ministry of Christ, and herself becomes the mystery of the theandric reality of Christ. The "priesthood" of the laity does not consist in their being some sort of priests of a second order in the Church—for the ministries are distinct and must never be confused—but in that being the *faithful*, i.e., the members of the Church, they are *ordained* into the ministry of Christ to the world, and they realize this, above all, through participation in the offering of Christ's sacrifice on behalf of the world.

Such, in the end, is the meaning of the exclamation "let us, the faithful." Through it the Church separates herself from the world, because, being the body of Christ, she is already "not of this world." But this separation is accomplished *for the sake of* the world, for the offering of Christ's sacrifice "on behalf of all and for all." If the Church did not have in herself the fulness of salvation, she would have nothing to witness to the world about. And if she were not to witness, if her calling and service were not the offering of Christ's sacrifice, then Christ would not be the savior of the world, but the savior *from the world*. And, finally, with this exclamation we are reminded that the meaning of the liturgy is not that in it the priest serves for the laity, or that the laity participates in the service each "for himself," but that the entire assembly, in the mutual submission of all ministries one to another, constitutes a single body for the realization of the priesthood of Jesus Christ.

And thus, when we hear these words, let us ask ourselves: are we confessing ourselves to be the *faithful*? Are we agreeing to fulfil the ministry to which each of us was ordained on the day of our baptism? Here there is no place for false humility or for separating ourselves from the gathering on the pretext of our sins. No one has ever been worthy of this participation, and no amount of righteousness can make a man able to offer the sacrifice of Christ for the world. But he himself has ordained, sanctified and placed us in this ministry, and he himself accomplishes it in us. We must remember, finally, that we do not go to church *for ourselves* and for our own desires, but for the service of Christ's work in the world.

For there is no other way of *our* salvation than to give our lives
over to Christ—"who loves us and has freed us from our sins by his
blood and has made us a kingdom, priests to his God and Father"
(Rv 1:5-6). We are gathered in the eucharist for the fulfilment of
this service, and we now proceed to its first liturgical act, to the
offering.

4

THE SOLEMN ACT THAT SIGNIFIES THE END OF THE LITURGY OF
the word and the beginning of the liturgy of the faithful is the
unfolding of the *antimension* on the altar. This Greek word, which
literally means "in place of a table," refers to the linen or silk
rectangle that usually has a picture of the Lord being placed in the
tomb, as well a particle of a relic sewn into the middle in a special
pocket, and the signature of the bishop who consecrated this particular antimension on the bottom.

The history, development and usage of the antimension in the
Orthodox Church is fairly complex and even contradictory. For
example, while the chief meaning of the antimension among the
Russians is focused on the relics sewn into it, the Greek East uses
the antimension without relics—which alone points to a certain
contradiction in the understanding of its function in worship. As
its history is of interest to specialists, we shall submit our remarks
on it in a special note.[8] Here it is enough to emphasize that for the
entire Orthodox Church the common and therefore normative
feature of the antimension is its connection with the bishop. Like
the holy chrism, the antimension is blessed only by the bishop,
and his signature on it serves as the condition for its "validity."
And whatever further stratifications of the various meanings of
the antimension, it originally signified the bishop's "delegation"
to a presbyter of the right to perform the eucharist. As I already
pointed out above, the normal celebrant of the eucharist in the
early Church was the bishop. For, inasmuch as the eucharist is
realized and experienced above all as the sacrament of the assembly, the sacrament of the Church—i.e., of the unity of the people
of God—then it is obvious that its celebrant would be the one

[8]Fr Schmemann was unable to write this supplementary note before his death.

whose ministry consists in the creation, expression and preservation of this unity. That is why even when the Church ceased to be a relatively small group of believers and embraced practically the entire population of the empire, traces of this understanding and experience of the eucharist as a presupposed "gathering of all in one place" under the presidency of the bishop were preserved for a long time in church practice. In Rome, for example, even in the seventh century, although the number of Christians made several gatherings inevitable, only one eucharist was performed, and the consecrated gifts were distributed by the deacons to the other assemblies. This underscores the meaning of the sacrament as the sacrament of the unity of the Church—as the overcoming of the sinful shatteredness and division of the world. And even today, the interdiction in the Orthodox Church against one priest serving more than one eucharist on the same altar bears witness to the understanding of the eucharist, which goes back to Christian antiquity, as the sacrament of the Church and unity par excellence. It is precisely in this connection that we need to understand the meaning of the antimension.

Historically, the antimension arose from a necessity to coordinate in actual life, on the one hand, the meaning of the eucharist as an act of the entire Church, expressing her unity and therefore being the primary ministry of the bishop, and on the other hand, the necessity of a multitude of eucharistic assemblies. St Ignatius of Antioch had written: "You should regard that eucharist as valid which is celebrated either by the bishop or by someone he authorizes."[9] This indicates that already in those early times there were instances when a bishop could not serve it and delegated the responsibilty to one of his presbyters. In the later development and complication of church life, what began as an exception became a general rule. The bishop was gradually transformed from the leader of a concrete church community into an administrator of a more or less extensive ecclesiastical district (eparchy), and the "church," as a living community, became a "parish." For a brief moment the Church perhaps did not know which was better: to preserve the former immediate link of the bishop with the community, and thus to multiply the number of bishops so that one

---

[9]*Smyrneans* 8:1, tr. Richardson, 115.

would head each parish (such is the historical context of the short-lived and unsuccessful experiment with the so-called *chorepisko-poi*), or to preserve the regional and thus ecumenical significance of the episcopate and therefore grant new functions to the members of the episcopal council, or "prebyterium," and place presbyters at the head of parishes. Historically the second alternative triumphed and gradually led to the appearance of the ministry of the "parish priest," i.e., an individual leader of a more or less extensive church community, a performer of the services and sacraments and the immediate pastor of his flock.

One can hardly doubt that in current church consciousness the idea of pastorship is chiefly linked with the priest, and not with the bishop, who has been transformed into an "archpastor" and is much more strongly perceived as the head and superior of the clergy, an "administrator" of the Church, rather than the living bearer of church unity and the focus of church life. (Thus, it is characteristic that we call the priest, not the bishop, "father," while we greet the bishop as "master.") But, whatever the pluses and minuses of the change that took place in the Church, there is no doubt that the meaning of the contemporary "parish" does not coincide with that of the original community—the "Church." The early "church" possessed, in the unity of the bishop, clerics and people, the fulness of church life and church gifts. The parish, in contrast, lacks this fulness. Not only administratively, but mystically, spiritually, it is a part of the greater unity, and only in union with the other parts, the other "parishes," can it live in the entire fulness of the Church. Consequently, the calling and mystical essence of the episcopate consists in ensuring that no one community, no single "parish" becomes self-contained, shut up in itself, and ceases to live and breathe by the "catholicity" of the Church.

Thus, one of the chief causes of the change indicated above, precisely the separation of the bishop from the concrete community and his substitution by the parish priest, was the fear of reducing the bishop to the level of the leader of a purely local community and of completely identifying him with local "interests" and "needs." For the time when this change occurred was the time of the reconciliation of the Church with the empire, when Christianity was turned into the state religion. The local

Church—a community, in that era of persecution, separated from natural life—was the Church *in* a given city, but not the Church *of* the given city. Now it gradually began to merge with the natural city or provincial society, being transformed into its so-called "religous projection." And this in turn signified a deep change in the psychology and self-consciousness of the Christian. From a "third race" of people (in the expression of one of the earliest Christian documents, the *Letter to Diognetus*), who were living in a foreign land but whose true home was somewhere else, Christians now became full and equal citizens of the land, and their faith became the natural, compulsory and self-evident religion of all society. And it was precisely in hopes of averting the ultimate merger of the Church and the world, of the church assembly and "natural" society, that the Church was compelled in a certain sense to modify her original structure and place the bishop *over* the parishes, in order that each of them would always be transformed into the Church, in order to remind them of the otherworldly, universal calling of the Church.

Yet this also signified an essential change in eucharistic practice and even in the very order of the eucharistic assembly. The presbyter, who at first had been a "concelebrant" of the bishop in the eucharistic gathering and only in exceptional cases had substituted for him as the *president*, now became the president of the eucharistic gathering in the parish. We have already seen that this essential change is apparent to this very day in the eucharistic offices, particularly in the first part of the liturgy. But all the same, such is the organic link between the eucharist, the Church and the bishop, that even when the eucharist was for all purposes separated from the bishop as its natural celebrant and presider and became the basic lot of the parish clergy, it still remained linked with the bishop, and the witness to this link, its guardian, is precisely the antimension. From any truly deep point of view (and not reduced to only administrative or even canonical categories) the eucharist is today, always and everywhere accomplished *by the commission of the bishop*, or, speaking in juridical language, by the authority delegated by him. But this is not because the bishop bears authority as an individual. In the early, pre-Nicene Church he exercised his authority precisely with his "council" or "prebyterium," and the expression "monarchical episcopate," used so frequently in church history textbooks, very poorly expresses the spirit and structure of the early Church. The issue here is not "authority" but the nature of the eucharist as the sacrament of the Church, as an act in which the unity of the Church and her other-worldly and universal nature is fulfilled and realized. Not only "quantitatively," but "qualitatively," ontologicaly, the Church is *more* than the parish, and the parish is the Church only to the degree that it partakes of the fulness of *tserkovnost'*, that it "transcends" itself as a parish and overcomes the inner, natural "egocentrism" and narrowness peculiar to everything "local." Both Protestant congregationalism, which simply identifies any parish with the Church, and Roman centralism, which identifies the Church only with the "whole," with the sum of all "parishes," are equally foreign to Orthodoxy. In the Orthodox understanding, the Church exists so that each of her parts can live in fulness and be an incarnation of the fulness of the Church—so that, in other words, each part can live *by the whole* and *wholly*. The parish is, on the one hand, only a *part* of the Church, and only in the bishop and through the bishop is it linked with the fulness of the Church, always receiving this fulness and itself "revealing" it. This is the meaning of the dependence of the parish on the bishop and through him on the "whole" Church. On the other hand, the eucharist is a gift of the Church to the parish, and through it each parish partakes of the "whole Christ," receives all the fulness of the beneficent gifts and identifies itself with the Church. From this stems the dependence of the eucharist on the bishop, on his "commission," and along with this the self-evidency of the eucharist as the focus of the "parish" and all its life. Without the link with the bishop the eucharist would cease to be an act of the whole Church, the surmounting of the natural narrowness of the parish. Without the eucharist the parish would cease to be a part of the Church, living by the fulness of the Church's gifts.

All this is expressed in the antimension. I repeat, whatever were the developments and stratifications in its meaning, its fundamental significance lies in this: when the priest unfolds it upon the altar in preparation for the offering of the eucharistic sacrifice, and when he kisses the signature of the bishop on it, this altar is "fulfilled" not only as the altar of the given temple and local community, but as the one altar of the Church of God, as the place of the offering, presence and coming of the *whole Christ*, in whom we are all the body of Christ, in whom all "parts," all divisions, are overcome by the "whole" and given the gift and grace of the new life and above all the *fulness of life*. For this fulness is precisely preserved and fulfilled in the indissoluble bond of bishop, eucharist and the Church.

CHAPTER SIX

The Sacrament of Offering

*"...Christ loved us and gave himself
up for us, a fragrant offering and sacrifice to God."*

EPHESIANS 5:2

I

*B*READ AND WINE. BY BRINGING THESE HUMBLE HUMAN
gifts—our earthly food and drink—and placing them on
the altar, we perform, often without thinking of it, that most
ancient, primordial rite that from the first day of human history
constituted the core of every religion: we offer a sacrifice to God.
"Now Abel was a keeper of sheep, and Cain a tiller of the ground.
In the course of time Cain brought to the Lord an offering of the
fruit of the ground, and Abel brought of the firstlings of his
flock" (Gn 4:2-4).

A thousand books have been written on sacrifices and sacrificial offerings, and they still produce the most varied explanations.
Theologians, historians, sociologists, psychologists—all have
their own points of view, endeavoring to elucidate the essence of
the sacrifice, some finding it in fear, some in joy, some in "lower"
and some in "higher" causes. And whatever may be the value of
all these explanations, it remains indubitable that wherever and
whenever man turns to God, he necessarily senses the need to offer him the most precious things that he has, what is most vital
for his life, as a gift and sacrifice. From the time of Cain and Abel,

101

the blood of sacrifices has daily covered the earth and the smoke of burnt offerings has unceasingly risen to heaven.

Our "refined" sensibilities are horrified by these blood sacrifices, by these "primitive" religions. In our horror, however, do we not forget and lose something very basic, very primary, without which in essence there is no religion? For in its ultimate depths religion is nothing other than *thirst for God*: "My soul thirsts for God, for the living God" (Ps 42:2); and often "primitive" people know this thirst better, they sense it more deeply—as the psalmist declared once and for all—than contemporary man does, with all his "spiritualized" religion, abstract "moralism" and dried-up intellectualism.

To want God means above all to know with one's whole being that *he is*, that outside of him there is only darkness, emptiness and meaninglessness, for in him and only in him is the cause, the meaning, the goal and the joy of all existence. This means further to love him with one's whole heart, one's whole mind and one's whole being. And this means, finally, to feel and to recognize our complete and boundless alienation from him, our frightful guilt and loneliness in this rupture—to know that ultimately there is only one sin: not wanting God and being separated from him; and there is only one sorrow: "not being a saint,"[1] not having *sanctification*—unity with the One who is holy.

But where there is this thirst for God, this consciousness of sin and this yearning for genuine life, there necessarily is sacrifice. In the sacrifice man gives himself and his own over to his God, because, knowing God, he cannot but love him, and loving him, he cannot but strive toward him and toward unity with him. But as his sins stand on this road and encumber him, in his sacrifice man likewise seeks forgiveness and atonement; he offers it as a propitiation for sin, he fills it with all the pain and torment of his life, so that through suffering, blood and death he may finally *expiate* his guilt and be reunited with God. And however darkened and coarsened our religious consciousness may be, however crude, "utilitarian" or "pagan" is man's understanding of his sacrifice—as well as of him in whose name and to whom he offers it—at its basis necessarily remains man's primordial, indestructible

[1] Leon Bloy, *La femme pauvre*.

thirst for God. And in his sacrifices, in these innumerable offerings, invocations and holocausts, man, albeit in darkness, albeit
savage and primitive, seeks and thirsts for the one for whom he
cannot cease to seek, for "God created us for himself, and our
hearts will not rest until they rest in him."[2]

2

ALL THESE SACRIFICES, HOWEVER, WERE POWERLESS TO
destroy sin and restore the fulness of unity with God that man had
forfeited. All alike, and not only Old Testament sacrifices, could
be related to the words of the epistle to the Hebrews: "it [the law]
can never, by the same sacrifices which are continually offered
year after year, make perfect those who draw near. Otherwise,
would they not have ceased to be offered? If the worshipers had
once been cleansed, they would no longer have any consciousness
of sin" (10:1-2). They were powerless because, though filled with
thirst for God and for unity with him, they themselves remained
under the law of sin. And sin is not guilt, which can be smoothed
over and atoned for—albeit at a very high price. Sin is above all
the rupture from God of life itself, and that is why it is such a fall
and shattering, in which all life, and not just individual actions,
becomes sinful, mortal and under the "shadow of death." And
this fallen life, wholly subordinate to the law of sin, does not, and
cannot, have the power to heal and revive itself, to fill itself with
life again, to make itself sanctified once more. Separation, yearning, repentance remain, and man includes them in his "religion"
and in his sacrifices, but this religion and these sacrifices cannot
save man from slavery to sin and death, just as one who is falling
into an abyss cannot turn back upward, one who is buried alive
cannot dig himself up, a dead man cannot raise himself. Only
God can save—precisely *save*—us, for our life needs salvation, and
not simply help. Only he can fulfil that concerning which all sacrifices remain an impotent plea, of which they were all expectation, prefiguration and anticipation. And he fulfils this in the
ultimate, perfect and all-embracing sacrifice in which he gave his
only-begotten Son for the salvation of the world, in which the Son

[2]Augustine, *Confessions* 1:1.

of God, having become the Son of man, offered himself as a sacrifice for the life of the world.

In this sacrifice everything is fulfilled and accomplished. In it, above all, sacrifice itself is cleansed, restored and manifested in all its essence and fulness, in its preeternal meaning as perfect love and thus perfect life, consisting of perfect self-sacrifice: in Christ "God so loved the world that he gave his only Son," and in Christ man so loved God that he gave himself totally, and in this twofold giving nothing remains not given, and love reigns in all—"the crucifying love of the Father, the crucified love of the Son, and the love of the Spirit triumphing through the power of the cross."[3] In this sacrifice, furthermore, because it was made only through love and only in love, was forgiveness of sins granted. And finally, in it man's eternal thirst for God was fulfilled and slaked: the divine life became our food, our life. Everything that man, consciously or unconsciously, in darkness, partially, distortedly, included in his sacrifices, everything that man hoped for from them, and all that "the heart of man could not conceive," was fulfilled, perfected and granted *once*—once and for all—in this sacrifice of sacrifices.

The ultimate and most joyful mystery of all is that Christ gave this sacrifice to us, to the new humanity regenerated in him and united with him: the Church. In this new life, his life in us and our life in him, his sacrifice became our sacrifice, his offering our offering. "Abide in me, and I in you" (Jn 15:4). What does this mean, if not that his life, fulfilled by him in his perfect sacrifice, was granted to us as our life, as the only true life, as the fulfilment of God's eternal design for mankind? For if Christ's life is offering and sacrifice, then also our life in him and the whole life of the Church are offering and sacrifice—the offering of ourselves and each other and the whole world, the sacrifice of love and unity, praise and thanksgiving, forgiveness and healing, communion and unity.

And thus this sacrifice, which we have been given and commanded to offer and in the offering of which the Church fulfils herself as Christ's life in us and ours in him, is not a new sacrifice, something "other" in relation to the single, all-encompassing and unrepeatable one that Christ offered *once* (Heb 9:28). Embracing

---

[3]Filaret (Drozdov), Metropolitan of Moscow, *Homily on Holy Friday*, in *Sermons and Discourses*, 1 (St Petersburg, 1873).

and uniting in himself all "things in heaven and things on earth" (Eph 1:10), filling all things with himself, being the life of life, Christ offers all to the God and Father. In his sacrifice is forgiveness of all sins, all the fulness of salvation and sanctification, the fulfilment and therefore the completion of all "religion." And therefore other, new sacrifices are unnecessary and impossible. They are impossible, however, precisely because through the one and unrepeatable sacrifice of Christ our life itself was restored, regenerated and fulfilled as offering and sacrifice, as the possibility of always converting our bodies and our whole lives into "a living sacrifice, holy and acceptable to God" (Rm 12:1); "be yourself built into a spiritual house, to be a holy priesthood, to offer spiritual sacrifices acceptable to God, through Jesus Christ" (1 Pt 2:5). New sacrifices are not needed, for in Christ we "have access...to the Father" (Eph 2:18). This access, however, consists in the fact that in it our life has become offering and sacrifice, it "grows into a holy temple in the Lord" (Eph 2:21), through the joy of offering ourselves and each other and all creation to God, who has called us into "his wonderful light." The Church lives by this offering and fulfils herself in it. Each time we again offer this sacrifice, we know with joy that we offer it *through Jesus Christ*, that it is he who, giving himself to us and abiding in us, eternally offers the sacrifice that was once and forever offered by him. In offering our life to God, we know that we are offering Christ—for he is our life, the life of the world and the life of life, and we have nothing to bring to God except him. We know that in this offering Christ is "the Offerer and the Offered, the Receiver and the Received."

3

THE EUCHARISTIC OFFERING BEGINS WITH A SOLEMN RITE THAT is now usually called the "Great Entrance." This is a secondary name, for it is absent from the service books. It was introduced and came into fixed usage when the original meaning of this rite, as precisely the bringing of the sacrifice to the sacrificial table, became somewhat obscured, and the entrance into the sanctuary with the gifts became overgrown with the illustrative symbolism already familiar to us and began to be interpreted as an image of the Lord's royal entrance into Jerusalem or the burial of Christ by Joseph and Nicodemus, etc.

We must acknowledge that the chief source of this symbolic complication of the Great Entrance was the gradual detachment of the preparation of the eucharistic gifts, i.e., the offering in the immediate, literal sense of the word, from the liturgy itself and its disjunction into a separate rite, which acquired the name *pro-thesis* or *proskomidē* (from the Greek, meaning the carrying or conveying of something to a certain place). In contemporary practice this service is performed *before* the liturgy, at the side of the sanctuary, by the clergy alone. The participation of the laity in it is reduced to giving ("outside," by the way, through third parties) their personal prosphora with lists of names to be mentioned —"For the Health of..." and "For the Repose of..."—and even this is not done everywhere.

What is most noteworthy in the proskomidē from the theological point of view is its *order*, which consists of a certain *symbolic sacrifice*. The preparation of the eucharistic bread is likened to an immolation of the lamb, and the pouring of wine and water into the cup recalls the effusion of blood and water from the ribs of the crucified Christ, etc. At the same time it is evident that this sufficiently complex symbolical rite is in no way a substitute for the liturgy itself, for which it is a preparation.

Thus, the question inevitably arises: what is the meaning of these symbols? What is the connection between this, as it were, "preliminary" sacrifice and the offering that, as we already were saying, constitutes the essence of the eucharist? These questions are of tremendous importance for an understanding of the liturgy, and yet they are simply ignored by our school theology. And as far as liturgists are concerned, their answers consist entirely of references to that "symbolism," as though it were inherent to our worship, that explains precisely nothing. And yet this is the whole point: in its essence, in the fact that it is rooted in the divine incarnation and in its orientation to the coming kingdom of God manifested in power, the liturgy rejects and excludes the contraposition of "symbol" and "reality." But meanwhile, every day over the course of centuries, thousands of priests, while making cross-shaped incisions in the eucharistic bread, recite, reflecting with reverence and faith, the hallowed words: "Sacrificed [i.e., offered as a sacrifice] is the Lamb of God, who takes away the sin of the world."

What is this? "Simply a symbol," in which "as a matter of fact" nothing happens, nothing is accomplished, there is no "reality"? But then we venture to ask: precisely why is it needed? Performed in the solitude of the sanctuary, removed from the presence of the laity, it cannot be attributed even to pedagogical considerations, as a certain "lesson." It is imperative to analyze this question more deeply, for a correct understanding of the eucharist and the sacrificial offering accomplished therein depends on it.

4

WHILE NOT REDUCING THIS QUESTION TO HISTORY ALONE, IT does require first of all an understanding of the historical factors that determined the development of our contemporary proskomidē. The point of departure of this development is without any doubt the participation, self-evident for early Christianity, of all members of the Church in the eucharistic offering. In the consciousness, in the experience and in the practice of the early Church, the eucharistic sacrifice was offered not only on behalf of all and for all, but *by all*, and therefore the real offering by each of his own gift, his own sacrifice, was a basic condition of it. Each person who came into the gathering of the Church brought with him everything that, "as he has made up his mind" (2 Co 9:7), he could spare for the needs of the Church, and this meant for the sustenance of the clergy, widows and orphans, for helping the poor, for all the "good works" in which the Church realizes herself as the love of Christ, as concern of all for all and service of all to all. The eucharistic offering is rooted precisely in this sacrifice of love, therein lies its origin. And this was so self-evident for the early Church that, according to one witness, orphans who lived at the expense of the Church and did not have anything to bring participated in this sacrifice of love by bringing water.

In the early Church, the appointed ministers of charity and thus of this sacrifice of love were the *deacons*. Concern not only for the "material prosperity" of the community (a concern that in our day is reduced almost entirely to the activity of all manner of church committees and, in effect, of the entire church organization) but precisely for love, as the very essence of church life, for the Church, as the sacrificial and active service of all for all, lay primarily with them. And just as in the early Church the place and ministry of each in the eucharistic gathering expressed the place and ministry (*leitourgia*) of each in the church community, so to the deacons fell the responsibility for receiving the gifts from those who came, for sorting them out and for preparing that portion of them that, as an expression of this offering, of this sacrifice of love, was to constitute the "matter" of the eucharistic mystery. The performance of the proskomidē by the deacons—and not, like today, by the priests—was preserved in the Church right up to the fourteenth century, as was the bringing of the holy gifts precisely by them to the presider at the beginning of the eucharistic oblation, the eucharist proper. And while we shall still speak further about the change that occurred at that time, we can already note that if in our day the presence of a deacon in *every* church community has ceased to be perceived as necessary and self-evident, as one of the conditions of the *fulness* of church life, and the "diaconate" has been converted into a certain "decorative" appendage (particularly in the hierarchical service) and likewise a "step" on the way to the priesthood, then is that not because the experience of the Church herself as the love of Christ and the liturgy as the expression and fulfilment of that love has been weakened in us, if not entirely dissipated?

Gradually, however, this original, as it were "family" practice of the participation of all in the offering of the gifts became complicated and modified. The sudden increase of the numbers of Christians—especially after the conversion to Christianity of the whole empire, with practically the entire populace becoming Christian—made it impossible in practice to bring to the eucharistic gathering of the Church everything necessary for church "philanthropy" and for the living needs of the community. Not only was she recognized by the government, but with all "charitable" activity being gradually concentrated in her hands, the Church could not but have been transformed into a complex organization, overcome by an "apparatus." And this in itself led to the eucharistic gathering, which in the early Church had been the focus of the *entire* life of the Church—teaching and proclamation, philanthropy and administration—ceasing to be such. "Good works," being gradually isolated into a special sphere of church activity, ceased outwardly to "depend" on the eucharistic offering. Here, however, we approach the most important element for an understanding of the proskomidē. For so obvious was the *inner* link between the eucharist and the "sacrifice of love," the inner dependency of one on the other in the consciousness of the Church, that the preparation of the gifts, on ceasing to be an expression of practical needs, remained as a rite, expressing this inner dependency, realizing this inner link.

Here we find a vivid example of that law of liturgical "development" according to which changes in outward *form* are frequently determined by the necessity of preserving inner *content*, of preserving intact the succession and identity of the experience and faith of the Church under all changes in the outward circumstances of her existence. However complex and specifically "Byzantine" in many respects was the development of the proskomidē, reaching its present form only in the fourteenth century, for us it is important that it remained and still remains an expression of that *reality* from which it was born, a witness to the organic link between the eucharist and the essence of the Church herself as love, and *therefore*, sacrifice and offering, as the fulfilment in time and space of the sacrifice of Christ. And now, having considered the historical meaning of the development of the proskomidē, we may go on to its theological meaning.

5

THIS MEANING CONSISTS IN THAT, FIRST OF ALL, BY WHOMEVER and however the "matter," i.e., the bread and cup, of the eucharistic mystery is offered, from the very beginning we foresee and anticipate in them Christ's sacrifice of love, Christ himself, offered by us and in himself offering us to the God and Father. And this foreknowledge, our knowing *before the liturgy* and therefore "signifying" the predestination of the bread to be changed into the body of Christ and the wine into the blood of Christ, constitutes in essence the basis and condition of the very *possibility* of the eucharistic offering.

In actuality, we only serve the liturgy and only can serve it because the sacrifice of Christ *has already been offered* and in it was revealed and fulfilled the preeternal design of God for the world and mankind, their predestination, and therefore also their possibility of becoming a sacrifice to God and in this sacrifice finding their fulfilment.

Yes, the proskomidē is a *symbol*, but, like everything in the Church, it is a symbol completely filled with the *reality* of the new creation, which already exists in Christ but which in "this world" is known only through faith. Thus, for faith there are only transparent symbols. When, preparing for the eucharistic mystery, we take the bread into our hands and place it on the diskos, *we already know* that this bread, like everything in the world, like the world itself, has been sanctified by the incarnation of the Son of God, by his becoming man, and that this sanctification consists in Christ's restoration of the possibility for the world to become a sacrifice to God and for man to offer this sacrifice. What is destroyed and overcome is its "self-sufficiency," which constitutes the essence of sin and which made bread only bread—the mortal food of mortal man, a partaking of sin and death. In Christ our earthly food, which is converted into our flesh and blood, into our very selves and our lives, becomes that for which it was created—participation in the divine life, through which the mortal is clothed in immortality and death is swallowed up in victory.

Precisely because the sacrifice of Christ, which includes all things in itself and was offered *once*, occurred *before* all our offerings, which have their principle and content in it, likewise the proskomidē, the preparation of the gifts, takes place *before* the liturgy. For the essence of this preparation lies in referring the bread and wine, i.e., our very selves and our whole life, to the sacrifice of Christ, their conversion precisely into *gift* and *offering*. Here is precisely the *reality* of the proskomidē—the identification of the bread and wine as the sacrifice of Christ, which encompasses all our sacrifices, our offering of our very selves to God. Hence the *sacrificial* character of the office of the proskomidē, the preparation of the bread as if it were the immolation of the Lamb, the wine as the effusion of blood; hence, the assembling on the diskos each time of everything around the Lamb, the inclusion of everything in his sacrifice. Only when this preparation is completed, when all is *referred* to the sacrifice of Christ and included in it, and our lives, "hid with Christ in God," are placed on the diskos in a way visible to the eyes of faith, can we begin the liturgy—the eternal offering of him who offered himself and in himself all that exists to God, the ascent of our life to that place, the altar of the kingdom, where the Son of God, who has become the Son of man, has lifted it.

6

OF COURSE, LIKE MANY OTHER THINGS IN OUR WORSHIP, THE proskomidē stands in need of a cleansing—but precisely not of its *order*, its form, but of that perception of it that has made it in the consciousness of the faithful "only a symbol," in the unchurchly, nominal meaning of this word. What is needed to cleanse it (or, to put it better, restore it) is a sense of the genuine meaning of the *commemoration*, which is performed in the proskomidē while the pieces are taken out of the prosphora, and which is reduced in the understanding of the faithful and the clergy to one aspect of the prayers "for the health of" and "for the repose of," i.e., to an utterly individualistic and utilitarian understanding of church worship. The fundamental meaning of this commemoration, however, lies precisely in its sacrificial character, in referring all of us together and each of us individually to the sacrifice of Christ, in the gathering and formation of the new creation around the Lamb of God. In this is the power and the joy of this commemoration, that in it is overcome the partition between the living and the dead, between the earthly and the heavenly Church, for all of us—both living and fallen asleep—"have died and our lives are hid with Christ in God," for the whole Church, with the Mother of God and all the saints at her head, is gathered on the diskos, for all are united in this offering by Christ of his glorified and deified humanity to the God and Father. Thus, in taking out particles and pronouncing names, we are caring not simply for the "health" of ourselves or certain of our neighbors, nor for the fate of the dead "beyond the grave"; we offer and return them to God as a "living and well-pleasing" sacrifice in order to make them participants in the "inexhaustible life" of the kingdom of God. We immerse them in the forgiveness of sins, which shines forth from the grave, in that healed, restored and deified life for which God has created them.

Such is the meaning of commemoration in the proskomidē. In offering our *prosphora* (offering), we offer and return "ourselves and each other and all our life" to God. And this offering is *real*, because Christ has already accepted this life and made it his own, he has already offered it to God. In the proskomidē this life, and through it the entire world, is realized again and again as sacrifice and offering, as the "matter" of that sacrament in which the Church fulfils herself as the body of Christ, "the fulness of him who fills all in all" (Eph 1:23).

That is why the proskomidē concludes with a joyous confession and affirmation. Covering the gifts—and thus signifying that in "this world" the reign of Christ, the manifestation of the kingdom of God in him, remains mysterious, known and visible only to faith—the priest recites the words of the psalm: "The Lord reigns; he is robed in majesty...Thy throne is established...the Lord on high is mighty." And he blesses God, who is "thus well-pleased," who desired all this, who fulfilled all this, who granted and is granting us in our earthly bread to joyously anticipate and desire "the Heavenly Bread, the food of the whole world, our Lord and God Jesus Christ." And only now, having grasped the meaning of the proskomidē, can we return to the Great Entrance, to the *sacrament of offering*.

7

IN THE FIRST APOLOGY OF ST JUSTIN MARTYR, IN ONE OF THE earliest descriptions of the liturgy to have reached us, we read: "Then bread and a cup of water and mixed wine are brought to the president of the brethren."[4] And from the *Apostolic Tradition* of St Hippolytus of Rome we know that these gifts were brought by the deacons: "offerent diacones oblationem..."[5] As we can see,

---

[4]65:3, tr. Richardson, 286.
[5]Ed. Dom B. Botte, 4, Sources Chrétiennes, 11 bis (Paris, 1968) 90.

between this simplest form of the offering and our present Great Entrance an extensive and complex development of the eucharistic order occurred, about which it is proper to say a few words at this time. For while the general course and succession of this development has been made sufficiently clear by liturgists, next to nothing has been said about its theological meaning, of the elucidation in it of the faith and experience of the Church.

In the current order of the liturgy the procession includes the following rites: the reading by the priest of the prayer "No one is worthy"; the censing of the altar, the gifts and the people assembled; the hymn of the offering; the solemn transfer of the gifts; the exclamation by the celebrant of the commemorative formula "May the Lord God remember all of you in His Kingdom"; the placing of the gifts on the altar, their being covered by the aer and a repetition of their censing; and the reading by the priest of the "Prayer of the Offering after the Deposition of the Gifts on the Altar." Inasmuch as in each of these rites one aspect of the *whole*, i.e., the Church's offering, finds its expression, each of them demands an explanation, however brief.

8

IN EARLY MANUSCRIPTS THE PRAYER "NO ONE IS WORTHY" (and we find it already in the well-known eighth-century *Codex Barberini*) is called "the prayer that the priest says for himself while the entrance of the holy gifts is being performed." And, in fact, the formal peculiarity of this prayer lies in the fact that, in contrast to all other prayers of the liturgy, the priest offers it *personally* and for *himself*, and not on behalf of us, who comprise the gathering of the Church: "Look down on me, a sinner, Thine unprofitable servant, and cleanse my soul and my heart from an evil conscience; and by the power of the Holy Spirit enable me, who am endowed with the grace of the priesthood, to stand before this, Thy holy table, and perform the sacred mystery of Thy holy and pure Body and precious Blood..."

This peculiarity deserves attention because, if not properly understood, one may find in it a confirmation of that contraposition of the priest and the assembly, that identification of *ministry* only with the clergy, that long ago penetrated our theology from the West and, alas, became firmly accepted in everyday piety. Has it not become generally accepted to relate the words "serving," "performing," "offering," only to the priest, and to understand the laity as a *passive* element in relation to this service, taking part in the service only through a pious presence? This use of words is not accidental. It reflects a gross distortion of church consciousness itself, of its understanding not only of the liturgy but of the Church herself. It finds its expression in the fact that, with each passing century, an understanding of the Church has intensified in which she is experienced above all as the clergy's "serving" of the laity, the satisfaction by the clergy of the "spiritual needs" of the faithful. It is precisely in this perception of the Church that we must seek the cause of those two chronic illnesses of church consciousness that run like a red thread through the entire history of Christianity: "clericalism" and "laicism," which usually takes the form of "anticlericalism."

In the present context, however, it is important for us to note that this "clericalization" of the Church, the reduction of "ministry" to the clergy alone and the consequent atrophy in the consciousness of the laity, led to the gradual demise of the *sacrificial* perception of the Church herself and of the sacrament of the Church—the eucharist. The conviction that the priest serves *on behalf of* the laity and, so to speak, *in their place* led to the conviction that he serves *for* them, for the satisfaction of their "religious needs," subordinate to their religious "demand." We have already seen this in the example of the proskomidē, where the extraction of particles during the commemoration came to be perceived not as the transformation by ourselves of ourselves and each other into a "sacrifice, living and well pleasing to God," but as a method of satisfying certain personal needs—"for the health of...," "for the repose of..." But this example could be extended to the entire life of church society, to all its psychology. The overwhelming majority of the laity (supported in this, alas, all too often by the clergy and the hierarchy) sense the Church as existing for themselves but do not sense themselves as the Church transformed and eternally being transformed into a sacrifice and offering to God, into participants in the sacrificial ministry of Christ.

We have already spoken of this in the chapter on "the faithful," and if we return to it now, it is only because, with an incorrect understanding of the priest's prayer "for himself," with which the eucharistic offering begins, it is possible to conclude that this offering is performed only by the priest. This is why it is so important to understand its genuine meaning. This meaning lies not in contraposing the priest to the gathering, to the "laity," and not in any separation of one from the other, but in the *identification* of the priesthood of the Church with the priesthood of Christ, the one Priest of the New Testament, who through his own offering of himself sanctified the Church and granted her participation in his priesthood and in his sacrifice: "Thou art the Offerer and the Offered, the Receiver and the Received, O Christ our God."

Let us note, first of all, that, again in distinction from the eucharistic prayer as a whole, which, as we shall see, is offered to God the Father, this prayer is directed *personally* to Christ. Why? Because, of course, precisely at this moment of the eucharistic ceremony, when *our* gifts, *our* offering, are brought to the altar, the Church affirms that this offering is accomplished by Christ ("Thou art the Offerer") and that it is an offering of the sacrifice that was offered by him once and is eternally being offered ("and the Offered"). It is *only* the priest who is called and ordained to affirm this identity, to manifest and fulfil it in the mystery of the eucharist. This is the whole point, the whole meaning of this astonishing prayer: that he can fulfil this service only because the priesthood of the priest is not "his," not "other" in relation to the priesthood of Christ, but the one and same indivisible priesthood of Christ, which eternally lives and is eternally fulfilled in the Church, the body of Christ. And in what is the priesthood of Christ constituted, if not in the unity in him of all who believe in him, if not in the gathering and the creation of his body, if not in the offering of all in him and in all of him? Thus, in confessing the priesthood, in the grace of which he is "clothed," to be the priesthood of Christ, in preparing himself to celebrate the sacred mystery of the body of Christ, i.e., to manifest the identity of our offering with the sacrifice of Christ, not only does the priest not separate himself from the gathering, but, on the contrary, he manifests his unity with it as the unity of the head with the body.

That is precisely why his *personal* prayer *for himself* is not only appropriate but also necessary and, so to speak, self-evident. For (and we most strongly stress this) both the Latin reduction of the sacraments to *ex opere operato*—i.e., that understanding of them under which the *person* of the priest (as distinct from the "objective" gift of the priesthood, that is, the "right" to perform the sacraments) has no significance whatsoever in relation to their "validity"—and their reduction to *ex opere operantis*—to dependency on the subjective qualities of their performer—are equally foreign to Orthodoxy. For Orthodoxy this is a false dilemma, one of those impasses to which theological rationalism inevitably leads. In the Orthodox perception of the Church, both the absolute non-dependence of the gift that God has given on any earthly, human "causality" whatsoever, and the *personal* character of this gift, whose reception depends, consequently, on the person to whom it is given, are equally self-evident. "God gives the Spirit without measure...," but man can "assimilate" it only through personal endeavor, and only to the "measure" of this assimilation is the gift of grace actualized in him. And the very distinction of gifts and ministries in the Church ("Are all apostles? Are all prophets? Are all teachers?" 1 Co 12:29) is an indication of the correspondence of the gift to the person receiving it, to the mystery of choosing, appointing, calling, which is directed to each to fulfil *his* vocation, to "earnestly desire the higher gifts" and "a still more excellent way" (1 Co 12:31). And if, obviously, the Church does not make the "validity" of the sacraments dependent on the qualities of the person appointed to perform them—for in such case no single sacrament would be "possible"—then the dependence of the fulness of church life on the measure of the growth of her members in the reception and assimilation of the gifts received by them is equally obvious to her. The fundamental and eternal defect of any scholasticism, of any theological rationalism, lies precisely in the fact that it would be "satisfied" by this question concerning "validity" and "objectivity" and reduce the entire teaching on the sacraments (and on the Church herself) to it, whereas genuine faith, and therefore also the essence of each vocation, each gift, consists in the thirst for *fulness*, and this means the fulfilment by each and by the whole Church of the grace that God granted without measure.

The uniqueness of the ministry of the priest consists in that he is called and appointed in the Church, the body of Christ, to be the *image* of the Head of the body—Christ—and this means to be the one through whom the *personal* ministry of Christ is continued and realized. It is not simply Christ's authority—for his authority is the authority of love and is not separated from his *personal* love for the Father and for mankind—and it is not simply his priest-hood—for Christ's priesthood consists in his *personal* self-sacrifice to God and to mankind—and it is not simply his teaching—for his teaching is inseparable from his *person*—but it is precisely the very essence of this ministry as love and self-sacrifice to God and to mankind, as *pastorship* in the deepest sense of that term: the shep-herd's laying down of "his life for the sheep." And this means that the calling to the priesthood itself is directed to the *person* of the one called and is inseparable from it, and that any difference be-tween "priesthood" and "personality," by which priesthood would prove to be something self-contained and having no rela-tion to the personality of the bearer, is false, for it distorts the essence of priesthood as the continuation in the Church of the priesthood of Christ. The crude popular expression "as is the priest, so is the parish" has greater truth than all the cunning reasoning about *ex opere operato* and *ex opere operantis*. The Church does not reject the "validity" of a sacrament performed in love by any parish priest, whether bad or good, yet she knows the full, actually frightening dependence of church life on the adequacy or inadequacy of those to whom the "stewardship of the mysteries of God" is handed over.

And that is why, at the onset of that moment in the eucharis-tic mystery when it falls to the priest to *become Christ*, to take the place in the Church and in all creation that belongs only and per-sonally to Christ and which he has transferred and "delegated" to no one, when through the hands, voice and whole being of the priest Christ himself will function, how can the priest not turn to Christ with this *personal* prayer, how can he not confess his unwor-thiness, how can he not pray for help and for "clothing with the power of the Holy Spirit," how can he not give his *person* back to Christ, who chose him in order to manifest and fulfil in him his presence and his eternal priesthood? How can he not feel precisely a *personal* trembling, a need precisely for *personal* help from above and, chiefly, a *personal* responsibility—and not just for the "objective reality" of the sacrament but also for its "validity" in the hearts and life of the faithful? For if "no one is worthy" to perform this ministry, if it is entirely and completely a gift of the grace of God, then it is only in our humble consciousness of this unworthiness that the possibility of receiving and assimilating it is revealed to us.

9

WE HAVE ALREADY SPOKEN ABOUT THE MEANING OF CENSING in the services. To what was said we will add only that the censing during the offering of the gifts, i.e., *before* their transformation into the body and blood of Christ, and likewise their identification from the very beginning of the liturgy as *holy* and *divine*, expresses the very same "foreknowledge" of them as the sacrifice of Christ of which we were just speaking in the section devoted to the proskomidē. The gifts are holy and divine, just as the humanity of Christ is holy and divine, the beginning and gift of the "new creation," the new life. In the new life, which the Church is called to manifest and fulfil in "this world," creation is transformed into a gift and sacrifice, and only thus can it be carried up to heaven and become the gift of the divine life and communion in the body and blood of Christ. That is why it is not to perishable "matter" and not to "flesh and blood" of mortal people that we render reverence with the incense, but to the "living and well-pleasing" gift and sacrifice that they are predestined to become through the divine incarnation and which the Church sees beforehand in them. That is why it is not "simply" bread that lies on the diskos. On it all of God's creation is presented, manifested in Christ as the new creation, the fulfilment of the glory of God. And it is not "simply" people who are gathered in this assembly, but the new humanity, recreated in the image of the "ineffable glory" of its Creator. To it, to this humanity, which is eternally called to ascend to the kingdom of God, to participation in the paschal table of the Lamb and to the honor of the highest calling, we also show reverence with the censing, signifying by this ancient rite of preparation, sanctification and purification that it is "a living sacrifice, well pleasing to God."

10

THIS SAME FOREKNOWLEDGE, THIS SAME JOYOUS AFFIRMATION of the cosmic essence of the offering that is beginning we find also in the "hymn of the offering," which accompanies the movement of the gifts to the altar. Today we almost always sing the Cherubic Hymn. Only twice in the entire year is it replaced with another hymn: on Holy Thursday with the prayer "Of Thy mystical supper..." and on Holy Saturday with the ancient hymn "Let all mortal flesh keep silent..." And although in antiquity the Church also knew other "hymns of the offering," their meaning lies not so much in the various words as much as in their tonality or key, which is common to all. We can define this key best of all with the word *royal*. It is precisely a royal doxology: "That we may receive the King of all..." "For the King of kings and the Lord of lords comes to be slain..." The offering of the gifts is understood here as a triumphant royal entrance, as a manifestation of the glory and power of the kingdom. This "royal" tonality is not limited to the Great Entrance and the "hymn of the offering" alone. We already find it at the end of the proskomidē: while covering the gifts, the priest pronounces the words of the royal psalm: "The Lord reigns, he is clothed in majesty." We hear it furthermore in the priest's prayer for himself, which we have just analyzed: "No one is worthy... to serve Thee, O King of Glory." We also see it, finally, in the gradual Byzantine "staging" of the offering as precisely a "great entrance" through the *royal doors*. From here, of course, stem the beginning and the relatively early appearance of the explanation of the Great Entrance in Christian writing as a "symbol" of the entrance of the Lord into Jerusalem.

Historians of the liturgy explain the introduction and development of this royal "key" and royal "symbolism" as the influence exerted on Christian worship by Byzantine court ritual, in which processions, "exits" and "entrances" occupied a particularly important place. While not denying this influence, which actually explains many things in the particulars of Byzantine worship, we would stress, however, that the *theological* meaning of this royal "key" is rooted above all in the Church's original *cosmic* understanding of Christ's sacrifice. By his offering of himself as a

sacrifice, Christ established his *reign*, he restored the mastery over
"heaven and earth" that was "usurped" by the prince of this
world. The faith of the Church knows Christ as the conquerer of
death and Hades, as the King, who has already been manifested,
of the kingdom of God, which has already "come in power." She
knows him as the *Lord*, whom the Father of glory raised from the
dead and sat down "at his right hand in the heavenly places, far
above all rule and authority and power and dominion, . . . and he
has put all things under his feet and has made him the head over
all things" (Eph 1:20-22). In contrast to our contemporary piety,
utterly individualized and essentially minimalistic, which easily,
in the name of "spiritual comfort," hands the world over to the
devil, the joy over the lordship and reign of Christ imbued the
faith of the early Church with such strength that she breathed
precisely through this cosmic joy, through the experience of the
kingdom that was granted in Christ. And thus, whatever the outward influences and borrowings, it is precisely from this faith and
this experience that the *royal* tonality both of the hymn of the
offering and the entire Great Entrance comes. From here stems
the breakthrough of the Church into the *glory* of the age to come,
her entering into the eternal doxology of the cherubim and seraphim before the "King of kings and Lord of lords."

II

AND, FINALLY, WE COME TO THE GREAT ENTRANCE ITSELF.
Let us immediately note that in contemporary practice it has two
orders. When the liturgy is served by a bishop, he does not take
part in the actual carrying of the gifts, which is done by the clergy
celebrating with him, but, standing at the royal doors and facing
the assembly, he receives the gifts and then places them on the
altar. In the priestly liturgy the priest and deacon carry the gifts,
but only the priest places them on the altar.

We need to note this difference because, although the idea of
the *correlation* between the place and function of each member of
the Church in the eucharistic celebration and his ministry and
calling in the Church has been almost entirely effaced from
church consciousness, for early Christianity it was self-evident.

Quite often contemporary Orthodox are extremely zealous about preserving and observing "ancient rites," without, however, imparting to them any theological, or, as one would now say, existential meaning. Early Christian consciousness saw in the rites above all the Church's revelation and fulfilment of her essence, and therefore also of the essence of every ministry and every calling. In the liturgy is revealed that *image* of the Church that she has been summoned to realize in her life. And, conversely, all ministries—and the entire life of the church community—find their crowning and "fulfilment" in the liturgy. From this stems not only the "symbolic" but also the real correlation between what a member of the Church *does* in the life of the community and what he *does* in the eucharistic liturgy.

As we were saying above, in the early Church the ministers of the proskomidē, the preparation of the gifts, and likewise of their conveyance to the celebrant, were the deacons, for inside the church community their appointed vocation, their *leitourgia*, was the ministry of love, of the life of the Church as the love of all for all and the concern of all for all. That is why it was precisely the deacons who accepted from those who came into the church assembly the gifts through which the Church would realize her ministry of love. They distributed these gifts and singled out those that, *pars pro toto*, were to be offered in the eucharistic mystery. The contemporary "priestly" practice, i.e., the participation of the priest himself in the Great Entrance, arose, as we have already noted, when the *deacon*, or, to put it better, the ministry of the diaconate itself, ceased to be sensed as necessary and self-evident, when the experience of the Church as a community, linked through common life and active love, weakened, and the community was as it were dissolved into the "natural" society—the city, the village—became a "parish" or "congregation," "those who congregate" in the temple for the satisfaction of their religious needs, but who cease to live apart from the world through the life of the Church. In this new experience of the Church the deacon proved to be in essence unneeded, certainly not obligatory; and with his gradual disappearance his liturgical functions were for the most part transferred to the priest. From what has been said, it follows that of the two contemporary "orders" it is precisely the pontifical order of the Great Entrance that is closer to the ancient practice and that more fully expresses the essence of the eucharistic offering. Precisely in it is revealed the place of each, the participation of the whole Church, in this offering.

We know already that it begins—in the proskomidē—with each offering his own prosphora, his own sacrifice, with the inclusion of each in the offering of the Church. Alas, this rite is also threatened with almost total disappearance today, and it needs to be regenerated in every way possible, especially, of course, with the disclosure of its genuine meaning as precisely the participation of each member of the Church in the eucharistic offering. Inasmuch as in our day the *real* sacrifice of the members of the Church, their *real* participation in her life consists chiefly in monetary donations, it would be appropriate for our "collection basket" to be joined with the offering of prosphora, to make the latter again obligatory for all. To realize this would not be difficult: let the money that each person who comes to the liturgy intends to place in the "basket" be used *for a prosphora*, and in such manner make the prosphora an expression of his offering, his sacrifice. In any case, precisely here is the beginning of our offering, which, in the *movement* of the bread and the cup—from us to the table of oblation, from the table of oblation to the altar, from the altar to the heavenly sanctuary—is revealed as our entrance into the sacrifice of Christ, our ascent to the table of the Lord in his kingdom.

The second act of this movement is the transfer of the gifts from the table of oblation to the altar, which, as we have just seen, comprises the express *leitourgia* of the deacons. Even now, when the table of oblation, on which the proskomidē is performed, is found inside the sanctuary, and not, as in the early Church, in a special location called the prothesis (only the altar was called a "table" of oblation), the gifts are first brought out into the assembly and only from the assembly are they brought to the sanctuary, do they "enter" the altar. The Greek practice of bringing the gifts around the whole church, the whole gathering, needs to be acknowledged as a better expression of the meaning of the Great Entrance than the Russian practice, where the gifts are only brought around the solea and then directly to the royal doors. For the meaning of this consists in the fact that the offering of *each*, included in the offering of *all*, is now being realized as the

Church's offering of her very self, and this means Christ, for the Church is his body, and he is the head of the Church.

And, finally, the third and concluding moment of the entrance consists of the reception of the gifts by the celebrant and their deposition on the altar. That which *we* offer is now manifested as being offered by Christ and being taken up by him into the heavenly sanctuary. Our sacrifice is the sacrifice of the Church, which is the sacrifice of Christ. Thus, in this triumphant and royal entrance, in this movement of the gifts, is revealed the truly universal significance of the offering, the unification of heaven and earth, the raising up of our life to the kingdom of God.

12

"MAY THE LORD GOD REMEMBER ALL OF YOU...IN HIS KINGdom always, now and ever and unto ages of ages." These words, this *commemoration*, accompany the Great Entrance and the offering accomplished in it. The deacon pronounces them while bringing the gifts; the celebrants direct them to each other and to the gathering; the faithful answer the presider with them.

"Remember, O Lord..." Without any exaggeration one can say that the commemoration, i.e., the referral of everything to the *memory* of God, the prayer that God would "remember," constitutes the heartbeat of all of the Church's worship, her entire life. Not yet speaking of the sacrament of the eucharist, which Christ commanded us to "do...in remembrance of me" (we shall speak further of the precise meaning of this remembrance), the Church constantly, every day, almost every hour, "celebrates the memory" of a certain event, a certain saint, so that the essence of each of her "holy days" and all her services lies precisely in this "celebration of the memory," in this constant remembrance.

And if this is so, then we must ask: in what does the essence of this commemoration consist? This is necessary all the more because on this question our school theology maintains an almost total silence. Is it because the very concept of *memory* seems insufficiently objective to this theology, whose avowed single criterion is the "scientific method," and seems a surrender to the subjectivism and psychologism so hateful to "science"? Is it because, in the

interpretation and reconstruction of the faith of the Church as a
certain "objective" doctrine, constructed above all on "texts,"
memory, and even experience in general, simply has no place?
Whatever the case, commemoration, so fundamental to the life,
prayer and experience of the Church, appears to remain outside of
the theological field of vision. And, strangely enough, this theological obliviousness leads in fact precisely to the "psychologiza-
tion" of worship, which, like a splendid flower, blossoms in its
reduction to outward "illustrative" symbolism and so greatly
interferes with a genuine understanding of and genuine participation in worship. If, on the one hand, the liturgical "remembrance," the "celebration of the memory" of this or that event, is
perceived today entirely as a psychological, intellectual focus on
the "meaning" of that event (which inevitably abets its "symbol-
ization"), and if, on the other, commemoration in prayer is simply identified with a prayer *on behalf of* another human being,
then it is of course because we forget the genuine meaning of
memory and commemoration, which is manifested in the
Church. And we forget above all because of that theology that
itself is rooted not so much in the experience and memory of the
Church as in "texts." That is why we must recall this meaning
before we can understand the place of the commemoration in the
eucharistic offering.

13

THOUSANDS OF BOOKS HAVE BEEN WRITTEN, FROM ALL POSS-
ible points of view, on *memory*, this mysterious gift present only in
man, and it would be impossible here to simply enumerate all the
explanations and theories they provide. But this is unnecessary,
for however much man would strive to understand and explain its
meaning and "mechanism," the gift of memory would remain ultimately inexplicable, mysterious and even ambiguous.

One thing is without doubt: memory is man's capacity to
"resurrect the past," to preserve knowledge of it within himself.
But we must say precisely that this capacity is ambiguous. Actually, does its essence not lie in that if, on the one hand, in memory the past is surely resurrected—through it, in it I *see* a man who

some time ago passed from life, I *feel* in all particularities that morning when I met with him or the last time I saw him, and thus I can "collect" my life—then, on the other, it is resurrected precisely as past, that is, as unreturnable, so that in being realized through my memory the knowledge of this past is simultaneously a discovery of its *absence* in the present? Hence the sorrow inherent in memory. For, in the end, memory in man is nothing other than the *knowledge*, peculiar only to man, of *death*, of the fact that "death and time rule on the earth." This is why the gift of memory is ambiguous. Through it man simultaneously "resurrects" the past and comes to know the shatteredness of his own life, which "circling, vanishes in the mist"; he comprehends the shatteredness and unreturnability of time, in which, sooner or later, memory itself will darken, weaken and be snuffed out, and death will reign.

Only in relation to this "natural" memory—to the most human but therefore also the most ambiguous of all human gifts, thanks to which even before death man recognizes his own mortality and life as dying—can man not so much understand as feel the entire *newness* of that memory, that remembrance, which it is appropriate to call the essence of the new life given to us in Christ.

Here we should recall that in the biblical, Old Testamental teaching on God, the term memory refers to the attentiveness of God to his creation, the power of divine providential love, through which God "holds" the world and *gives it life*, so that life itself can be termed abiding in the memory of God, and death the falling out of this memory. In other words, memory, like everything else in God, is *real*, it *is* that life that he grants, that God *"remembers"*; it *is* the eternal overcoming of the "nothing" out of which God called us into "his wonderful light."

And this gift of memory, as the power that transforms love into life, into knowledge, communion and unity, has been given to man by God. Man's memory is his responding love for God, the encounter and communion with God, with the life of life itself. Out of all creation it is given to man alone to *remember* God and through this remembrance to truly live. If everything in the world witnesses to God, declares his glory and renders him praise, then only man "remembers" him and, through this memory, through this living knowledge of God, comprehends the world as God's world, receives it from God and raises it up to God. To God's remembrance of him, man answers with his remembrance of God. If God's remembrance of man is the gift of life, then man's remembrance of God is the reception of this lifecreating gift, the constant *acquisition* of and increase in life.

But then it also becomes understandable why the very essence and depth and horror of *sin* are most perfectly expressed not in a multitude of "scientific-theological" definitions but in the common, popular expression: *man has forgotten God*. For in relation to what has just been demonstrated, to the biblical and, so to speak, ontological (and not simply "psychological") understanding of memory, to *forget* means above all to cut what has been forgotten off from life, to cease to live by it, to fall away from it. It is not simply to "stop thinking" about God—for the militant atheist is often "obsessed" with his hatred for God, and there are many on earth who, while sincerely convinced of their "religiosity," nevertheless seek in religion everything imaginable, but not God. It is precisely a *falling away* from him, from life, ceasing to live through him and in him. And it is precisely in such *obliviousness* toward God that the fundamental—"original"—sin of man consisted and consists. Man forgot God because he turned his love, and consequently his memory and his very life, to something else, and above all to himself. He turned away from God and ceased to *see* him. He forgot God, and God ceased to exist for him. For the terror and irreparability of obliviousness lie in the fact that, like memory, it is *ontological*. If memory is lifecreating, then obliviousness is death or, more precisely, the beginning of death, the poison of dying, which poisons life and converts it inexorably, inevitably, into dying. The absence of one whom I forget for me is *real*, he is actually *not* in my life, not a part of my life—he is dead for me, and I for him. If it is God, the giver of life and life itself whom I have forgotten, if he has ceased to be *my* memory and *my* life, my life itself becomes dying, and then memory, which is the knowledge and power of life, becomes knowledge of death and the constant tasting of mortality.

As man cannot annihilate himself, return himself to that non-existence from which God called him to life, so it is not given to him to annihilate his *memory*, i.e., his knowledge of his own life.

But just as man's life in separation from God was filled with death and became dying, so also his memory became knowledge of death and its kingdom in the world. Through memory he wants to overcome time and death, to "resurrect the past," to not allow it to be absorbed without a trace by the "abyss of time," but this resurrecting itself turns out to be a pitiful knowledge of the unreturnability of this past, of the smell of corruption that fills the world. In religion, in art, in all the culture of this fallen life—for it is the life of fallen man—"life, like a wounded bird, wants to soar off and cannot." These upward flights can be infinitely beautiful, but on earth what is really beautiful is *only* the sorrow for genuine life, only the memory of what is lost and the yearning for it, only "holy melancholy." These flights can remain in the "memory" of man as thirst, appeal, repentance, entreaty, and all the same, in the final analysis, they are devoured by oblivion, just as after the death of the last relatives, the last of those who "remember," wild grass begins to grow over the grave over which they not so long ago sang "memory eternal." The gravestone crumbles, and it is no longer possible to decipher the faded letters of the name it bears. All anyone can make out are two terrifying and senseless dates of a forgotten life, no longer of use to anyone.

14

HERE IS WHY THE SALVATION OF MAN AND THE WORLD—WHY the renewal of life—consists in the restoration of *memory* as a lifecreating power, *remembrance* as the overcoming of time and of the destruction of life and the reign of death that it entails. This salvation is accomplished in Christ. He is the incarnation in man and for man, in the world and for the world, of God's remembrance, of the divine and lifecreating love directed toward the world. And he is the perfect manifestation and fulfilment in man of his remembrance of God, as the content, the power and the life of life itself.

The incarnation of the memory of God: if man has forgotten God, God has not forgotten man, he has not "turned himself away" from him. He has transformed the fallen and mortal time of "this world" into the history of salvation. He has revealed its meaning as expectation of and preparation for salvation, the gradual restoration in man of *memory* of himself, and in this memory, knowledge and anticipation and love, so that at the coming of the fulness of time, i.e., at the accomplishment of this preparation, man could recognize God in the Savior who had come, *remember the forgotten*, and in it find his lost life. The restoration, through God's remembrance of man, of man's remembrance of God—such is the meaning of the Old Testament, and it is impossible to separate Christ from it, to know him otherwise than through the Old Testament, because it is nothing other than the gradually disclosed *recognition* of Christ, the "creation" of his "memory" before his coming in time. And when Simeon took Christ into his elderly hands and called him the "salvation prepared before the face of all people," when the forerunner John pointed him out in the Jordan wilderness as the lamb of God who takes upon himself the sins of the world, when Peter, on the road to Caesarea Philippi, confessed him as the Christ, the Son of God, it was not a puzzling and inexplicable "miracle" but the apex and fulfilment of that *memory* of the Savior and salvation, that *recognition*, in which God's remembrance of man is *fulfilled* as man's remembrance of God.

Salvation consists in this: that in Christ—perfect God and perfect man—memory comes to reign and is restored as a lifecreating power, and, in *remembering*, man partakes not of the experience of the fall, mortality and death, but of the overcoming of this fall through "life everlasting." For Christ himself is the incarnation and the gift to mankind of *God's memory* in all its fulness—as love directed toward each man and toward all humanity, toward the world and all creation. He is the Savior because in his memory he "remembers" all, and through this memory he receives all as his own life, and he gives his own life to all as their life. But being the incarnation of the memory of God, Christ is likewise the manifestation and fulfilment of man's perfect remembrance of God, for in this *memory*—love, self-sacrifice and communion with the Father—is his *entire* life, the entire perfection of his humanity.

The essence of our faith and the new life granted in it consists in *Christ's memory*, realized in us through our *memory of Christ*. From the very first day of Christianity, to believe in Christ meant to *remember* him and keep him always *in mind*. It is not simply to "know" about him and his doctrine, but to *know him*—living and abiding among those who love him. From the very beginning the faith of Christians was memory and remembrance, but memory restored to its lifecreating essence—for, as opposed to our "natural," "fallen" memory, with its illusory "resurrection of the past," this new memory is a joyous recognition of the one who was resurrected, who lives and therefore is present and abides, and not only recognition but also encounter and the living experience of communion with him. While directed to the "past"—to the life, death and resurrection, in the time of Pontius Pilate, of the man Jesus—while rooted in this "past," faith eternally knows that the one who is remembered *lives*. He "is and shall be" among us. Faith could not be this recognition were it not a remembrance, but it could not be a remembrance were it not *knowledge* of the one remembered. We were not alive "in the days of his flesh," in the time of Pontius Pilate, and therefore we can neither remember nor recall what occurred at that time. Yet if we not only know *about* what happened—from "texts" that have reached us—but actually *remember* and *recall* it; if, moreso, our faith and our life in essence consist in this memory and in this remembrance, then it is because the one whom we remember lives, and everything that he has accomplished "for the sake of us men and for our salvation"—his life and death, his resurrection and glorification—he has given us and eternally gives to us, and through them he eternally communes with us. That is why it is no longer the "past" that we remember, but *Christ himself*, and this remembrance becomes our entry into *his* victory over time, over its collapse into "past," "present" and "future." It is an entry not into some abstract and motionless "eternity" but into "life everlasting," in which all is *alive*, everything lives through the lifecreating memory of God, and *everything is ours*—"the world or life or death or the present or the future"—all is ours, for we "are Christ's; and Christ is God's" (1 Co 3:22-23).

Such is the essence of that *remembrance*, which, as was said above, comprises the basis of the life of the Church and which is realized above all in her worship. The services are the entry of the Church into the new time of the new creation, *gathered* by the memory of Christ, transformed by him into life and the gift of life, salvation from the collapse into "past," "present" and "future." In the worship of the Church—the body of Christ, which

lives by his life, by his memory—it is necessary for us to again and
again recall, and this means to comprehend and realize, how for
us, in us and with us "what was accomplished," what was given
to us—the creation of the world and its salvation in Christ and the
kingdom of God, which is coming in glory but in Christ is already revealed—has already been granted. We *recall*, in other
words, both the past and the future as *living* in us, as given to us,
as transformed into our *life* and making it life in God.

15

ONLY IN THE LIGHT OF WHAT HAS BEEN SAID CAN WE NOW
understand the meaning of this *commemoration*, which appears as a
sort of verbal expression of the Great Entrance, the bringing of
the eucharistic gifts to the altar. Through this commemoration
we include the ones being remembered in the lifecreating memory of Christ: God's memory of man, man's memory of God, that
diune memory which is eternal life. We return each other, in
Christ, to God, and in this giving back we affirm that the one
remembered and given back is *alive*, for he abides in God's
memory.

The commemoration is united with the offering, and together
they constitute one whole. It is its verbal fulfilment, because
Christ offered himself "on behalf of all and for all," because in
himself he offered and gave back all of us to God, he united all in
his memory. The remembrance of Christ is the entry into his
love, making us brothers and neighbors, "brethren" in his ministry. His life and presence in us and "among" us is certified *only* by
our love for each other and for all whom God has sent into, has
included in our life, and this means above all in the *remembrance* of
each other and in the commemoration of each other in Christ.
Therefore, in bringing his sacrifice to the altar, we *create the memory of each other*, we identify each other as living in Christ and
being united with each other in him.

In this commemoration there is no distinction between those
who live and those who have fallen asleep, for God "is not God of
the dead, but of the living" (Mt 22:32). In this is the whole joy
and the whole power of this commemoration, that, in including

the remembered ones in the lifecreating memory of God, the borders between the living and the dead are erased, for all are recognized and manifested as living in God. That is why the serving of a special "liturgy for the departed" (and in black vestments, no less!) would have been incomprehensible and impossible in the early Church—incomprehensible because in each liturgy, and precisely in this inclusion of all in God's memory, we celebrate the union of all, both of the living and of those who have fallen asleep, in the "life everlasting." In this sense, every liturgy is "of the departed," and in every liturgy the memory and love of Christ that has been given to us triumphs over death, over separation and obliviousness. "There will be no separation, O friends..."

Thus, in the commemoration of our very selves, of each other and all our life, in its return through this commemoration to God, our offering is fulfilled. The offering by ourselves of Christ, and in Christ of ourselves, makes possible and fulfils our commemoration.

CHAPTER SEVEN

The Sacrament of Unity

> *"Greet one another with a holy kiss..."*
>
> I CORINTHIANS 16:20

I

*I*N THE CONTEMPORARY ORDER OF THE LITURGY THE EXCLA-
mation "Let us love one another!" takes up so little time that
it is almost impossible for us to truly hear it—to hear it not only
with our outer but also our inner ear. For us today it is just one of
the exclamations that precede the symbol of faith. But in earlier
times this was not so. We know from the liturgical evidence of
the ancient Church that a *kiss of peace* was actually performed after
this exclamation, and the entire Church, the entire gathering,
took part in it. "When the time comes for the exhortation of the
mutual reception of the peace," writes St John Chrysostom, "we
all kiss each other." And "the clerics greet the bishop, the laymen
the men, the women the women..."[1] This rite is preserved to this
day in the liturgical practices of the Nestorians, Copts and Arme-
nians, which were not exposed to late-Byzantine influences and
thus often reflect an earlier form of the eucharistic celebration.
And this rite is not only eucharistic, for the kiss of peace comprised an important and inalienable part of all Christian worship.
Thus, it was performed after a baptism, when the bishop kissed

[1] *Homily on II Corinthians* 18:3, PG 61:527.

133

the anointed with the words "The Lord be with you." At the consecration of a new bishop the entire assembly, both clerics and laity, likewise greeted him with a "holy kiss," after which he would preside over the eucharistic offering for the first time.

It is obvious from the history of this moment in the liturgy that it underwent a substantial change. From an *action*—and, moreover, a common action—it was transformed into an *exclamation*. And with this change the content of the summons contained in this exclamation also changed, at least in part. The contemporary exclamation "Let us love one another!" is a call to a certain condition, while in its ancient forms it summoned the gathering to a specific act: "greet one another." And we have evidence that this act was performed even without any exclamation: several documents describe a kiss being performed during the giving of the peace. It is obvious that, as has occurred more than once in the history of worship, an exclamation that itself was derived from an action then gradually displaced or, more precisely, narrowed the action to the sanctuary alone, where to this day it is performed between the celebrating priests and deacons.

At first glance this gradual replacement of a common action with an exclamation and all these "technical" details would not seem to present any particular interest. The exclamation itself would not require any explanation, inasmuch as everyone knows that love is the highest Christian commandment, and thus a reminder of it would be appropriate before this most important of all church ceremonies. But if so, what does it matter whether this reminder consists in a call to love or in a symbol of love (and in the kiss of peace the commentators see, of course, just one more "symbol")? One may suppose moreover that the disappearance of the action was linked with the growth of the Church, with the appearance of crowded assemblies in huge churches, where no one knew each other and where this rite, from our contemporary point of view, would be simply a formality.

But all this is so only "at first glance," when we have not yet considered the genuine and precisely liturgical meaning of these words and actions—and above all the meaning of the very expression "Christian love."

In fact, we have become so accustomed to this expression, we have heard preaching about love and the summons to it so many times that it is difficult for us to be struck with the eternal *newness* of these words. And yet Christ himself pointed out this newness: "A *new* commandment I give you, that you love one another" (Jn 13:34). Even before Christ, however, the world in fact knew about love, about the value and height of love. Do we not find in the Old Testament the two commandments—regarding love for God (Dt 6:5) and love for neighbor (Lv 19:18)—that Christ said contain the entire law and the prophets (Mt 22:40)? In what, then, lies the newness of this commandment, the newness not only at the moment of the pronunciation of these words by the Savior, but for all time, all people—the newness that never ceases to be new?

In order to answer this question it is enough to recall one of the fundamental signs of Christian love, as it is indicated in the gospels: *"Love your enemies."* These words contain nothing less than an unheard-of demand for love toward someone whom we precisely *do not love.* That is why they do not cease to disturb us, to frighten us and, above all, to *judge* us, as long as we have not become thoroughly deaf to the gospel. Precisely because this commandment is unheard of and new, we for the most part substitute our own cunning human interpretations of it. Already for centuries, and apparently with a pure conscience, not only individual Christians but also whole churches have affirmed that in reality Christian love must be directed toward *one's own*—that to love essentially and self-evidently means to love neighbors and family, one's own people, one's own country—all those persons and things that we would usually love anyway, without Christ and the gospel. We no longer notice that in Orthodoxy, for example, religiously colored and justified nationalism long ago became a genuine heresy, crippling church consciousness, hopelessly dividing the Orthodox East and making all of our profuse talk about the ecumenical truth of Orthodoxy a hypocritical lie. We have forgotten the other, no less strange and frightening words that the gospel contains about this merely "natural love": "He who loves father or mother...son or daughter more than me is not worthy of me" (Mt 10:37), and "If anyone comes to me and does not hate his own father and mother and wife and children and brothers . . . he cannot be my disciple" (Lk 14:26). If coming to Christ signifies the fulfilment of his commandment, then, obviously, Christian love not only is not a simple increase, "crown-ing" and religious sanction of natural love, but is radically distin-guished from it and even contraposed to it. It is really a *new* love, of which our fallen nature and fallen world are incapable and which is therefore impossible in it.

But how can we fulfil this commandment? How can we love those whom we do not love? Is not the mystery of any love that it can never be the fruit of only the will, of self-education, of practice, even of askesis? Through the exercise of the will and self-education one can attain "good will," toleration and evenhanded-ness in relations with others, but not love—which St Isaac the Syrian says is even "merciful to the demons." And what then can this impossible commandment of love mean?

There can be only one answer to this question. Yes, this com-mandment would actually be impossible and, consequently, monstrous if Christianity consisted only in the commandment to love. But Christianity is not only the commandment but also the *revelation* and the *gift* of love. And love was commanded only be-cause, before the command, it was revealed and given to us.

Only "God *is* love." Only God loves with that love of which the gospels speak. And only in the divine incarnation, in the uni-fication of God and man, i.e., in Jesus Christ, the Son of God and the Son of man, is the love of God himself—or, better yet, God himself who is love—manifested and granted to human beings. In this is the staggering *newness* of Christian love—that in the New Testament man is called to love with the divine love, which has become the divine-human love, the love of Christ. The newness of Christianity lies not in the commandment to love, but in the fact that it has become possible to fulfil the commandment. In union with Christ we receive his love and can love with it and grow in it. "God's love has been poured into our hearts through the Holy Spirit which has been given to us" (Rm 5:5), and through Christ we have been commanded to abide in him and in his love: "Abide in me, and I in you. As the branch cannot bear fruit by itself, unless it abides in the vine, neither can you, unless you abide in me...He who abides in me and I in him, he it is that bears much fruit, for apart from me you can do nothing...*abide in my love*" (Jn 15:4,5,9).

To abide in Christ means to be and to live in the Church,

which is the life of Christ, communicated and granted to humanity, and which therefore lives through Christ's love, abides in his love. The love of Christ is the origin, content and goal of the Church's life, and this love is in essence the only *sign* of the Church, for all the rest is embraced by it: "By this all men will know that you are my disciples, if you have love for one another" (Jn 13:35). Love is the essence of the *holiness* of the Church, for it "has been poured into our hearts through the Holy Spirit"; the essence of the *unity* of the Church, which "upbuilds itself in love" (Eph 4:16); and, finally, the essence of *apostolicity* and catholicity (*sobornost'*), for the Church is everywhere and always the same single apostolic union, "joined with the yoke of love." Therefore, "If I speak in the tongues of men and of angels... if I have prophetic powers, and understand all mysteries and all knowledge, and if I have all faith, so as to remove mountains, but have not love, I am nothing. If I give away all I have, and if I deliver my body to be burned, but have not love, I gain nothing" (1 Co 13:1-3). For only love gives every "sign" of the Church—unity, holiness, apostolicity and catholicity—its significance and actuality.

The Church is a union of love—or, as Khomiakov put it, "love as an organism"[2]—not only in the sense that her members are united by love, but above all in that through this love of all for each other, through love as life itself, she manifests Christ and his love to the world, she witnesses to him and loves and saves the world through the love of Christ. In the *fallen* world, the mission of the Church, as salvation, is to manifest the world as regenerated by Christ. The essence of the fallen world is that division, the separation of each from all, reigns in it. This is not overcome by the "natural" love of certain people for certain others, and it triumphs and is fulfilled in the ultimate "separation"—death. The essence of the Church lies in the manifestation and presence in the world of love as life and life as love. Fulfilling herself in love, she witnesses in the world to this love. She bears it to the world and with it she "ministers to creation," which had been subordinated to the law of division and death. In it each person mysteriously obtains the power to "yearn [ἐπιποθέω]... with the affection

[2]A. Khomiakov, *Complete Works* 1 (Moscow, 1900), chapter 21, cited by A. Gratieux, *A.S. Khomiakov et le mouvement slavophile* (Paris, 1939) 109.

[σπλάγχνον] of Christ Jesus" (Phil 1:8) and to be a witness to and bearer of this love in the world.

But then the *assembling as the Church* is above all the sacrament of love. We go to church *for love*, for the new love of Christ himself, which is granted to us in our unity. We go to church so that this divine love will again and again be "poured into our hearts," so that again and again we may "put on love" (Col 3:14), so that, *constituting* the body of Christ, we can abide in Christ's love and manifest it in the world. But that is why our contemporary, utterly "individualized" piety, in which we egotistically separate ourselves from the gathering, is so grievous, so contradictory to the age-old experience of the Church. Even while standing in the church, we continue to sense some people as "neighbors" and others as "strangers"—a faceless mass that "has no relevance" to us and to our prayer and disturbs our "spiritual concentration." How often do seemingly "spiritually" attuned and "devout" people openly declare their distaste for crowded gatherings, which disturb them from praying, and seek empty and quiet chapels, secluded corners, separate from the "crowds." In fact, such individual "self-absorption" would hardly be possible in the church assembly—precisely because this is not the purpose of the assembly and of our participation in it. Concerning this individual prayer the gospels say: "When you pray, go into your room and shut the door and pray..." (Mt 6:6). Does not this mean that the *assembling as the Church* has another purpose, already contained in the very word "assembly"? Through it the Church fulfils herself, accomplishes our communion with Christ and with his love, so that in participating in it, we comprise "out of many, one body."

And thus the *kiss of peace* is disclosed to us in its full significance. I have said above that it constituted an inalienable part of the church assembly from the first day of the Church's existence. This was because for the early Christians it was not simply a symbol and a reminder of love, but a *sacred rite of love*—the visible sign and rite in which and through which the effusion of divine love into the hearts of the faithful, the vesting of each and all together in the love of Christ is invisibly but really accomplished. In our current, utterly individualistic and egocentric approach to the Church this rite is inevitably perceived as a hollow "form." I really don't know the man who is standing across from me in church; I can neither love him nor not love him, for he is a "stranger" to me and thus *no one.* And we are so afraid of this hollow form, so utterly "sincere" in our individualism and egocentrism that we forget the chief thing. We forget that in the call to "greet one another with a holy kiss" we are talking not of our personal, natural, human love, through which we cannot in fact love someone who is a "stranger," who has not yet become "something" or "somebody" for us, but of the *love of Christ,* the eternal wonder of which consists precisely in the fact that it transforms the *stranger* (and each stranger, in his depths, is an *enemy*) into a *brother*, irrespective of whether he has or does not have relevance for me and for my life; that it is the very purpose of the Church to overcome the horrible *alienation* that was introduced into the world by the devil and proved to be its undoing. And we forget that we come to church for this love, which is always granted to us in the gathering of the brethren.

This is why in antiquity the assembly of the faithful was called not to a verbal answer but precisely to an *action.* For we know that we cannot of ourselves attain this love, just as we cannot acquire the peace of Christ—which "surpasses all understanding"—forgiveness of sins, eternal life and union with God. All this is given, granted to us in the sacred mystery of the Church; and the entire Church is one great sacrament, the sacred rite of Christ. Christ is at work in all our gestures, actions and ceremonies, and everything visible becomes "the visibility of the invisible," each symbol is fulfilled in the sacrament. Thus, in the "holy kiss" we express not our own love—rather, we embrace each other through the new love of Christ. And is this not the joy of communion, that I receive this love of Christ from the "stranger" standing across from me, and he from me? And that in it we are both "revealed" to each other as participants in Christ's love, and this means as *brothers in Christ?*

We can only desire this love and prepare ourselves for its reception. In antiquity those who had had fallings out had to be reconciled and forgive each other before taking part in the church assembly. Everything human had to be fulfilled, so that God could reign in the heart. And to prepare ourselves means to ask ourselves: do we go to the liturgy for this love of Christ, do we go as people who hunger and thirst not only for help and consolation but for the fire that burns away all our weaknesses, all our limitations, and illumines us through the new love of Christ? Or are we afraid that this love will weaken our hatred for our enemies, all our "principled" condemnations, our discrepancies and divisions? Do we not more often desire from the Church peace only with those with whom we already have it, love for those whom we already love, self-affirmation and self-justification? But if so, we are not acquiring that gift that allows us to actually renew and eternally renew our lives, we do not venture beyond the limits of our personal "alienation" and we are not really taking part in the Church.

Let us bear in mind that in antiquity the giving of the peace and the kiss of love were the first actions of the liturgy of the faithful, i.e., the eucharistic celebration itself. For they not only began the eucharist, but in a certain sense made it *possible*, for it is the sacrament of the New Testament, the kingdom of the love of God. Therefore, only when we are "clothed" in this love can we perform the remembrance of Christ, be partakers of his flesh and blood, await the kingdom of God and the life of the age to come.

"Make love your aim," says the apostle (1 Co 14:1). And where can we attain this, if not in the sacrament in which Christ himself unites us in his love?

2

THE RECITATION AND LATER THE SINGING OF THE SYMBOL OF faith was introduced into the order of the liturgy relatively late— toward the beginning of the sixth century. Up to that time its appointed place in Christian worship was in the sacrament of baptism. The "handing back of the creed" (*redditio symboli*), that is, the solemn confession of faith, concluded the preparation of the catechumens for their baptismal entry into the Church. The symbol of faith arose in connection with baptism, and only later, at the time of the great dogmatic disputes, did it more often come to be used in its capacity as a measure of orthodoxy, as an *oros*, a "limit," guarding the Church from heresy. As far as the eucharist is concerned—which, as we already know, was a closed assembly of the *faithful*, i.e., those who already have come to believe, who have been reborn through "water and the Spirit," who have received the anointment from above—in the consciousness of the early Church it presupposed, as something self-evident, the unity in the faith of all who take part in the gathering. Therefore, the inclusion of the symbol of faith in the order of the liturgy, which became universal relatively quickly, was nothing more than the confirmation of the originally obvious, organic and inalienable link between the *unity of faith* and the Church and her self-fulfilment in the eucharist. And this link constituted the heartbeat of the experience and life of the early Church.

We must dwell on this link, however, for it comprises, if you will, the chief difference between our contemporary experience and the experience of the early Church. In our time this link is not sensed as self-evident; and neither is unity, of which so many speak and argue in our day, sensed as being rooted in it and flowing from it.

I shall stipulate immediately that formally everything remains in place, as it were, and this link abides as an immutable law for the Orthodox, protected by the canons and church discipline. Thus, in accordance with this discipline, heterodox are not admitted to participation in the Orthodox liturgy, because according to Orthodox doctrine "communion in the sacraments" presupposes unity of faith, on which in turn is founded and which expresses the unity of the Church. Thus, on the strength of this discipline, Orthodox are forbidden to take part in sacraments performed by heterodox. However, this law is all the more obviously perceived as a formality, for in our official, school theology and in the consciousness of the believers it was long ago severed from the reality from which it arose, of which it testifies and outside of which it is, in essence, unintelligible.

This reality is the primordial, absolutely fundamental experience of the eucharist as the *sacrament of unity*, and this means the sacrament of the Church, which St Ignatius of Antioch defined as the "unity of faith with love."[3] "And unite all of us to one another

---

[3] Cf *Philadelphians* 4 and 6:2; *Ephesians* 4:2, 14:1, 20:2; and *Magnesians* 1:2: "I sing the praises of the churches, even while I am a prisoner. I want them to confess that Jesus Christ, our perpetual Life, united flesh with spirit. I want them, too, to unite their faith with love—there is nothing better than that." Tr. Richardson, 94.

who become partakers of the one Bread and Cup in the communion of the Holy Spirit." It is precisely this experience, engraved
in these words of the eucharistic prayer of St Basil the Great,
precisely this understanding and perception of the eucharist that
is utterly weakened in contemporary church consciousness. But
then, what can the prohibition against partaking of the sacraments of the heterodox mean, in a real, living and "positive"
sense, if the eucharist has long since ceased to be perceived by the
Orthodox themselves as communion and "union with each other," if not only for simple believers but also in theological definitions it has become a particular, individual "means of personal
sanctification," to which each resorts or from which each abstains
according to the measure of his personal and self-understood
"spiritual needs," frame of mind, preparation or unpreparation,
etc.? It is obvious that, if the earlier meaning of such a prohibition lay in the fact that it defended the real experience of the
Church as unity of faith and, in this manner, in fact affirmed this
unity and witnessed to it, then with the reduction of the eucharist, and likewise all the sacraments, to the category of one of the
"means of sanctification," it became merely a prohibition alas devoid for an ever greater number of the faithful of self-evident spiritual cogency.

3

THIS WEAKENING, THIS—WE CAN EVEN SAY—DEGENERATION OF
the original eucharistic experience, is, I repeat, in fact sanctioned
both by our formal theology and by that utterly individualistic
piety that is almost universally dominant in the Church and thus
passes itself off as something age-old and traditional. This sanction is already installed in formal theology in its very method.
Being borrowed from the West, and thus appearing to our
learned theologians as the height of science, this method consists
in the isolation of each element of faith and church tradition into a
self-sufficient object, if not into a separate "discipline," as though
the degree of comprehension of each of them depends precisely on
one's ability not to coordinate it with the others but, on the contrary, to apportion and "isolate" it. Thus, each of the three reali-

ties of which we are speaking here—i.e., faith, the Church, the eucharist—proves to be a subject of special study in a separate "division," removed from any ties with the other two. This, in turn, actually leads to a paradoxical result. What falls out of the theological field of vision is precisely the thing that unifies these three realities, that manifests them as a triune reality: *unity*, which in the experience of the Church constitutes the genuine content of the new life that we receive through faith, live in the Church, and are granted as "communion of the one Spirit" in the eucharist.

One is easily convinced of this paradox. Thus, for example, one of the best of our dogmaticians, while correctly interpreting faith as a "main condition of salvation," maintains complete silence on the matter of the Christian faith itself embracing the experience of unity, the experience of faith itself as unity. Why? Because, of course, constrained by his method of isolating and apportioning—in the present case, through the reduction of faith to a "subordinate and perceived principle in man"—he proves to be incapable of recognizing in unity simultaneously the fruit and content of faith, its life, its fulfilment in man. The same thing happens with regard to the Church. "Isolating," defining the Church as the "mediator in the sanctification of man," school theology inevitably reduces the doctrine of the Church to its divinely established order, its hierarchical structure, as the condition and form of this mediation, but leaves out of its field of vision nothing less than the Church herself, the Church as the new life in the "unity of faith and love," as the constant fulfilment of this unity. And, finally, isolating, on account of this hopelessly onesided and thus depraved method, the sacraments in general and the eucharist in particular into a certain self-sufficient department—"on the means existing in the Church for the sanctification of man"—this theology is simply unaware of the eucharist as above all the sacrament of the Church, as the gift and fulfilment of that "unity of faith and love," "communion of the one Spirit," in which the essence of the Church is revealed.

4

IF THE "DROPPING" OF UNITY FROM SCHOOL THEOLOGY IS THUS explained by the very method of this theology, torn away as it is from the living experience of the Church, then the cause of its falling out from contemporary piety needs to be sought in the gradual dissolution of faith into what can best be defined as "religious feeling." This statement may seem strange, even senseless, to many, inasmuch as in our day these concepts have become virtually equivalent. In the Christian experience and understanding of faith, however, the differences between them are indeed enormous. Faith is always and above all a *meeting* with the Other, conversion to the Other, the reception of him as "the way, the truth and the life," love for him and the desire for total unity with him, such that "it is no longer I who live, but Christ who lives in me" (Ga 2:20). And because faith is always directed to the Other, it is man's exodus from the limits of his "I," a radical change of his interrelations above all within himself. Meanwhile, "religious feeling," which in our day again dominates in religion, is so distinct from faith because it lives and is nourished *by itself*, i.e., through the gratification that it gives and which, in the final analysis, is subordinated to personal tastes and emotional experiences, subjective and individual "spiritual needs."

Faith, to the degree that it is indeed faith, cannot but be an inner struggle: "I believe; help my unbelief..." (Mk 9:24). Religious feeling, on the contrary, "satisfies" precisely because it is passive, and if it is oriented toward anything, it is primarily toward help and consolation amidst life's adversities. Although its subject is always the person, faith is never individualistic, for it is directed to that which is revealed to it as absolute truth, which by its very nature is incapable of being "individual." Faith therefore invariably requires confession, expression, attraction and conversion of others to itself. Religious feeling, on the contrary, being utterly individualistic, feels itself to be inexpressible and shies away from any attempt at expression and comprehension, as if it were an unnecessary and unhealthy "rationalizing," which would put "simple faith" at risk of destruction. True faith aspires to the integral illumination of the entire human composite by subordinating to itself the reason, the will, the whole of life. Religious feeling, on the contrary, easily accepts a rupture between religion and life and gets along happily with ideas, convictions, sometimes entire worldviews that are not only alien to Christianity but frequently openly contradictory to it.

It is precisely "religious feeling," and not faith in the original Christian perception of the word, that dominates if not altogether reigns in contemporary Orthodox piety. Its gradual substitution for faith usually goes unnoticed, because externally, on the surface of church life, it often appears as the most absolute, one-hundred-percent bulwark of genuine "churchliness" and "true Orthodoxy." In its Orthodox variant it expresses itself, to be sure, chiefly in a uterine attachment to rituals, customs, traditions—all the outward forms of church life. And here, thanks to this outward "churchliness" of religious feeling, so many do not understand that the conservatism inherent to it is in fact pseudo-conservatism, deeply alien—one can even say inimical—to the original Christian tradition. It is a conservatism of form, but one that not only fails to relate the form to its content—i.e., the faith incarnate in it, revealed and granted through it—but in fact denies the very presence of such content. If religious feeling is so "conservative," so devoted to form that any, even the most insignificant change in the latter troubles and irritates it, then it is precisely because it is bewitched by the form, "form-in-itself," its immutability, sacredness, beauty. It is nourished by the form, it finds in it that gratification, the quest of which is its very essence. And thus it is even more troubled and irritated by any attempt to comprehend the form, to seek the truth incarnate in it and manifested by it—and quite rightly so, for here religious feeling can smell the mortal danger that hangs over it from the judgment of faith.

In reality, the newness—the absolute and eternal newness—of Christianity lies *only in faith*, only in the truth, which is ascertained through faith and transformed into salvation and life. Therefore, without referring themselves to faith, without a constant "identification" of themselves as the incarnation and fulfilment of faith, no "forms" in Christianity are real, all the more so in that they themselves become idols and idolatry, for they create a violation of the worship of God "in Spirit and truth" that was commanded and granted to us by Christ. It is not difficult to demonstrate that Christianity has created no new forms, but has embraced and inherited the "old" forms present in human religion and life from time immemorial. However, in this is its eternal newness, that it not only filled the ancient forms with new

content, new meaning, but indeed transformed and eternally
transforms them into the very manifestation, the very gift of
truth, into communion with it as the new life. But this transformation, I repeat, is accomplished *only* through faith. "It is the
spirit that gives life, the flesh is of no avail" (Jn 6:63). Only
through faith, because it is from the Spirit and knows the truth, is
given the power to create life out of the flesh of the form, to transform it into "communion of the one Spirit."

But "religious feeling" does not know this transformation
above all precisely because it *does not want to*. It does not know and
does not want to know because in its very essence it is *agnostic*.
Not oriented toward the truth, it is nourished and lives not by
faith, as knowledge and possession of the truth, as the life of life,
but by itself, by its own self-delight and self-sufficiency. The best
witness to this is the startling indifference to the content of faith,
the complete lack of interest in what *faith believes*, on the part of
the overwhelming majority of people who call themselves believers and who are most sincerely devoted to the Church. The radiant revelation of the triune God, of the trinitarian divine life, of
the mystery of Christ's God-manhood, of the union in him—
"without confusion, without change, without division, without
separation"—of God and man, the descent of the Holy Spirit into
the world, and in the Spirit "the beginning of another life, new
and eternal"—everything by which the early Church literally
lived, in which she rejoiced as the "victory that overcomes the
world," and which therefore became the subject of strained attempts at comprehension and passionate disputes—all this holds
no interest for the contemporary "religious man." And this is not
the result of a sinful laziness or weakness. The content of faith,
the truth to which it is directed, holds no interest for him because
it is not necessary for his "religiosity," for that religious feeling
that gradually substituted itself for faith and dissolved faith in
itself.

But then, of what *unity of faith* can one speak? What can this
very concept—so important, so central to the early Church and to
her understanding of tradition—mean? To what experience can it
correspond? If both theology, in its formal, rationally and juridi-
cally saturated form, and piety, in its thorough reduction to "individualized" religious feeling, are "not occupied" with unity, for

it dropped out of their field of attention and interest, then what is the content of this concept, which nevertheless remains one of the chief poles, the chief nerves of Christianity?

Actually, there is much talk today—in all likelihood immeasurably more than in times past—about Christian unity, about the unity of the Church. But here the whole fact of the matter, I am not afraid to say, lies in the *heretical* temptation of our day, that this unity is something *other* than the unity that constituted the heartbeat and chief joy, the very content of Christian faith and Christian life from the first day of the Church's existence. Almost imperceptibly to religious consciousness, a substitution has occurred, and in our day this substitution manifests itself all the more obviously as a betrayal.

The essence of this substitution lies in the fact that, instead of understanding, recognizing and experiencing the Church as simultaneously the source and gift of a unity that is always new—for it is a unity neither extracted from the world nor reduced to its level—the Church has herself come to be perceived as the expression, form and "sanction" of an already existing, earthly, "natural" unity. Or, to put it another way, the Church as *unity from above* has been replaced by the Church as *unity from below*. When, in the service of this unity from below, the chief, if not the only, calling and purpose of the Church becomes the expression and preservation of this unity of flesh and blood, the substitution becomes a betrayal.

I am convinced that, precisely in our day and precisely because our epoch, as no other, is literally possessed by the cult and pathos of "unity," this substitution is especially dangerous, threatening to become betrayal and heresy in the full meaning of these words—although this is something to which the majority of believers and "church" people are blind. They are blind to it because they neither have nor know any experience of unity and, consequently, they do not want it, for the heart can only want that which, though only partly—"in a mirror, dimly"—it has sensed, gotten to know, come to love and already cannot forget. But here, not knowing, not remembering, they want and seek unity from below. To it they transfer man's unquenchable thirst for unity. And they fail to understand that, outside the unity from above given to us by Christ, any unity from below not only becomes inwardly senseless and useless, but inevitably becomes an idol and, strange as it may seem, draws religion itself, Christianity itself, backward—into idolatry.

Therefore the Church—and first of all Orthodox theology—now has no more urgent and pressing task than the elucidation of the experience and knowledge of unity from above, i.e., the very essence of the Church, which sets her apart from everything in "this world," but which therefore manifests her as the salvation of the world and mankind.

5

THE LOFTIER THE WORD, THE MORE AMBIGUOUS IT IS, THE more insistently it demands from Christians who use it not simply its most precise definition but also its *liberation*, exorcism and cleansing from the lie that perverts it from within. The discernment of spirits, to which the apostle John the Theologian calls us, is above all a differentiation of words, for not only did the word, with the world and all creation, fall, but the fall of the world began precisely with the perversion of the word. Through the word entered that lie whose father is the devil. The poison of this lie consists in the fact that the word itself remained the same, so that when man speaks of "God," "unity," "faith," "piety," "love," he is convinced that he knows of what he is speaking, whereas the fall of the word lies precisely in that it inwardly became "other," became a lie about its own proper meaning and content. The devil did not create new, "evil" words, just as he did not and could not create another world, just as he did not and could not create anything. The whole falsehood and the whole power of this falsehood lie in the fact that he made the *same* words into words *about something else*, he usurped them and converted them into an instrument of evil and that, consequently, he and his servants in "this world" always speak in a language literally stolen from God.

This is why all attempts to reduce the question of words, their content and meaning, to a question of their definition are vain. For in any case, a definition is made up of words, and this means that it does not and cannot escape from its own vicious circle, which enslaves all fallen creation. Therefore the fallen word, like all of the fallen world, requires not definition but *salvation*, and it awaits this salvation not from itself and not from other words but from the cleansing and revivifying power and grace of God.

Theology, whose essence lies in the search for "words appropriate to God" (θεοπρεπεῖς λόγοι), is called to be such a salvation of words through the power of God. But it fulfils its mission not with the help of definitions, not through "words about words," but by referring words to that reality and to that experience of it that is more primary than the word itself and in relation to which the word is a *symbol*: manifestation, gift, partaking, possession. For it is precisely as a symbol—i.e., not as a definition of reality, which in the end is undefinable, but as its manifestation and gift, as partaking in it and as possession of it—that the word was created. Through the symbol the word frees itself from its fall and rises to that encounter with reality and that reception of it that we call faith.

The flaw of contemporary theology (including, alas, Orthodox theology) and its obvious impotence lies in the fact that it so often ceases to refer words to reality. It becomes "words about words," definitions of a definition. Either it endeavors, as in the contemporary West, to *translate* Christianity into the "language of today," in which case—because this is not only a "fallen" language but truly a language of renunciation of Christianity—theology is left with nothing to say and itself becomes apostasy; or, as we often see among the Orthodox, it attempts to thrust on "contemporary man" its own abstract and in many respects "archaic" language, which, to the degree that it refers neither to any reality nor to any experience for this "contemporary" man, remains alien and incomprehensible, and on which learned theologians, with the aid of all these definitions and interpretations, conduct experiments in artificial resuscitation.

But in Christianity, faith, as experience of an encounter and a gift received in this encounter, precedes words, for only from this experience do they find not simply their meaning but their power. "Out of the abundance of the heart the mouth speaks" (Mt 12:34). And thus words that are not referred to this experience or that are turned away from it inevitably become *only* words—ambiguous, easily changed and evil.

6

ALL THAT HAS BEEN SAID RELATES IN THE FIRST PLACE TO A
truly key term for Christianity: *unity*. I am convinced that there is
no word in human language more divine—but therefore also more
diabolical, in that it has fallen and has been "stolen" from God.
And this is true because in this case both the primary meaning
and the substitution, the "theft," concern not something related
to life but *life itself*, genuine life in its quintessence.

The word "unity" is divine because in the experience of Christian faith it is *referred* above all to God himself, to the revelation of
divine life as unity and of unity as the content and fulness of divine life. God revealed himself in his triunity and triunity as his
life, and this means as the source and principle of all life, as truly
the life of life. Perhaps nowhere is the Church's *knowledge* that this
unity is far above any reasoning and definition better and more
fully expressed—incarnated—than in that icon of icons, Rublev's
Holy Trinity, the miracle of which lies in the fact that, while being a representation of the three, it is in the deepest sense of the
word an icon, i.e., a revelation, manifestation and vision, of unity
as divine life itself, as the Real.

Because the entire Christian faith, in all its depth, is directed
toward the triune God—the knowledge of God in his triunity—
through this knowledge it knows also the creaturely life created
by him. It knows it in its *original state*, it knows it in its *fall*, it
knows it in its *salvation*. First of all, this is knowledge and experience of creation, i.e., as created by God and granted life as unity
with God, and in him, only in him, with all creation, all life.
Secondly, this is knowledge and experience of the fall, i.e., of the
very essence of evil and sin as division, separation from God and
therefore the disintegration and decomposition of life itself, the
triumph of death in it. Finally, this is knowledge and experience
of salvation, i.e., the restoration of unity with God and in him
with all creation, in which lies the essence of the new and eternal
life, coming in power but already granted, already anticipating
the kingdom of God: "that they may be one even as we are one"
(Jn 17:22).

This means that to the Christian faith, unity is not something important and desired but nevertheless "supplementary," distinct from faith, as if there could be faith without "unity," and as if unity were not contained, manifested and living by faith. In unity is the very essence, the very content of faith, which also is entrance into unity, the reception of the unity forfeited by the world in its fall, and the experience of unity as salvation and new life. Thus it is said of faith that "He who through faith is righteous shall live" (Rm 1:17), that "He who believes in the Son has eternal life" (Jn 3:36) and "shall never die" (Jn 11:26). Faith is the partaking of the *unity from above*, and in it of the "beginning of another life, new and eternal." And the Church is manifested in this world as the gift, the presence, the fulfilment of this *unity from above*, and thus of faith. The Church is not something "other" in relation to faith, although linked with faith, but precisely the fulfilment of faith itself—that unity the reception of which, the entrance into which, the partaking of which, is faith. In the Christian tradition and experience, faith is that which leads us, which introduces us into the Church, which *knows* the Church herself as the fulfilment of faith, as the new creation and the new life. The man who says, as is so often the case in our day, "I am deeply faithful, but my faith does not need the Church," may possibly believe, and even deeply, but his faith is something *other* than that faith that from the first day of Christianity was the thirst for baptismal entry into the Church and the constant quenching of this thirst in the "unity of faith and love" at Christ's table in his kingdom. The whole life of the Church is "illumined by the Holy Trinity in a mystic unity" (first matins antiphon, tone 4). Conversely, there is no life of the Church that does not shine through and commune in this divine unity. It is through this light that an ascetic such as St Serafim of Sarov, in his "remote hermitage," in an external sense distant from the Church's "visible reality," can nevertheless live in the Church and through the Church. At the same time, a man fully immersed in this "visible reality," in the externals of church life, may not live by this light. For the whole order of the Church, her whole "structure," her whole "visible reality" is alive, real, lifecreating, only to the degree that it is referred and related to this divine *unity from above*, and related not only as a "means" to an ultimate end, when "God will be all in all" (1 Co 15:28), but as the image, gift, light and power, *here and now*, of the kingdom of God, as truly the visibility of the invisible and the realization of that which is anticipated.

It is *only* through this unity from above, in which we find the Church's genuine life and grace and the newness of this life, that the Church is separated from "this world," and it is only through the knowledge and experience of this unity that she knows it as the "fallen world," whose image passes away (1 Co 7:31) and which is doomed to death. For, if the "visible" Church, in her members and in her whole "external" life, is flesh of the flesh and blood of the blood of "this world," then in her genuine life—invisible to the world, for it is "hid with Christ in God" (Col 3:3) and recognizable only to faith—she is, in relation to it, of an entirely *different nature*. It is "this world" because its fall consists in this: that through sin its life was torn away from this unity from above and in this rupture became itself corruption, decay and hopeless enslavement to death and time, which reign upon earth.

It is precisely this comprehension of the Church's being of a different nature in relation to "this world," of her essence as unity from above, that discloses to us the genuine meaning of that substitution we spoke of earlier: that the chief and most frightening danger poisoning contemporary church consciousness is the substitution of *unity from below* for unity from above.

7

IN ORDER TO UNDERSTAND THE DEPTHS OF THIS DANGER AND its genuine horror, one must first of all sense the essence of what we have termed "unity from below," in contradistinction to the "unity from above." It is that unity that, however much it is fallen, dead and "lying in evil," lives to the same degree that "this world" lives and that, however much it obscures and distorts, is placed in it by God. The devil could turn man, and in him, the world, away from God, he could poison and enfeeble life through sin, permeate it with mortality and death. One thing he could not and cannot do: change the very essence of life as unity. He could not and cannot because only God is the creator and giver of life. Only from him is there life, the law of which, however much life is perverted by sin, remains the law of unity. Everything that lives, in every pulse of life, lives through unity, awaits it and strives toward it.

The substitution, the victory of the "prince of this world," however, lies in the fact that he has torn this unity away from God, its source, content and goal, and thus has made unity an end-in-itself or, in the language of faith, an *idol.* Unity, which is *from* God, has ceased to be unity with God and in God, who alone fulfils it as genuine unity and genuine life. Unity becomes its own content, its own "god."

Here, on the one hand, because unity is *from* God, it continues to shine in "this" fallen world and to create its life: in family and friends, in the sense of belonging to a particular people and of responsibility for its fate, in love, compassion and charity, in art, its flights and transports to the eternal, heavenly and beautiful, in the highest quests of the mind, in the divine beauty of goodness and humility—in everything, in other words, that exists in man and in the world from the image and likeness of God, darkened but not destroyed. And, on the other hand, to the degree that it ceases to be unity with God and in God and is transformed into an end-in-itself and an idol, it becomes not only "easily transformable," unstable and easily shattered, but also the generator of every new division, evil, violence and hatred. Itself being turned *downward*—to the earthly and natural, to things below—and regarding flesh and blood as its principle and source, this unity from below begins to divide in the same measure that it unifies. Love for one's own, unity among one's own, revolves around enmity toward the "foreign," what is not one's own, and separation from it, so that unity itself proves to be above all a type of chauvinism, self-affirmation and self-defense *against* something or someone. Everything in the world lives through unity, and everything in the world is divided by this unity and constantly divides itself into collisions and struggles of "unities" that have become idols. And nowhere does the truly diabolical essence of this substitution become more apparent than in those *utopias of unity* that constitute the content and inner motivation of all contemporary *ideologies* without exception, both "left" and "right"—ideologies in which the diabolical lie sells itself as the ultimate dehumanization of man, as the offering of man as a sacrifice to the "unity" that has become a complete idol.

Here is why the ever more obvious penetration into the Church of the temptation of "unity from below," its gradual poisoning of church consciousness, is so horrible. We are not talking about outward changes, about some revisions of dogmas or canons, about a "reappraisal" of tradition. On the contrary, in contrast to western Christians, who spontaneously "capitulate" to the spirit of "our time," the Orthodox remain deeply conservative, attached to everything covered by the halo of antiquity. Moreover, in this time of a profound spiritual crisis, provoked by the triumph of secularism, of impersonal and inhuman technology, of ideological utopianism, etc., this nostalgic attraction to "antiquity" is growing stronger in Orthodox "religious feeling," becoming itself its own form of a utopianism of the past.

We are speaking of the inner orientation of church consciousness, of that *treasure*, of which the gospels say that there where the heart is, man's treasure is also (Mt 6:21), and which comprises the inner nerve, the inner inspiration of church life. For the Church of Christ, the kingdom of God, i.e., the unity from above, unity with God in Christ through the Holy Spirit, has always been, always will be and cannot but be such a treasure. It is only to manifest it in "this world" and through it to save the world that the Church remains and "sojourns" on earth. Her witness and proclamation concern only the kingdom, her life is only in it. We can even say further that the coming of Christ and, in him, of the unity from above into this world, his commandment to the apostles, and thus to the Church, to preach the gospel to all creation, baptizing them "in the name of the Father and of the Son and of the Holy Spirit," and thus, to enter into the Church and to create it, brought into "this world" the final and ultimate *division*— "not...peace, but a sword" (Mt 10:34). "For I have come to set a man against his father, and a daughter against her mother, and a daughter-in-law against her mother-in-law;...and a man's foes will be those of his own household" (Mt 10:35-36).

But the whole power of this truly saving division, the whole absolute, radical distinction between it and the destructive division brought into the world by the devil, which comprises the very essence of sin and the fall, is that it is the *exposure* (and I mean this in the literal sense of this word: the manifestation, revelation, the "unmasking") of the devilish substitution, the lie, the conversion of the "unity from below" into an idol, and the service to it in idolatry, in separation from God, in the division of life, in destruction and death. Only because the divine unity from above came into the world, was manifested and granted and abides in it, can man finally come to *believe* in it, i.e., to see, to accept its entire essence, to love, to know it as the heart's treasure and the one thing needful, but in the same manner to see and comprehend the utter depths, the entire horror, the whole dead-end of the fall, of the "unity from below" that the devil has kept secret from us under cunning and seductive makeup. The *conversion* that necessarily lies at the foundation of Christian faith is first of all a conversion from the "unity from below" to the "unity from above," the rejection of the one for the reception of the other, for without renunciation it is impossible to receive, without "repudiating the devil and all his angels and all his service" the baptismal unity with Christ is impossible. "And a man's foes will be those of his own household." What are these words about if not the "unity from below," any "unity from below," i.e., unity that has become an idol and idolatry, existing in itself, self-oriented and consequently a division of life? "Do not love the world or the things in the world. If anyone loves the world, love for the Father is not in him. For all that is in the world, the lust of the flesh and the lust of the eyes and the pride of life, is not of the Father but is of the world" (1 Jn 2:15-16). What is this commandment of the apostle of love about if not the renunciation of "unity from below" in the name of the "unity from above," of "this world," which has become an idol, in the name of the world as communion in the divine unity from above, as life in God?

Here is why the unity from above, in which the salvation of the world lies, comes into the world through the cross and is granted to us as the cross, through which, in the words of the apostle Paul, "the world has been crucified to me, and I to the world" (Ga 6:14), as a real struggle with the temptation of "unity from below," which has permeated all life, both the most private, most "personal," and the most "external." But just as death—which God did not create and which the apostle calls the "last enemy" (1 Co 15:26)—is destroyed in its very "mortality" in the free death of Christ, fulfilled only through love, only through self-sacrifice, and the tomb is thus made a bearer of life, so also

the division brought into the world by Christ, since he is the ex-
poser of the devil, the liar and the divider, destroys the devil's
work, for through this division the one real (for it is divine) unity
enters into the world, and reigns in everyone who receives and
lives by it. Through it every division is overcome and shall be
fully conquered, so that God may be all in all.

Yet Christians do not bear this gift, they do not endure their
lofty and saving calling in "this world." This unity from above is
all that is necessary; the world itself, without knowing it, hungers and thirsts for it from the Church. And all people have always wanted—for ages!—to compel the Church herself to serve all
manner of "unities from below," to bless, to consecrate, to "religiously" sanction them, to be their expression and justification.
Precisely these "unities from below"—natural, national, ideological, political—have become the treasure of the heart, although the
substitution is also often hidden from the very ones who accomplish it, for this treasure is clothed in church vestments and
speaks so often in a particularly traditional, particularly "Orthodox" language. But here, even if bewitched with churchliness,
antiquity and all their splendor, the heart that has given itself
over to this treasure will not utter words that resound with such
joy—and above all such self-evidency—as, for example, those in
the early Christian *Letter to Diognetus*: "Every foreign land is their
fatherland, and yet for them every fatherland is a foreign land."[4]
Such a heart does not find Christians to be a "third race," wander-
ers and strangers on earth—for they have already come to know,
already beheld the full joy of the homeland of the heart's desire.
Such a heart will not breathe by this freedom in Christ that alone
bears the transfiguration of the world, the return to God of all
"unities," all "values," which have been estranged from him by
the devil.

8

ONLY NOW, HAVING SAID THIS, CAN WE RETURN TO THAT
confession of faith that from the first day of the Church was and
remains the condition of the baptismal entry into church life and

⁴5:5, tr. Richardson, 217.

which in the current order of the liturgy introduces, as it were, the eucharistic canon, the very sacrament of thanksgiving and oblation.

"For man believes with his heart and so is justified, and he confesses with his lips and so is saved" (Rm 10:10). We spoke earlier of the decisive significance of the *word* for the Christian faith. Christianity itself is above all the *good news*, the proclamation of the Word of God, and thus the salvation and revivification of the word, its transformation into what God made it to be: into the word not only about reality but word-reality, word-life, word as manifestation, gift and "great power." The confession of faith in words and through words is thus so fundamental in Christianity that the "unity from above," which constitutes the essence of the Church herself as the "unity of faith and love," is realized, granted and received above all through its *naming*, through its genuine manifestation and incarnation in the word. If the entire life of the Church and the entire life of each of her members is called to be a confession, then the principle, the source of this confession is always in the word, for in it and through it God's gift to us—and our acceptance of this gift, the communion, the unity that also constitutes the essence and life of faith—is identified, named and fulfilled. As the evangelical word about Christ manifests and grants to us Christ himself, the incarnation of the Word of God, so the confession of faith in words—the naming of the divine truth, to which faith is directed and of which it is the knowledge—is, by the same token, the gift of and communion in the truth. Therefore the Church never ceases, never tires of, again and again, and each time as if the first, "with one heart and with one mind," pronouncing the most astonishing, the most inexhaustible of all human words: "I believe"—and thus identifying, naming that divine truth, through the knowledge and light of which she lives. Therefore, being the very realization of the "unity of faith," the confession of faith contains and grants the joy of this unity: it is a joyful rite of the Church. And thus, finally, it is precisely this naming of the unity from above that introduces us into the sacrament of this unity, that itself begins the eucharistic ascension to the table of Christ in his kingdom.

But the confession of faith is likewise a judgment of the Church, and of each of us who are members of the Church. "For by your words you will be justified and by your words you will be condemned" (Mt 12:37). In it is the criterion and in it is the indictment of all of our substitutions and betrayals. In it is the unfailing test of where and in what is the treasure of our hearts, the test of our faith itself.

Everything in the Church, all her forms and structure, and even worship and piety, can be "reinterpreted," for there is no limit to the guile and cunning of the "prince of this world"; everything in the world—even religion, even "spirituality," even visible splendor—can become an idol and idolatry. But as long as the Church, and each of us with her and in her, repeats the *confession of faith* and by it judges herself and again and again is enlightened by the truth, the "gates of hell" shall not prevail against her, shall not dry up the eternally revivifying, the eternally healing power of her life, "illumined by the Holy Trinity in a mystic unity."

CHAPTER EIGHT

The Sacrament of Anaphora

"Lord, it is good that we are here..."
MATTHEW 17:4

I

"*L*ET US STAND ARIGHT! LET US STAND WITH FEAR! LET US attend, that we may offer the Holy Oblation in peace." When, after the confession of faith, we hear this summons, something happens in the liturgy that is difficult to express in words, occurring only from within, perceptible only spiritually—a "passing over into another level." Something has been completed, and now something is obviously beginning.

What? The generally accepted answer to this question goes something like this: we now begin the *eucharistic canon*, that chief part of the liturgy, during which the sacrament, i.e., the change or the transubstantiation of the eucharistic gifts of bread and wine into the body and blood of Christ, is accomplished. But, although formally correct, this very answer gives rise to further questions, demands refinement, for, as I shall try to demonstrate, one can understand it in different ways, and on these various understandings depends in turn one's entire conception of the liturgy, of its place not only in our life, and not only even in the life of the Church, but in the mystery of the salvation of the world, as the return and the ascent of the creation to the Creator.

So, first of all, what do we mean by defining this part of the liturgy as the "chief part," or, more precisely, what can and what

159

must we mean? This word presupposes a certain correlation, a certain link between the "chief" and the "non-chief," and outside of
this link it makes no sense. But "scholastic," school theology,
from whose example this definition arose and became generally
accepted and as it were self-evident, was itself never really occupied and is not concerned with any other part of the liturgy. On
the contrary, at first in the West and then, by imitation, also in
the East, it was precisely scholastic theology that reduced the entire sacrament of the eucharist to one of its parts (the "eucharistic
canon"), and as if that were not enough, to one single moment
within it (the transubstantiation). And it is precisely because of
this "reduction" that all the remaining parts of the liturgy, which
we have been discussing in the preceding chapters, proved to be,
in relation to this no-longer-chief but one-and-only part, of a different nature and therefore *unnecessary* for the theological definition and comprehension of the sacrament of the eucharist.
Finally, it is precisely their "superfluity" for theology that has
destined them only for, on the one hand, the "liturgists" and "ru-
bricists" and, on the other, "religious feeling" and the unrestrained efforts peculiar to it to find everywhere in worship
"illustrative symbolism," which usually has no relation whatsoever to the sacrament.

To anyone who has paid the slightest attention to the preceding chapters it should be clear that if such is the meaning of the
word "chief" in this definition of what is nevertheless in fact the
chief part of the liturgy, the elucidation of which we are now approaching, then I categorically reject this meaning. I reject it because in it I see the most glaring example and evidence not only of
the onesidedness or insufficiency but, speaking to the point, the
depravity of our still-born, western school theology—a depravity
that nowhere reveals itself so obviously as in its approach to the
holy of holies of the Church: the eucharist and the sacraments.
Therefore it was not to sound more solemn but perfectly consciously and responsibly that I have entitled each of the chapters
devoted to the first parts of the liturgy—entrance and assembly,
reading and proclamation of the word of God, offering, kiss of
peace and confession of faith—with the word *sacrament*. For I see
the entire task at hand in demonstrating as fully as possible that
the divine liturgy is a single, though also "multifaceted," sacred

rite, a single sacrament, in which all its "parts," their entire sequence and structure, their coordination with each other, the necessity of each for all and all for each, manifests to us the inexhaustible, eternal, universal and truly divine meaning of what has been and what is being accomplished.

Such in any case is the tradition of the Church, such is her living experience, in which the sacrament of the eucharist is inseparable from the divine liturgy. For its setting, its entire sequence, order and structure consist in manifesting to us the meaning and the content of the sacrament, in bringing us into it, in converting us into its participants and communicants. Meanwhile, it is precisely this unity, this integrity of the eucharist, the indissoluble link of the sacrament with the liturgy, that school theology destroys through its arbitrary isolation of one "moment" (act, formula) in the liturgy and the identification of it alone with the sacrament. We are speaking here not of discrepancies in abstract definitions, not of theological "niceties," but of something very profound and essential: of how and where to seek the answer to the question, *what is accomplished in the eucharist?* If for the Church not only the answer to this question but also the question itself, i.e., its correct "context," is rooted in the liturgy, it is because for her the eucharist is the crowning and fulfilment of the liturgy, just as the liturgy is the crowning and fulfilment of the entire faith, the entire life and the entire experience of the Church. School theology, however, does not "inquire" of the liturgy about the meaning of the sacrament. Its fallaciousness, its tragedy lies in this: that it creates in fact a *substitute* for the question itself, it replaces it with another question, rooted not in the experience of the Church, but in the "seekings of this age"—in the questions, categories of thought, one can almost say in the curiosity of our fallen reason, which has not been reborn and enlightened by faith. Thus, having created its own particular, a priori and "self-sufficient" definition of the sacrament, it directs and attaches to it the questions and "problematics" that in reality should be referred to the experience of the Church and evaluated in the light of that experience.

2

OVER THE COURSE OF THE CENTURIES THIS "PROBLEMATICS" has come to be reduced to two questions: *when* and *how*. When— i.e., at what moment are the bread and wine transformed into the body and blood of Christ? How—i.e, what is the causality by which this is accomplished? Literally hundreds of books have been written in answer to these questions, and even to this day they constitute the subject of intense disputes—between Catholics and Protestants, between East and West. But one need only to attempt to *refer* all these conjectures and theories to the immediate experience of the liturgy, to that *service* that is performed in church, and it becomes obvious to what degree these explanations turn out to be external to this experience, falling outside it and thus not only not really explaining anything but in the end simply *unnecessary*.

What in fact does the distinction of *essence* and *accidents*, which goes back to Aristotle and which the scholastics made use of to answer the question of how the transubstantiation of the bread and wine into the body and blood of Christ is accomplished, mean—not philosophically, not abstractly, but really—for our faith, our communion in the divine, our spiritual life, our salvation? Does transubstantiation consist, according to this experience, in the change of the "substance" (essence) of the bread into the essence of the body of Christ, while the "accidents" of the body remain the accidents of the bread? To faith, which confesses every Sunday, in the fear of God and with love, that "this is truly Thine own most pure Body... this is truly Thine own precious Blood," this explanation is unnecessary, and for the mind itself it remains an equally incomprehensible violence to those very "laws" on whose foundations the explanation is supposedly constructed.

It is the same with the question *when*, that is, at what moment, by the force of what "causality" is the transubstantiation accomplished. The western scholastics' answer is at the moment when the priest pronounces the *words of institution*: "this is my body... this is my blood"—words that thus constitute the "consecratory formula," the formal, "necessary and sufficient" cause of the transubstantiation. In rejecting—and rightly, as we shall see later—this Latin doctrine, Orthodox theology in turn affirms that the transformation is accomplished not through the words of institution but through the *epiklesis*, the prayer of the invocation of the Holy Spirit, which in our order of the liturgy immediately follows these words. But since it is in fact constrained by the same method and the same "problematics," this theology does not reveal what ultimately is the meaning and importance of this dispute. One "consecratory formula" is replaced with another, one "moment" is replaced by another "moment," but without disclosing the very essence of the *epiklesis*, its true significance in the liturgy.

The point of all that has been said—and I shall emphasize this over and over—is not that, having become convinced of the uselessness or the impossibility of theological comprehension, we should simply dismiss these questions and as a result explain the eucharist with that hackneyed but fundamentally blasphemous formula: "it is impossible to understand; it is only necessary to believe." I believe and I confess that for the Church, for the world, for mankind there is no more important, more urgent question than *what is accomplished in the eucharist*. In reality this question is most natural to faith, which lives by the thirst for entry into the wisdom of truth, by the thirst for the logical (λο-γική), i.e., reasonable, service of God that manifests and is rooted in the divine wisdom. It is truly the question of the ultimate meaning and purpose of all that is real, of the sacramental ascent to where "God will be all in all," and thus it is the question that, through faith, was constantly radiating as a mysterious burning in the hearts of the disciples on the road to Emmaus. But that is exactly why it is so important to liberate this urgent question, to cleanse it of everything that obscures, diminishes and distorts it, and this means, first of all, those "questions" and "answers" whose depravity lies in the fact that instead of explaining the earthly through the heavenly, they reduce the heavenly and the otherworldly to the earthly, to their own "human, only human," impoverished and feeble "categories."

Indeed, with the summons "let us stand aright" we actually do enter into the "chief" part of the divine liturgy. But it is chief in relation to its other parts, and not in isolation and separation from them. It is chief because in it the entire liturgy finds its *fulfilment*, everything that it witnesses to, that it manifests, to which it leads and ascends. It begins that sacrament of anaphora that would be *impossible* without the sacrament of the gathering, the sacrament of offering and the sacrament of unity, but in which—and precisely because it is the fulfilment of the entire liturgy—we are given the understanding of the sacrament that surpasses all comprehension but nevertheless manifests all and explains all. It is precisely this "relation," the wholeness and unity of the eucharistic celebration, that we are reminded of, that we turn our spiritual attention to when the deacon summons us to "stand aright," to "stand straight" or even to "be good."[1]

3

"RIGHT," "WELL," "GOOD"...SUCH WORDS, LIKE ALL WORDS, like fallen human language itself, have been effaced, watered down, weakened. "Good," for example, has come to mean more or less "anything you like": pleasing to us, pleasing to "this world," pleasing to the devil. Only sometimes, and then only partly—in poetry, in the language of art—does it flare up in its primordial purity and power, in its original, divine meaning. For "good," like any real word, is from God, and to hear it in its liturgical resonance and sense, to understand what it means, what it manifests at the beginning of the eucharistic anaphora, it must be raised to God. It must be heard there, where it resounded for the first time as a certain primordial revelation.

"And God saw that it was good" (Gn 1:10). Here is this word in its initial resonance, here it is as beginning itself. But how do we hear it, how do we understand and receive it? How do we explain it with the use of other words, if they are all secondary in relation to this primary word, themselves only receiving their meaning and power from it? Of course, "culture," "science," "philosophy" are all sufficiently literate, all *know* enough to formally define it: something is good or right when it conforms to its nature, purpose, conception, when its "form" or fulfilment corre-

---

[1]The Greek Στῶμεν καλῶς or the Slavonic *Stanem dobre* suggests a range of meanings that cannot be rendered succinctly in English.

sponds to its "content" or plan. Applied to the biblical text, consequently, it appears as such: and God saw that what he had created corresponded to his conception and therefore was right and good. All true enough, all correct according to the correctness of the words used, but what impoverished words these are, as they are powerless to convey the main thing: the very *goodness of the good*, the revelation about the world, about life, about us ourselves, that this divine *good* bears and manifests in itself—the fulness of joy, the *rapture*, through which it radiates and gives life. But where then are we to find, not the explanation, not the definition, but above all the very experience, the firsthand knowledge of this primordial, imperishable good?

We find it, we hear and we receive this word where it resounded anew in all its power and fulness, where it rang out as the human answer to the divine *good*. "Lord, it is good that we are here" (Mt 17:4). Through this answer, on the mount of the transfiguration, was witnessed forever, for all time, man's reception of the divine *good* as his life, as his calling. There, in that "cloud of light" that overshadowed him, man saw "that it is good," and accepted and confessed. And it is by this vision, this knowledge, this experience that the Church, in her deepest depths, lives. In this *experience* is her beginning and fulfilment, as well as the beginning and fulfilment of everything within her. One can actually "discuss" the Church ad infinitum, one can endeavor to "explain" her, one can "study" ecclesiology, one can argue over "apostolic succession," the canons and the principles of church structure, but without this experience, without this secret joy, without the orientation of everything to this "it is good that we are here," all remains simply words about words.

The divine liturgy—the continual ascent, the lifting up of the Church to *heaven*, to the throne of glory, to the unfading light and joy of the kingdom of God—is the focus of this experience, simultaneously its source and presence, gift and fulfilment. "Standing in the temple of thy glory we think we are in heaven." These words are not pious rhetoric, for they express the very essence, the very purpose both of the Church and of her worship as above all precisely a *liturgy*, an action (ἔργον), in which the essence of what is taking place is simultaneously revealed and fulfilled. But in what is this essence, in what is the ultimate meaning of the divine liturgy if not in the manifestation and the granting to us of this divine good? From where, if not from our "Lord, it is good for us to be here," comes its simultaneously otherworldly, heavenly and cosmic beauty, that *wholeness*, in which *all*—words, sounds, colors, time, space, movement, and the *growth* of all of them—is revealed, realized as the renewal of creation, as ours, as the ascent of the entire world on high, to where Christ has raised and is eternally raising us? And therefore, if it is at all appropriate to speak here of *causality*, of "when" and "how," then this causality, binding together the liturgy, making each of its parts precisely a part, a stage, and thus a condition and "cause" of further ascent, is contained in this *good*, through the knowledge and experience and partaking of which the Church *lives*. This divine good *assembles* the Church as the new creation, renewed by God; it transforms this gathering into *entrance* and *ascent*; it opens the mind to the hearing and reception of the *word of God*; it *includes* our sacrifice, our *offering* in the one, unrepeatable and universal sacrifice of Christ; it fulfils the Church as the *unity of faith and love*; and, finally, it brings us to that threshold we have now approached, to that truly *chief* part, in which all this movement and growth will find its completion and fulfilment at Christ's table in his kingdom. And therefore, unless we see the entire liturgy as the gift and fulfilment of this divine *good*, we will never know what is fulfilled in this *chief* part, we will not know *what is accomplished in the eucharist* and in its summit: the transformation of the bread and wine, with us, with the Church, with the world, with *all and through all*.

The words of the deacon also witness to this "good" and call us to stand in it, as they now begin the chief—for everything is about to be fulfilled in it—part of the liturgy.

4

THREE EXCLAMATIONS OF THE CELEBRANT AND THREE SHORT replies from the gathering comprise an introductory dialogue by which the sacrament of the anaphora begins.

The first is the solemn blessing. It exists in every eucharistic prayer, without exception, that has come down to us, although it comes in various formulas—from the simple "the Lord be with you" of the Roman and Alexandrian liturgies to our trinitarian formula, which is almost identical with the one we find in the apostle Paul: "The grace of the Lord Jesus Christ and the love of God the Father and the fellowship of the Holy Spirit be with all of you " (2 Co 13:13). The meaning of this blessing is always and everywhere the same: the triumphant affirmation and confession that the Church is gathered in *Christ* and in him offers the eucharist. And this means that we are in such unity with him that everything done by us is accomplished by him, and everything accomplished by him has been granted to us.

It is precisely this that is emphasized by the irregularity of this blessing's trinitarian formula. Its irregularity lies of course in its contrast to the formula that is always otherwise used: Father, Son and Holy Spirit. The eucharistic blessing begins with Christ, with the bestowal of his grace, because in this moment of the liturgy the essence of the blessing lies not in the confession of the Most Holy Trinity in its eternal essence but in the revelation, the testimony, one can even say the *experience* of it as knowledge of God, which is life eternal (Jn 17:3), as the reconciliation, union and communion with him that has been granted and is eternally being granted to us as our salvation. This salvation is granted to us in Christ, the Son of God, who became the Son of man, in whom "we have peace with God...we have obtained access to this grace" (Rm 5:1-2), "we have access in one Spirit to the Father" (Eph 2:18). For we have "one mediator between God and men, the man Christ Jesus" (1 Tm 2:5), who has said: "I am the way, and the truth, and the life; no one comes to the Father, but by me" (Jn 14:6). Christian faith begins with the encounter with Christ, with the reception of him as the Son of God, who manifests the Father and his love to us. This acceptance of the Son, this union in him with the Father, is fulfilled as salvation, as the new life, as the kingdom of God in the communion of the Holy Spirit, which is the divine life itself, divine love itself, communion with God. And thus, the eucharist is also the sacrament of our *access* to God and knowledge of him and union with him. Being offered in the Son, it is offered to the Father. Being offered to the Father, it is fulfilled in the partaking of the Holy Spirit. And therefore the eucharist is the eternally living and lifecreating source of the Church's knowledge of the Most Holy Trinity. This is not the abstract knowledge (of dogmas, doctrine) that it unfortunately remains for so many of the faithful, but knowledge as a genuine *recognition*, as meeting, as experience, and thus as partaking of life eternal.

5

THE NEXT EXCLAMATION OF THE CELEBRANT, "LET US LIFT UP our hearts," we find in no other service—it belongs entirely and exclusively to the divine liturgy. For this exclamation is not simply a call to a certain lofty disposition. In the light of all that has been said above, it is an affirmation that the eucharist is accomplished not on earth but in heaven. "But even when we were dead through our trespasses, God made us alive together with Christ (by grace you have been saved), and raised us up with him, and made us sit with him in the heavenly places with Christ Jesus" (Eph 2:5-6). We already know that this ascent to heaven began with the very beginning of the liturgy, with our very entrance and "assembly as the Church," when our true life was "hid with Christ in God." And need we demonstrate and explain that this heaven has nothing in common with that "heaven" that Bultmann and his followers, with their condescending scientificity, debunk for the sake of "demythologization" and an explanation of it to "contemporary" man that would supposedly save Christianity, and of which St John Chrysostom already said over 1500 years ago: "what is heaven to me, when I contemplate the Master of heaven, *when I myself become heaven?*"[2]

We can lift our hearts "on high" because this "on high," this heaven is within us and among us, because it has been returned, restored to us as our real homeland of the heart's desire, to which we returned after an agonizing exile, for which we have always groaned with homesickness, and through the memory of which all creation lives. If we speak of the earthly, of ourselves, of the Church in categories of *ascent*, then we speak of the heavenly, of God, of Christ, of the Holy Spirit in categories of *descent*. But we are saying the same thing: we speak of heaven on earth, of heaven as having transfigured the earth, and of the earth as having ac-

[2]Unidentified quotation.

cepted heaven as the ultimate truth about itself. "Heaven and earth will pass away" (Mk 13:31)—they will pass away in their opposition, in their rift from each other; they will pass away because they shall be transformed into "a new heaven and a new earth" (Rv 21:1), into the kingdom of God in which "God will be all in all." For "this world" it is as yet in the future, but in Christ it is already revealed and in the Church it is already "anticipated," and the eucharist raises and elevates us to this heavenly kingdom of God from on high, and in it the eucharist is accomplished.

But that is why the call "let us lift up our hearts" also sounds like a solemn and ultimate warning. "Let us beware that we do not remain on the earth," says St John Chrysostom. We are able, we are free to remain down below, and not hear, not see and not receive this truly *difficult* ascent. But if we remain on earth we have no place in this heavenly eucharist, and in that case our presence at its celebration becomes our condemnation. And when each of us, through the lips of the choir, answers "we lift them up unto the Lord," i.e., when we have turned our hearts on high, to the Lord, a judgment is made on us. For one who, albeit fallen and sinful, has not turned his whole life to heaven, who does not always measure the earth next to heaven, cannot turn his heart on high for just this moment alone. Thus, when we hear this *ultimate* summons let us ask ourselves: are our hearts turned to the Lord, is the ultimate treasure of our heart in God, in heaven? If so, then in spite of all our weakness, all our fallenness, we have been received into heaven, we behold now the light and the glory of the kingdom. If not, the sacrament of the coming of the Lord to those who love him shall be for us the sacrament of the coming judgment.

6

"LET US GIVE THANKS UNTO THE LORD . . . IT IS MEET AND right..." These words are the beginning of the traditional Hebrew prayer of thanksgiving, and the Lord doubtlessly uttered them when he began, with this prayer, his own *new* thanksgiving, which was necessary to bring man to God and save the world. And likewise the apostles no doubt answered with the prescribed "it is meet and right." And each time the Church celebrates the remembrance of this thanksgiving she repeats after them and with them: it is meet and right.

Salvation is complete. After the darkness of sin, the fall and death, a man once again offers to God the pure, sinless, free and perfect thanksgiving. A man is returned to that place that God had prepared for him when he created the world. He stands at the heights, before the throne of God; he stands in heaven, before the face of God himself, and freely, in the fulness of love and knowledge, uniting in himself the whole world, all creation, he offers thanksgiving, and in him the whole world affirms and acknowledges this thanksgiving to be "meet and right." This man is Christ. He alone is without sin, he alone is Man in all the fulness of his purpose, calling and glory. He alone in himself restores the "fallen image" and raises it to God, and thus we now offer the thanksgiving of Christ, hear it and take part in it, when the celebrant begins the eucharistic prayer commanded to us by Christ, who has united us for all ages with God.

CHAPTER NINE

The Sacrament of Thanksgiving

"Give thanks for all things."
I THESSALONIANS 5:18

I

*I*N THE LITURGICS TEXTBOOKS THE PRAYER OF THANKS-
giving, to which the eucharistic celebration leads as its summit and fulfilment, is usually considered according to its parts,
which have long been designated by Latin or Greek titles: *praefatio, sanctus, anamnesis,* etc. This division, moreover, does correspond to the structure and order of the eucharistic prayer and
could be useful for its comprehension precisely as the *fulfilment* of
the liturgy. One must suppose that it did arise in liturgical studies with this aim in mind. In fact, however, it has led, strange as
it may seem, literally to the opposite result. In the consciousness
of liturgists and theologians, and after them the faithful themselves, this phenomenon indeed divided the eucharistic prayer,
shattered it as it were into several prayers, which, although following one after another, were no longer perceived as a whole, as
one, single prayer. Moreover, if all of these parts, their historical
"genesis," the similarities and distinctions between them in the
many eucharistic texts that have come down to us from antiquity,
remain a subject of study for liturgists, then theologians have
long ago concentrated their entire interest on the part they have
identified with the "consecratory formula," i.e., the moment and
the mode of the transformation of the eucharistic gifts.

171

The fragmentation of the eucharistic prayer led of course to the predominant practice of the priest reading it *secretly*, i.e., "to himself." I intend to speak of the origins of this practice, which was absolutely unknown to the early Church, in a special excursus, inasmuch as it is a complex question and its discussion in the present context would take up too much space.[1] For now I will say only that already for several centuries now, the laity, the people of God, whom the apostle Peter called "a chosen race, a royal priesthood, a holy nation, God's own people" (1 Pt 2:9), have simply *not heard* and thus *do not know* this veritable prayer of prayers, through which the mystery is completed and the essence and calling of the Church herself are fulfilled. All the faithful hear are individual exclamations and fragmented phrases, whose interconnection—and sometimes even simple meaning—remain unintelligible, as in: "...singing the triumphant hymn, shouting, proclaiming and saying..." If we add to this the fact that in many Orthodox churches these prayers, being "secret," are moreover read behind closed royal doors, and sometimes even behind a drawn altar curtain, then it would be no exaggeration to say that the prayer of thanksgiving has for all practical purposes been dropped from the church service. I repeat, the laymen simply do not know it, theologians are not interested in it, and the priest, who is forced to glance over it while the choir is singing—and frequently even giving a "concert"—is hardly capable of perceiving it in its fulness, unity and integrity. And, finally, in the service books themselves it has long been printed in broken fragments, separated by ellipses that have no reason at all for being where they are, and likewise with various insertions that crept into it from purely accidental sources.

Considering this situation, in which I honestly cannot but see a deep decadence, we need to begin any discussion of the eucharistic prayer with the revelation of its unity, i.e., how all of those parts into which it was dismembered by both liturgical studies and, alas, liturgical practice are mutually joined in an indivisible whole. For, I repeat, only in this whole is its meaning and power revealed as precisely the act *completing the sacrament*, as the fulfilment of the sacrament of the eucharist.

---

[1] Fr Schmemann was unable to write this excursus before his death.

Let us note right away that the multiplicity of eucharistic prayers that have come down to us in no way contradicts this unity. In antiquity almost every ecclesiastical province had its own *anaphora*, i.e., its own form and text of the prayer of thanksgiving. The early Church, being free from the obsession with uniformity that later developed, in no way identified such uniformity with unity. Even today there exist in the Orthodox Church two liturgies—of St John Chrysostom and of St Basil the Great—and the chief difference between them lies in the text of the prayer of thanksgiving. Thus, when we speak of the unity of this prayer, we do not mean an outward, linguistic unity, which never existed in the Church, but of something immeasurably deeper. We are speaking of the unity of the faith and experience of the Church, from which all these prayers were born. For, whatever the semantic differences between them, they all manifest and incarnate one and the same integral experience, one and the same knowledge, one and the same witness. It is an experience of which one can say for identical reasons that all human words fail to suffice for its definition and that, for those who have it, it lives, grows and bears fruit in the briefest, fewest and simplest words.

2

WHAT, THEN, GIVES THIS CHIEF, TRULY "CONSUMMATE" prayer of the liturgy its unity, transforms it into that *whole*, in and through which we affirm that this sacrament of sacraments is accomplished? The Church has answered this first and fundamental question literally from the first day of her existence by naming not only this prayer itself but also the entire liturgy with one word. This word is *eucharist, thanksgiving*. Thus, with the word eucharist the Church has named and still calls the offering of the gifts, the prayer, their consecration, and the partaking of them by the faithful. In communing of the holy mysteries, we pray that they may be for us "thanksgiving, health and happiness." Hence it follows that both the call of the celebrant—"let us give thanks unto the Lord"—and the response of the gathering—"it is meet and right"—obviously relate not just to a single "introductory" section of the eucharistic prayer, the "praefatio" in the language of liturgists, but are essentially the beginning, the foundation and the key to its entire contents, outside of which the most holy mystery of the eucharist remains hidden from us. The entire *oblation*, *anaphora*, which this part of the liturgy was long ago named, is from beginning to end a thanksgiving. However, in order to understand *today*, after centuries of forgetting, the meaning of this affirmation, to understand what for the early Church was joyfully self-evident, in no need of explanation, we must first make our way through the piles of interpretations in which this self-evidency became lost and only then go on to the original Christian meaning and experience of *thanksgiving*.

It would be better to simply say: thanksgiving is the experience of paradise. But the word "paradise" has also become weakened and stale in contemporary Christian consciousness—the learned interpreters of Christianity shun it as "naive" and "primitive"—and needs to be, in a way, exhumed. Perhaps, however, it has become weakened because it came to be torn away from its churchly "ring," from that experience of paradise in the gift and anticipation of which consists the first and deepest meaning of church worship. "Standing in the temple of thy glory, we think we are in heaven." And thus, on the day of the Nativity of Christ, when we celebrate the advent of God into the world, the Church sings: "and the Cherubim withdraw from the tree of life, and I partake of the delights of paradise" (vespers, first stichera on "Lord, I Call"). Thus, from the radiant depths of the paschal night we address the risen Christ with the exultant affirmation: "You have opened to us the gates of paradise" (matins canon, ode 6,1). And again we come to know that paradise is the primordial state of man and all creation, our state before the fall, before our "banishment from paradise," and our state upon our salvation by Christ, the eternal life that was promised by God and in Christ is already granted, already opened to man. Paradise is, in other words, the *beginning* and the *end*, to which is oriented and through which is defined and determined the entire life of man and in him of all creation. It is in relation to it that we comprehend the divine source of our life and of our fall from God, our enslavement to sin and death, our salvation by Christ, and our eternal destiny. We were created in paradise and for paradise, we were exiled from paradise, and Christ "leads us again into paradise."

If with our spiritual vision and with our spiritual ear we contemplate and hearken to the Church's experience of paradise, to the harmonious witness of the word of God and the worship and sanctity that never runs low in the Church, then the essence of this experience, the content of eternal life, of eternal joy, of eternal bliss, for which we were created, is revealed to us as the *triunity of knowledge, freedom and thanksgiving*. It is not, I emphasize, knowledge and freedom and then in addition thanksgiving as something separate from them, but knowledge and freedom themselves fulfilled in thanksgiving, thanksgiving as the fulness of knowledge and freedom, and thus communion, and thus possession.

3

"THIS IS ETERNAL LIFE, THAT THEY KNOW THEE THE ONLY true God" (Jn 17:3). All Christianity lies in these words of Christ. Man was created for knowledge of God, and in the knowledge of God is his true and thus eternal life. But this knowledge is not the knowledge through which our reason puffs itself up, convinced that it can know everything, including God, and all the while remaining ignorant of the fact that the entire depth and irretrievability of our fall lies precisely in the darkening of our mind and in the decay of genuine knowledge. Thus, the *knowledge of God* that Christ speaks of as eternal life, as paradise, is not the rational *knowledge about God* that, however "formally" and "objectively" correct, remains nevertheless within the limits and a part of that knowledge that is fallen and shattered, made feeble by sin, deprived of access to the essence of what is known and thus ceasing to be encounter, communion, unity. In his alienation from God, in his literally *senseless* choice of life not in God, but in itself and by itself, Adam did not cease to "know about God," which means to believe through that faith about which it is said that "even the demons believe and tremble." But he ceased to *know God*, and his life ceased to be that meeting with God, that communion with him—and in him with all of God's creation—all of which the book of Genesis depicts as the essence of paradise. And it is only for this meeting—with the living God, with God as the life of life—that the soul thirsts and cannot but thirst, for in its deepest depths it itself is this thirst: "my soul thirsts for the living God," says the psalmist.

Thanksgiving is the "sign," or better still, the presence, joy, fulness, of knowledge of God, i.e., knowledge as meeting, knowledge as communion, knowledge as unity. Just as it is impossible to know God and not give him thanks, so it is impossible to give him thanks without knowing him. Knowing God transforms our life into thanksgiving, and thanksgiving transforms eternity into life everlasting. "Bless the Lord, O my soul; and all that is within me, bless his holy name!" (Ps 103:1) If the entire life of the Church is above all one continuous burst of praise, blessing and thanksgiving, if this thanksgiving is raised up both out of joy and out of sorrow, out of the depths of both happiness and misfortune, out of both life and death, if the most bitter graveside lamentation is transformed by it into a song of praise, "Alleluia," then it is because the Church is the meeting with God, which has been accomplished in Christ. It is his—Christ's—knowledge of God that has been granted to us as the gift of pure thanksgiving and heavenly praise. Christ has "opened to us the gates of paradise." For, after all had been accomplished, when forgiveness of sins and victory over death had shone forth, when the "Cherubim withdrew from the tree of life," then there remained only praise, only thanksgiving. Thanksgiving, which before it became thanksgiving *for something*, for "all things of which we know and of which we know not, whether manifest or unseen," is granted to us as precisely a pure thanksgiving, as the blessed, heavenly fulness of the soul, "beholding the ineffable goodness [i.e., beauty] of the face of God," and in this knowledge finding the total joy of that little child of the gospels, about whom Christ said that if he does not arise in us, we cannot enter into the paradise of the kingdom of God.

4

IT IS THROUGH THIS PURE THANKSGIVING—AND PRECISELY because it is true knowledge, the fulness of the soul that has come to know God—that the integral *knowledge of the world*, which had

disintegrated in the sinful fall of man from God and become nothing more than only *knowledge about the world*, is restored. As Kant
has demonstrated once and for all, this "objective," *external*
knowledge is hopelessly closed off from access to "things in themselves," to the very essence of the world and life, and thus to
genuine possession of them.

And yet man was created for this possession, he was called to
it when in paradise God appointed him king of creation, invested
him with authority to *give names* to "every living creature," i.e.,
to know them *from within*, in their deepest essence. And thus the
knowledge that is restored by this thanksgiving is not knowledge
about the world, but of the world, for this thanksgiving is knowledge of God, and by the same token apprehension of the world as
God's world. It is knowing not only that everything in the world
has its cause in God—which, in the end, "knowledge about the
world" is also capable of—but also that everything in the world
and the world itself is a gift of God's love, a revelation by God of
his very self, summoning us in everything to know God, through
everything to be in communion with him, to possess everything
as life in him.

As the world was created by the word of God *by blessing*—in
the deepest, ontological significance of this expression—so is it
saved and restored by thanksgiving and blessing, granted to us in
the temple of Christ. Through them we recognize and comprehend the world as an icon, as communion, as sanctification.
Through them we transform it into what it was created for and
granted to us by God. "And when He had given thanks and
blessed it, and hallowed it . . ." Each time we pronounce these
words of the prayer of thanksgiving we "accomplish" the remembrance of Christ, who "took bread"— and this means matter, the
world, creation—"in His holy, pure, and blameless hands," and
again we witness to the world as a new creation, recreated as the
"paradise of delight," in which everything created by God is
called to become our partaking of the divine love, of the divine
life.

5

FINALLY, THANKSGIVING, BEING THE FULNESS OF KNOWLEDGE, is also the fulfilment of freedom, that genuine freedom of which Christ said: "you will know the truth, and the truth will make you free" (Jn 8:32). This is the freedom that man lost in his fall from God, in his banishment from paradise. Just as the knowledge that man struts around with, considering it all-powerful, is not genuine knowledge, so the freedom that he continually bewails is not genuine freedom, but a certain mysterious reflection of it that cannot be explained with scientific "precision," an unexplainable thirst in the human heart. It is astonishing how easily Christians themselves forget this, and how thoughtlessly, as something that goes without saying, they adopt the cheap "liberation" rhetoric that is smothering contemporary civilization. It is astonishing because Christians should know better than others that indeed in "this world," enslaved by sin and death, no one can ever define the essence of this freedom, which has become an idol, no one can describe that "kingdom of freedom," the struggle for the achievement of which supposedly defines human history.

And this is because here again we *know about freedom* but we *do not know freedom*. Indeed, we know something about it only relatively, only "by comparison." Of course, those who lived under an Orthodox government were freer than those living under a "totalitarian" government. For someone sitting in jail freedom begins beyond the walls of his cell. For someone living "in freedom" it begins with the overcoming of whatever "unfreedom" comes next, and so on ad infinitum. However, no matter how many layers of "unfreedom" we remove, each time we remove one, we inevitably find beneath it another, which turns out to be not less but more impenetrable. It would seem that we would finally be forced to see the illusoriness of the daydreams that torment us. The ordinary man, whose attention is entirely focused on the next "unfreedom," could easily fail to know this "illusoriness." The crowds storming the next Bastille would not know it; and it would not be known to the Ortega y Gasset "man of the masses," whose "liberators" change every hue and cry into "*hurrah* from the throat of the patriot, *down with* from the throat of the renegade," to use the words of one Russian poet. But those few who in their Promethean quest for freedom, freedom not only *from* someone and something but absolute "freedom in itself," smash themselves on the blank walls to which this search inevitably leads in "this world," according to its elements and logic, have come to know it and witness to it by their terrible fate. In Dostoevsky's *The Possessed* Kirillov commits suicide. And in "real life" Nietzsche, sinking into insanity, took his own life while hearing the "sinister laughter of the idiot," Arthur Rimbaud; "I'm staring at the walls," whispered the dying Valery; and the dark, Kafkaesque flame of absurdity and despair all the more clearly bursts through the cracks of a world supposedly constructed on freedom and reason and promising freedom.

But it is time we acknowledged that Christians themselves bear a large share of the responsibility for this tragedy of freedom, that it is not accidental that the roots of this tragedy stretch out into that world and that culture that not very long ago at all called itself Christian. On the one hand, the unheard of, impossible good news of freedom—the call, "For freedom Christ has set us free; stand fast therefore" (Ga 5:1)—came into the world with and only with Christianity. It is precisely Christianity, and only it, which has forever spoiled human consciousness with this unquenchable thirst. But on the other hand, who, if not Christians themselves, have substituted, or one can even say, handed down this good news while reducing it—for the world, for "those outside"—to facile, "scientific" and "objective" *knowledge about God*, to a knowledge *from without* that cannot define God other than in categories of power, authority, necessity and law. Precisely from here stems the terrible pathos of theomachy, inherent to all ideologies that promise freedom to mankind. And here there is no misunderstanding, for if God is what "knowledge about God" self-assuredly affirms about him, then man is a slave, in spite of all the stipulations and elucidations suggested in smooth apologetics and theodicy. And then, for the sake of freedom, it is necessary that God not exist, that he be killed, and through this murder of God contemporary man, deifying himself, advances to his lowest depths.

Hence, neither "this world" nor the "knowledge about God" constructed upon its logic and categories has the power to define the essence of freedom at its heart, not only in its negative but in its positive and absolute content. This is because freedom is not at all an "essence," something existing and consequently definable "in itself." God created us not for some kind of abstract "freedom" but for himself, for our communion, having been "brought" out of nonbeing into life and life in abundance, which is only from him, in him, *is* him. Man seeks and thirsts only for this life. It is only this life that man calls by that most incomprehensible—for it corresponds to nothing in the nature of "this world" and thus is always hardened—word *freedom*. It is only toward it that he strives, even when he is blindly and mindlessly struggling with God.

Thus we shall leave the "dead to bury the dead." We shall leave this joyless quest for squaring a circle, which any attempt to pose and resolve the "problem of freedom" inevitably becomes. We shall leave it and attend to the *thanksgiving* that we just spoke of, in which is fulfilled the genuine knowledge of God, in which is accomplished our meeting with him, and not with ideas about him. The Church lives in thanksgiving; it is the air she breathes. Let us listen and, to the measure of our acceptance of this thanksgiving, we shall grasp, and not by reason alone but with our entire being, that here and only here, only in this knowledge/thanksgiving, occurs our entrance into the sole true—for it is of God—freedom. It is the freedom that the Holy Spirit, the giver of life, who "blows where it wills, and you hear the sound of it, but you do not know whence it comes or whither it goes; so it is with every one who is born of the Spirit" (Jn 3:8), grants both as our breath, our royal nobility, and as power and perfection, fulness and beauty of life, or better still, *life in abundance*.

The one born of God, knowing him, gives thanks, and in giving thanks he is free, and the power and miracle of thanksgiving, as freedom and liberation, lies in the fact that it *makes the unequal equal*: God and man, creature and Creator, servant and Master. And it is not the "equality" inspired in man by the devil, whose secret impulse is in envy, in hatred for everything that is *above*, holy and lofty, in a plebeian repudiation of thanksgiving and worship, and therefore in a striving to make everything equal at the *lowest* point. Rather, it makes equal in that it *knows* man's dependence on God, objectively indisputable and ontologically absolute, *to be freedom*. It knows this inwardly, through the knowledge of God, from the meeting with God, from which thanksgiving itself was freely born. And if the itch for equality is, out of ignorance, the itch of the slave, then thanksgiving and worship come out of knowledge and vision, out of meeting with the holy and exalted one, out of entry into the freedom of being sons of God.

The Church manifests and grants this freedom to us each time that we ascend to the very summit of the divine liturgy and hear the call, directed to us and to all of God's creation, embracing everything in itself: "Let us give thanks unto the Lord!" And in the fulness of knowledge we answer: "It is meet and right!"

6

"IT IS MEET AND RIGHT TO HYMN THEE, TO BLESS THEE, TO praise Thee, to give thanks to Thee, and to worship Thee in every place of Thy dominion."

Here again this pure, free, blessed thanksgiving, restored and granted to man by Christ, is raised up over the world. It is his thanksgiving, his knowledge, his filial freedom, which has become and eternally becomes ours. Because it is of Christ and *from above*, this thanksgiving raises us up to paradise, as anticipation of it, as partaking while still on earth of the kingdom which is to come. And thus, each time it is raised up the *salvation of the world is complete*. All is fulfilled, all is granted. Man again stands where God placed him, restored to his vocation: to offer to God a "reasonable service," to know God, to thank and to worship him "in spirit and in truth," and through this knowledge and thanksgiving to transform the world itself into communion in the life that "was in the beginning with God" (Jn 1:2), with God the Father, and was manifested to us.

This Life was with the Father. It is infinitely important for understanding not only the liturgy but the very essence of the Christian faith to know and remember that *the eucharist is communion with the Father*. The daring *Thou* of the prayer of thanksgiving is directed to the Father, and the *knowledge of God,* in which, as we endeavored to show, the thanksgiving of the Church fulfils itself, is *knowledge of the Father*. But we have become so accustomed to

applying this word *Father* to God that we no longer feel how completely unheard of this is, how impossible it is for human lips, for
the mouth of a creature, to direct it toward the Creator. Therefore
we do not realize that this possibility "with boldness and without
condemnation" to call God Father, *to have access to the Father* (Eph
2:18), is not only the greatest of all Christ's gifts to us but is the
very essence of salvation—of ourselves and of the whole world—by
Christ.

"No one has seen God" (Jn 1:19). This is known to any genuine religious experience, which is always above all an experience
of the *holy*, in the original, primordial meaning of this word—
"holy" as *absolutely other*, incomprehensible, unknowable, unfathomable and ultimately even frightful. Religion was born and is
born simultaneously from attraction to the *holy*, from knowledge
that the absolutely other *is*, and from incomprehension as to *what*
it is. And thus there is nothing on earth more ambiguous and in
its ambiguity tragic than religion. It is only our contemporary,
fizzled-out and sentimental "religiosity" that is convinced that
"religion" is always something good, positive and useful, and
that in essence people have always believed in the same "good"
and condescending God, in a "Father," who in fact was created
"according to the image and likeness" of our own little goodness,
easy morality, commonplace pity, cheap complacency and shoddy
magnanimity. We have forgotten how close to "religion," in a
certain sense connatural to it, are the dark abysses of fear, insanity, hatred, fanaticism—all the sinister *superstition* that early
Christianity, seeing in it a devilish delusion, took such pains to
expose. In other words, we have forgotten that religion, as much
as it is from God, from the ineradicable thirst and seeking for him
in man, can also be from the "prince of this world," separating
man from God and submerging him in the horrible darkness of
ignorance. We have forgotten, finally that the most horrible of all
words that ever resounded on earth were spoken not to lukewarm
"agnostics" but to "religious" people: "your father is the devil"
(Jn 8:44).

Only in relation to this darkness, to the "valley of the shadow
of death" in which "this" fallen world abides, is the light of
knowledge that shines in Christ revealed to our spiritual consciousness as knowledge of the one true God and *knowledge of him*

as Father. For the fatherhood of God manifested to us by Christ is not the natural, anthropomorphic fatherhood, the knowledge of which, in relation to God, religion infers *from below,* and which God thus shares with various earthly "fatherhoods." This fatherhood is possessed only by God, and manifested and granted only by the only-begotten Son of God. "No one knows the Son except the Father, and no one knows the Father except the Son and any one to whom the Son chooses to reveal him" (Mt 11:27). Christianity did not begin with an "ecumenical," universal message of a Father-God common to all religions—in which the word "father," to cap it all off, is ambiguous, for God did not give birth to the world and man, but created them, and thus they are in no way an "emanation" from God. Christianity began with faith in the coming into the world, in the incarnation, of the only-begotten Son of God and in our *becoming sons*—in him and only in him—of his Father. Christianity is the gift of a double revelation: the revelation by the Father of the Son, whom "no one knows except the Father," and the revelation by the Son of the Father, whom "no one knows except the Son," but in whose manifestation to us, in our being brought to him, consists the matter of the salvation of man and the world, accomplished by Christ. "See what love the Father has given us, that we should be called children of God ...Beloved, we are God's children now!" (1 Jn 3:1-2) Consequently, to believe in Christ means above all to *believe him,* that he is the only-begotten Son of God and hence the manifestation in the world of *knowledge of God,* of love for the Father, of life through him and in him; and likewise the manifestation of the love of the Father, with which he "eternally loves the Son and has given all things to him." It is to believe further that the Son grants his unique, only-begotten sonship to us, making us sons of God the Father: "I am ascending to my Father and your Father, to my God and your God" (Jn 20:17). And finally, it is to believe and to know that in his beloved Son the Father, whom "the world has not known" (Jn 17:25), manifests and grants to us his Fatherhood, he loves us with the same love with which he loves his Son. And because all knowledge of the Father, all love for him, all unity with him, resides in the sonship of the Son, because the Son and the Father are *one* (Jn 10:30), he who knows the Son knows the Father, he has access to him and to eternal life.

The Church lives through this filial knowledge of the Father, through access to him in the Son, and she proclaims them as salvation and life eternal. And thus the sacrament of the eucharist, in which the Church fulfils herself as the new creation, as the body of Christ and as communion in the kingdom which is to come, is in its deepest depths the *sacrament of the knowledge of the Father*, of access, of ascent to him in his only-begotten Son. The apostle Philip asked him: "Lord, show us the Father, and we shall be satisfied" (Jn 14:8). And now, in the Son of God the Father is shown and manifested to us: "He who has seen me has seen the Father" (Jn 14:9)—and not only seen, but has access to him, knows him as the Father.

7

"THOU IT WAS WHO BROUGHT US FROM NONEXISTENCE INTO being..." Since it is knowledge of the Father, thanksgiving is every time *apprehension of the world*—apprehension of it as it was given to us by God and discovery about our very selves, as having been called by God "out of darkness into his marvelous light" (1 Pt 2:9) and as receiving "his precious and very great promises, that through these [we] may...become partakers of the divine nature" (2 Pt 2:4). Only when we are presented to the Father, in Christ, the Son of God, do we become cognizant both of ourselves and of the world with the knowledge that was impossible in the darkness of "this world" but is restored, returned to us through our sonship of the Father.

Actually, nowhere is the darkness of ignorance into which we were immersed with our fall from God more obvious than in man's staggering *ignorance of himself*, and this in spite of the insatiable interest with which, having lost God, man studies himself and endeavors in his "sciences humaines" to penetrate the mystery of man's being. We live in an era of unrestrained *narcissism*, universal "turning into one's self." But, as strange and even terrible as this may seem, the more elemental is this interest, the more obvious it is that it is nourished by some dark desire to *dehumanize* man. Levi-Strauss, one of the leaders of anthropological structuralism, declares himself convinced that the ultimate goal of the "science of men" is not the affirmation of man, but his dissolution. And, be it in different ways, contemporary linguistics, psychology and sociology all echo him. "The entire archeology of our thought," says Michel Foucault, another mental giant, demonstrates without difficulty that man is of recent invention, and it announces his end, possibly soon. The solution to the mystery of man is already turned into a negation not only of the mystery but of man himself, his dissolution into that monotonously gray and meaningless world that, in the words of the Nobel laureate Jacques Monod, is undividely ruled by the frigid law of "chance and necessity."

The thanksgiving offered by the Church each time answers and destroys precisely this not only contemporary but age-old lie about the world and man. Each time it is a manifestation of man to himself, a manifestation of his essence, his place and calling in the light of the divine countenance, and therefore an act that renews and recreates man. In thanksgiving we recognize and confess above all the divine source and the divine calling of our life. The prayer of thanksgiving affirms that God brought us from *nonexistence* into *being*, which means that he created us as partakers of *Being*, i.e., not just something that comes from him, but something permeated by his presence, light, wisdom, love—by what Orthodox theology, following St Gregory Palamas, calls the divine *energies* and which makes the world called to and capable of transfiguration into a "new heaven and a new earth," and the ruler of creation, man, called to and capable of theosis, "partaking of the divine nature."

8

"AND WHEN WE HAD FALLEN AWAY [THOU] DIDST RAISE US UP again..." Only now, only from the heights of the knowledge of God, man and the world to which thanksgiving has brought us, can we hear these two expressions—this double revelation given to us at each eucharist of the mystery of sin and salvation—in their full depth and power.

Why "only now"? Because for the *anthropological maximalism* inherent in Christianity, of which we were just speaking—the affirmation of the divine height of man, of his essence and calling—an ostensibly pious but in essence truly heretical *anthropological minimalism* is always being substituted in the consciousness even of faithful and devout people. It is heretical because in its false humility it constitutes nothing other than a deeply unchristian *normalization* of sin and evil. In point of fact, in our usual, everyday, lukewarm "religiosity" do we not perceive sin as something precisely normal, which arises self-evidently out of the weakness and imperfection supposedly inherent to our nature, while perfection and holiness, conversely, we see as something "supernatural"? And every word, every action of the eucharist exposes precisely this normalization of sin, this lowering of man to the level of the weakest—and in his weakness, most irresponsible—creature, this, speaking directly, defamation of God's creation. It exposes it in that it reveals sin as man's *falling away* not only from God *but also from himself*, from his true nature, from the "honor of the high calling" to which God has summoned him.

Even the very expression "when we had fallen away" presupposes and contains the experience of the heights from which the fall occurred. The fall is so horrible because it is not something naturally inherent to God's creation. It could never have been natural for one whom God "has chosen for glory and honor" when he placed him "over his handiwork." Because the Church knows these heights, because her whole life is the grace-filled experience of *restoration*, of return to these heights, of ascent to them, *the Church knows sin* in its full depth and power. But this knowledge is radically different from those facile, rational, discursive explanations whose fatal insufficiency consists in the fact that they all, in one way or another, give sin a "legal basis," making it, in philosophical terminology, a *phaenomenon bene fundatum*. In such explanations sin ceases to be precisely a *fall*. Considered in an "objective," cause-and-effect relationship, it turns out to be "legitimized," "normal," and it is no longer sin itself but the overcoming of it that is perceived as something that exceeds the "norm." But for the Church, in her experience and in her faith, sin and evil are essentially and above all a *mystery*, because evil does not and cannot have its own *existence* (for everything that exists is from God, and hence is "very good"), something that man could freely choose in preference to his own free essence as "good." Evil, according to one of the church fathers, is "unsown grass." But while it is not sown, not created by God, it *is*: it possesses a terrible destructive power, so that it can be said about the world itself that it "lies in evil" (1 Jn 5:19).

There is no explanation of this mystery in the Christian faith, because in the categories of our fallen and cunning reason explanation inevitably becomes justification, as one of the most false but, then, perhaps one of the most popular of sayings affirms: "to understand is to forgive." But it is not possible either to understand or justify sin. And the Church, while not explaining it, *convicts* sin, in the original, seminal meaning of the word "to convict": the Church, and only the Church, exposes sin *as* sin, evil *as* evil, to the full boundlessness of their inexplicability, *impossibility*, and thus, terror, nonexistence, irreparability.

How, when is this conviction accomplished? To this in essence singularly important question, fully aware that the learned interpreters of the "problem of evil" will hardly listen, we answer: above all, first of all, the Church convicts sin through her *thanksgiving*. Through it she recognizes the "vital essence" of evil, the source of sin as *unthankfulness*, as man's falling away from the "hymning, blessing, praising, giving thanks and worshiping" through which he lives—for man, and in him all creation, knows God and has communion with him. Not giving thanks is the root and the driving force of that *pride* in which all teachers of the spiritual life, that "art of arts," without exception see the sin that tore man away from God. For the subtlest spiritual essence of pride, properly distinguishable only in the spiritual effort of "discernment of spirits," lies precisely in the fact that, as opposed to all other causes ascribed to the fall, it alone is *not from below* but *from above*: it is not from imperfection but from completion, not from deficiency but from an overabundance of gifts, and not from weakness but from power. In other words, it comes not from some unexplainable "evil" of an unknown origin, but from the enticement and temptation of the divine "very good" of creation and man. Pride is opposed to thanksgiving precisely as unthanksgiving because it arose from the same causes as thanksgiving. It is another, opposite answer to the same gift; it is temptation by the same gift.

We know that, according to the testimony of all who follow

the path of struggle with sin, temptation is not yet sin. Christ himself was tempted, and precisely by the gifts he possessed: power, authority, miracle-working. In fact, every gift of God to man, his divine image and perfection itself, is a *temptation*—and above all the gift to man of his *I*, the miracle of his absolutely unique, eternal, unrepeatable and indivisible *personality*, which renders each man "like a king of creation." Temptation is *inherent* to the personality because out of all creation only man is called by God to love himself, i.e., to be conscious of his divine gift and the miracle of his *I*. It is actually only through this love for himself that man comprehends God as the Life of his life, as the absolutely desired *Thou*, in which he finds himself, his fulness, his happiness, his human *I*, created in the image and likeness of God, who is love. The human personality is love for oneself and *thus* love for God, love for God and *thus* love for oneself, the apprehension of oneself as a bearer of the divine gift of knowledge and ascent into the fulness of life. And here it is innate to convert this *love for himself* that is implicit in man into *love of oneself*, into *self-love*, which constitutes the essence of *pride*. No, man is not enticed by "evil" but by himself, by his own divine image, by the divine miracle of his *I*. He heard the serpent's whisper "you will be like gods" not from outside, but from within, in the blessed fulness of paradise, and wanted to have life in himself and for himself. He wanted all of God's gifts as his own and for himself: "I looked upon the beauty of the garden and my mind was deceived..." (Canon of St Andrew of Crete, ode 2,1)

The fall of man occurred here, at these heights and from these heights: "you will be like gods." But these words were in fact stolen from God. God created us and called us into "his wonderful light" so that we would become "like gods" and have abundant life. What then transformed these words into a lie, into the beginning of the fall, into the source of sin, decay and death? The answer to this question is given precisely by the eucharist, by the thanksgiving that returns us to the throne of the kingdom, grants us to see the face of God and his creation, heaven and earth, the fulfilment of his glory. The eucharist answers not with definitions, with words about words, but with its own light and power. For thanksgiving is the power that transforms desire and satisfaction, love and possession, into life, that fulfils everything in the world, given to us by God, into knowledge of God and communion with him. And thus only thanksgiving *convicts*, i.e., exposes, sin as the falling away of love from thanksgiving, as *unthankfulness*. Created in the image and likeness of God, who is love, man cannot cease to be love. Even in "unthankfulness" he nevertheless remains that same love, he "admires" all the same gifts. But it is a love that has ceased to be thanksgiving, i.e., the knowledge of the gift of life and everything in life as not only God's, from God, but as the revelation of God's love to man, as a call to man to transform all gifts and life itself into partaking of the divine life, *into knowledge of God.*

Life in oneself... But only the Father "has life in himself" (Jn 5:26), only God is Life and therefore the life of any life. The horror and finality of the fall lies in this: wanting life in himself and for himself, man fell away from life. Through sin *death entered the world* (Rm 5:12) and the world itself became "darkness and the shadow of death." Not transformed by thanksgiving into the "food of immortality," into communion unto life, it became communion unto death, and love for the world. Not transformed by thanksgiving into knowledge of God, it became a dim and self-devouring "lust of the flesh and lust of the eyes and the pride of life" (1 Jn 2:16). "Man is a passion, but a useless passion." In saying this Jean-Paul Sartre did not of course know what happened in the *falling away* of man, in that "original sin," in which, ceasing to be a sacrament of thanksgiving, the world died, and life became dying.

9

WE KNOW THAT ALL OF THIS, THE TERRIBLE LAWLESSNESS AND untruth of sin, the bottomless sorrow and death-dealing power of our fall from God, the power of evil, had once reigned in the world each time that, from the heavenly heights to which Christ's thanksgiving has raised us, these two expressions come forth: "when we had fallen away [Thou] didst raise us up again..." But we know it because *we have been restored*, because we have access to the Father and have been made partakers of the kingdom which is to come: "and [Thou] didst not cease to do all things until Thou hadst brought us up to heaven, and hadst endowed us with Thy Kingdom which is to come."

In Christ human nature is lifted up to heaven, sanctified, deified. "What no eye has seen, nor ear heard, nor the heart of man conceived, what God has prepared for those who love him, God has revealed to us through the Spirit. For the Spirit searches everything, even the depths of God" (1 Cor 2:9).

Paradise was on earth, but we have ascended to heaven, and even now our life "is hid with Christ in God" (Col 3:3). The revelation of this last and highest gift, its *endowment*, is precisely the Church. And this endowment is accomplished in the sacrament of thanksgiving, in which the Church fulfils herself as *heaven on earth*.

This fulfilment is also witnessed to by the *sanctus*, that angelic praise *holy, holy, holy*, which in almost every eucharistic text that has come down to us concludes the *praefatio* and through which, as we shall later see, the sacrament of thanksgiving introduces us into the sacrament of remembrance.

> For all these things we give thanks to Thee, and to Thine only-begotten Son, and to Thy Holy Spirit; for all things of which we know and of which we know not, whether manifest or unseen; and we thank Thee for this Liturgy which Thou hast deigned to accept at our hands, though there stand by Thee thousands of archangels and hosts of angels, the Cherubim and Seraphim, six-winged, many-eyed, who soar aloft, borne on their pinions, singing the triumphant hymn, shouting, proclaiming and saying: Holy! Holy! Holy! Lord of Sabaoth! Heaven and earth are full of Thy glory! Hosannah in the highest! Blessed is He that comes in the name of the Lord! Hosannah in the highest!

To what do these ancient angelic praises witness if not to *heaven*, which we are *seeing* and *hearing*, for we ourselves are lifted up to it? What are these words of the royal greeting if not an *icon*: the gift, vision, revelation of the kingdom of glory; if not meeting with God, fulfilled through thanksgiving, at his table, in his kingdom?

CHAPTER TEN

The Sacrament of Remembrance

*"...as my Father appointed a king-
dom for me, so do I appoint one for you
that you may eat and drink at my table in my kingdom."*

LUKE 22:29-30

I

WITH THE PROCLAMATION OF THE ANGELIC GLORIFICATION
"holy, holy, holy" the prayer of thanksgiving finds its
fulfilment as the ascent of the Church to *heaven*, to the throne of
God, to the glory of the heavenly kingdom. But here, at this
height, from this fulness of divine communion, knowledge and
joy, the prayer of thanksgiving, while embracing all creation, the
entire world visible and invisible, while manifesting the Church
as heaven on earth, realizes itself as it were in the remembrance of
one event: the *last supper*, which Christ performed with his disciples on the night in which he gave himself up to suffering and
death.

Here is this part of the eucharistic prayer, the so-called *remembrance* (ἀνάμνησις) in liturgical science, in the liturgy of St John
Chrysostom:

With these blessed powers, O Master who lovest mankind, we also cry aloud and say: Holy art Thou and all-
holy, Thou and Thine only-begotten Son and Thy Holy

191

Spirit! Holy art Thou and all-holy, and magnificent is
Thy glory! Who hast so loved Thy world as to give Thine
only-begotten Son, that whoever believes in Him should
not perish but have everlasting life; who when He had
come and had fulfilled all the dispensation for us, in the
night in which He was given up—or rather, gave Himself
up for the life of the world—took bread into His holy,
pure, and blameless hands; and when He had given
thanks and blessed it, and hallowed it, and broken it, He
gave it to His holy disciples and apostles, saying: Take!
Eat! This is My Body, which is broken for you, for the
remission of sins. And likewise, after supper, He took the
cup, saying: Drink of it, all of you! This is My Blood of
the New Testament, which is shed for you and for many,
for the remission of sins! Remembering this saving commandment and all those things which have come to pass
for us: the Cross, the tomb, the Resurrection on the third
day, the Ascension into heaven, the Sitting at the right
hand, and the second and glorious Coming, Thine own of
Thine own we offer unto Thee on behalf of all and for all.

What is the meaning of this *remembrance*, its place not only in the
prayer of thanksgiving but also in the totality of the divine liturgy, which is accomplished and fulfilled through this prayer?

2

DESPITE HUNDREDS OF TREATISES WRITTEN IN RESPONSE TO
this question, neither academic theology nor liturgical studies has
given, alas, a satisfactory answer. Here we see yet again the insufficiency of the method that I have already spoken of many times,
which consists in the *dismemberment* of the eucharistic prayer, and
essentially even the whole liturgy, into parts, which are then
studied and explained outside of their connection with the other
parts, without relating them to the whole. And this insufficiency
is particularly obvious precisely in explanations of the eucharist as
remembrance, for here it becomes clear to what degree the "reduc-
tionism" inherent to this method narrows and then ultimately

distorts the understanding not only of this "moment" itself but of the entire sacrament of the eucharist as well. We need to dwell on these "reductions," which for hundreds of years now have been perceived as seemingly self-evident, for, in the first place, without overcoming them, we cannot "break through" to the genuine meaning, embedded in the very experience of the Church, of the eucharist as the *sacrament of remembrance*.

The first of these reductions consists in the understanding and definition of *remembrance* as a "consecratory" *reference* to Christ's establishment, at the last supper, of the sacrament of the eucharist, i.e., the transformation of the bread and wine into the body and blood of Christ. The power of this transformation, the "actuality" of the sacrament, is attributed here to the remembrance. The remembrance is the "cause" of the actuality of the sacrament, just as the *institution* of the eucharist at the last supper is the cause of the actuality of the commemoration itself.

We find such a reduction in its "pure" form in the Latin doctrine of the transubstantiation of the eucharistic gifts through the *words of institution* of Christ, i.e., the words he pronounced at the last supper and which the priest repeats while performing the sacrament: "this is my body," "this is my blood." But inasmuch as these words are defined as "consecratory" and, consequently, both necessary and sufficient for the sacrament, the eucharistic commemoration of the last supper is essentially reduced to them.

This reduction, in such an extreme form, is rejected both by Orthodox and Protestant theologians. But it is rejected, however, precisely and only as an *extreme*. For its main point, the reduction of the commemoration to the institution, remains the singular and, I repeat, seemingly self-evident context for the explanation of this part of the eucharistic prayer. In the Orthodox East, for example, in spite of the fact that our theologians unanimously affirm that it is not the "words of institution" but the *epiklesis*, the invocation of the Holy Spirit, that accomplishes the transformation of the gifts, a special *isolation* precisely of the words of institution long ago was introduced and practiced everywhere. So, during the celebrant's generally accepted *secret*, i.e., "to himself," reading of the prayer of thanksgiving, only these words, and not the words of the epiklesis, are pronounced aloud. So, during their pronouncement, the celebrant (or the deacon) points his hand first

at the bread and then at the cup, as if to emphasize the particular-
ity, the exclusivity of precisely this moment. And, finally, at the
pronouncement of each of the two formulas of "institution"—over
the bread and over the cup—the assembly answers with a solemn
amen, a word that in worship always has precisely a "consecratory"
meaning.

As far as Protestant theology is concerned, although it generally dismisses any objective change of the eucharistic gifts as
needless and somewhat "magical" and places the reality of the
change in dependence not on liturgical formulas and rites but on
the personal faith of the communicant, this very "dismissal" takes
place *within* entirely the same reduction, for it applies the question not to the link between the last supper and the eucharist as
such, but to the "actualization," the "reality" of this link in the
Church.

In what does the insufficiency, the harmfulness of this approach consist? For what reason do we define it as a reduction?
Because, of course, the endlessly important—for our faith, for our
life—question of the eucharistic commemoration of the last supper, and hence of the connection of the eucharist with the last
supper, is brought down in this approach to a question of *how*, not
what: of *how* the institution at the last supper "operates" in the
eucharist, but not of *what* Christ accomplished through this last
act of his earthly ministry before his betrayal, cross and death.

In other words, the reduction here consists in the substitution
of the chief question with a derivative one. This substitution was
derived, without any doubt, in connection with another, far more
profound reduction, which, although it issues from the same
"dismembering" method, concerns the theological source no
longer of just the eucharist but of the entire saving work of
Christ. It is the identification, inherent to scholastic theology in
all its varieties, of the *sacrifice* that Christ offered for us and for our
salvation with Golgotha: with the cross, suffering and death. To
be sure, according to the Church's teaching, in the eucharist the
Church "proclaims the Lord's death, confesses his resurrection."
To be sure, the connection of Golgotha with the last supper, accomplished by Christ "before [he] suffer[s]" (Lk 22:15), and thus
of the sacrifice of Golgotha with the eucharist, is indisputable.
School theology, however, reduces its interpretation of the eucha-

rist almost exclusively to it. According to this interpretation, Christ established the eucharist at the last supper as a sacramental commemoration of his sacrificial immolation on the cross, the taking on himself of the sin of the world, which is redeemed by him through his suffering and death. Offered once on Golgotha, this sacrifice is eternally "actualized" in the eucharist, on our altars, since on our behalf and for us it has been offered and is offered.

As is well known, such a sacramental identification of the last supper and the eucharist with the sacrifice of Golgotha led the Protestants to the general repudiation of the sacrificial character of the eucharist as incompatible with the doctrine of the singularity, unrepeatability and "sufficiency" of the sacrifice offered by Christ ἅπαξ, i.e., once and for all. Among us Orthodox, it became entrenched in our school theology—albeit without the extremes inherent to the Latin "prototype" of this interpretation—and in part affected the very rites and prayers of the liturgy. But above all, to a significant degree it colored the *symbolical* interpretations of the liturgy, of which I have spoken repeatedly in the first chapters of this investigation.

What we ultimately need to say of these "reductions" is that they have led, both in theology and in the very liturgical life of the Church, to an almost total rupture between the teaching on the eucharist as *sacrifice* and the doctrine of it as being the sacrament of *partaking of communion*. In our school theology these two doctrines have simply coexisted, as it were, but without any inner connection. As far as our liturgical practice, which undoubtedly reflects the theology, is concerned, we perceive the eucharist-sacrifice and the eucharist-communion in two completely different "keys." Thus, for example, as both theologians and pastors and even directors of the "spiritual life" have taught the faithful, one can—and it appears even that one must—take part in the eucharist-sacrifice while not partaking of communion: by being present, by prayer, by offering prosphora, by receiving the antidoron, or even by simply "requesting" one or several liturgies. This is possible because in the consciousness and piety of church people, communion has for a long time not been linked to the eucharist as sacrifice, but has been subordinated entirely to another "law": the law of individual "spiritual needs"—sanctification, help, consolation, etc.—and correspondingly to the question of personal "pre-paredness" or "unpreparedness."

All these reductions, I repeat, have their origin and are rooted in a theology, in a liturgical science, which takes as its basis for the study and interpretation of the eucharist not the *lex orandi*, not the rule of the Church's prayer in all its integrity, where all the parts that comprise the eucharistic celebration are subordinat-ed one to another, but, on the contrary, its dismemberment in the name of a priori criteria, i.e., criteria located outside the eu-charist itself, outside its "self-witness."

3

TO BE FAIR, ONE MUST RECOGNIZE THAT OVER THE PAST decades there has occurred a significant and in general positive thrust in the study of the eucharist. This was furthered, on the one hand, by the so-called *liturgical movement*, with its intense fo-cus on the early, prescholastic understanding of the place of the eucharist in the Church, and, on the other, by the new, deepened study of the link between the Christian liturgical tradition and its Jewish roots. The works of such scholars as Dom Gregory Dix, Oscar Cullmann, Joachim Jeremias, Jean Daniélou and many others has broadened our knowledge of the religious forms of later Judaism (*Spätjudentum*), within which Christianity and the Church were born and the preaching of the gospel—the good news of the coming into the world for its salvation of the messiah prom-ised by God and the fulfilment in him of all the prophets, all that was promised—began to be proclaimed.

Thus, we now know that, along with its absolute singularity, the last supper was *in its form* a traditional religious meal with prescribed rites and prayers, and that Christ fulfilled all these pre-scriptions. And we likewise know that these prescriptions, this "form"—precisely because Christ fulfilled them, referred them to himself, to his saving work—became the original, fundamental "form" of the Church, her self-witness, her fulfilment in the world.

This knowledge itself, however, no matter how useful and necessary, cannot give us the *complete* answer to the question we posed at the beginning of this chapter: of the meaning of the *commemoration* of the last supper, which from the beginning constituted an inalienable part of the prayer of thanksgiving. Moreover, now that historical investigation has helped free us from the *scholastic* reduction, we are now threatened with a new, this time *historical* reduction. This latter consists in the conscious or unconscious conviction that the historical method is capable by itself of revealing the meaning and content of the eucharist—and also that it alone can realize this. In contemporary "historicism," inasmuch as it pretends to fulness of knowledge (but, alas, only pretends to it), we are thus dealing with the same rationalism as in the case of the scholastics—i.e., with the certainty that human reason in itself possesses a guarantee of its infallibility. But need we once again demonstrate that no kind of history, even the most scientific, is ever in the end free of "presuppositions," but always, both in its questions and in its answers, depends on the convictions, even if they are often unconscious, of the "questioner," i.e., the historian? As far as Christianity is concerned, the best demonstration of this is the conglomeration of "scientific-historical" interpretations of the early Church, her faith and her life, which marked the era of the triumph of "historicism," its triumph precisely as a "reduction." For it is precisely seeing it as such a "reduction" that explains the fact that each of these theories, self-assuredly proclaiming itself as the last word of science, was soon debunked by its successor, which was just as self-assured and just as doomed.

Therefore, unreservedly acknowledging the full indisputable use and, moreover, absolute necessity of historical research into liturgical theology, which I wrote of with—I hope—sufficient clarity in my *Introduction to Liturgical Theology*, I consider the lowering of the liturgy to a *history* of the worship services, which replaced the earlier imprisonment of theological scholasticism, to be wrong and harmful. I am convinced, for example, that this historical reduction explains, in the first place, the helplessness, confusion and discordance of the "liturgists" in the face of the profound liturgical crisis that has erupted within Christianity in our day. It is as if they have nothing to say to the liturgical experiments of every description that are carried out with the aim of bringing the services "closer" to the "needs," "ideas" and even "demands" of the contemporary world, or, simply put, dissolving them into contemporary life. They have nothing to say precisely because, by "dissolving" worship into history in the first place, they supplied the means for its dissolution in contemporary life today. They have stripped of meaning the very question of the eternal and unchanging essence of the liturgy, of its significance for the Church, for man, for the world. And at the same time they have prompted a sterile, liturgically illiterate "integrism" in reaction against all these experiments.

4

ALL THIS NEEDED TO BE SAID IN ORDER TO AGAIN JUSTIFY, THIS time in relation to the eucharistic *remembrance*, the method that lies at the basis of this entire investigation and which, in my deepest conviction, is the only one that corresponds to and answers both the essence and the goal of liturgical theology. We must seek the complete answer to the question of the meaning of this commemoration, of the meaning of the liturgy as the *sacrament of remembrance*, in the eucharist itself—and this means in the continuity, in the identity of that *experience*, not personal, not subjective, but precisely *ecclesial*, which is incarnated in the eucharistic celebration and is fulfilled each time the eucharist is celebrated.

We must most strongly stipulate that the *integral* answer does not stand for the whole answer, all the knowledge that it reveals. It is not given us to know the *whole* answer to any genuine question, and this is so not only because of our limitations but also because of the inexhaustibility of the depths of the divine mystery, of the divine economy concerning the world and man, and thus the inexhaustibility of our seekings, our questionings, both here on earth and in eternity as well. Indeed, here and now, in this earthly life, we are called to participation in the heavenly mystery, to communion with heaven. But all the more our knowledge is still only *partial*: "For our knowledge is imperfect and our prophecy is imperfect; but when the perfect comes, the imperfect will pass away.... For now we see in a mirror dimly, but then face to face. Now I know in part; then I shall understand fully, even as I have been fully understood" (1 Co 13:9-10, 12).

But here the entire depth, the entire joy of the Christian faith and of the whole experience of the Church lies in the fact that this *partly* stems from the *whole*. It is referred to it, it witnesses to it, it shines with its light and functions through its power. If we are not given in "this world" to know the *entire* answer, then in the Church, which is "in this world" but not "of this world," we have been granted the way of the full approach to it, of growth into it. This way is in the entrance into the experience of the Church and in partaking of it above all in the *sacrament of sacraments*, in which each time the Church performs it, even if no one is ever able to wholly perceive it, the fulness of this experience is granted. And it is precisely this contact with it that gives birth in us to the desire to always more truly, more fully, more integrally, more perfectly partake of it and comprehend it.

5

THE FIRST THING THAT IS REVEALED TO US ABOUT THE LITUR-gical remembrance of the last supper in the light of the eucharistic experience is precisely that, being a part of the thanksgiving, it not only is inseparable from the thanksgiving, not "isolated" from it, but only in reference to it, within it, is its true meaning disclosed to us.

We already know that through thanksgiving the meaning of the eucharist as the ascent of the Church to the heavenly altar, as the sacrament of the kingdom of God, is fulfilled. We likewise know that the entire liturgy, through its successive self-realization as the sacrament of assembly, sacrament of entrance, sacrament of the word, sacrament of offering and, finally, sacrament of thanksgiving, is oriented toward this ascent. We know, finally, that in this sense the whole liturgy is a *remembrance* of Christ. It is all a sacrament and experience of his presence: of the Son of God, who came down from heaven and was incarnate that he might in himself lead us up to heaven. He "gathers us as the Church," he transforms our gathering into an entrance and ascent, he "opens our mind" to the hearing of his word, he, as "the offerer and the offered," makes his offering ours and ours his, he fulfils our unity as unity in his love, and, finally, through his thanksgiving, which has been granted to us, he leads us up to heaven, he opens to us access to his Father.

What can all this mean except that the *remembrance*, into which thanksgiving now converts itself, having attained this goal, having through itself fulfilled the ascent of the Church to heaven, *is* the very *reality* of the kingdom—which we are precisely able to *remember*, and thus comprehend as *real*, as present "in our midst," because Christ manifested it and appointed it then, on that night, at that table.

"As my Father appointed a kingdom for me, so do I appoint one for you that you may eat and drink at my table in my kingdom" (Lk 22:29-30). In the night of the fallen world, enslaved to sin and death, the last supper manifested the otherworldly, divine light of the kingdom of God. Here is the eternal meaning and the eternal reality of this singular event, which can be compared with and reduced to no other. The eucharistic experience of the Church discloses precisely this meaning of the last supper. The Church apprehends it as her own ascent to the heavenly reality, which Christ has manifested and granted, once and for all time, on earth at the last supper. And when, approaching for communion, we pray, "Of Thy Mystical Supper, O Son of God, accept me *today* as a communicant," this identification of what is accomplished *today* with what was accomplished *then* is *real*, and precisely in the full meaning of the word, for *today* we are gathered in the same kingdom, at the same table, where *then*, on that festal night, Christ was present among those whom "he loved to the end."

"He loved them to the end" (Jn 13:1). In the eucharistic experience and in the gospels the last supper is the *end* (τέλος), i.e., the completion, the crowning, the fulfilment of Christ's love, which constitutes the essence of all of his ministry, preaching, miracles, and through which he now gives himself up, as love itself. From the opening words, "I have earnestly desired to eat this passover with you" (Lk 22:15), to the exit to the garden of Gethsemane, everything at the last supper—the washing of the feet, the distribution to the disciples of the bread and the cup, the last discourse—is not only concerned with love, but is *Love itself*. And thus the last supper is the τέλος, the completion, the fulfilment of the *end*, for it is the manifestation of that kingdom of love, for the sake of which the world was created and in which it has its τέλος, its fulfilment. Through love God created the world. Through love he did not abandon it when it fell into sin and death. Through love he sent his only-begotten Son, his Love, into the world. And now, at this table, he manifests and grants this love as his kingdom, and his kingdom as "abiding" in love: "As the Father has loved me, so have I loved you; *abide in my love*" (Jn 15:9).

6

SUCH IS THE ANSWER OF THE LITURGY ITSELF, OF THE EUCHA-ristic experience of the Church, to the first of the "reductions" that we pointed out, which explains the eucharistic commemoration of the last supper as a reference to the institution of the sacrament and by the same token reduces this very institution to the granting to the Church of the authority and power to transform the bread and wine of the eucharistic offering into the body and blood of Christ.

It is precisely in the light of what has been said that this interpretation's entire insufficiency, its entire incompatibility with the experience of the Church is revealed. The insufficiency is not that this interpretation affirms the *reality* of the body and blood of Christ in the eucharistic gifts but that it excludes what, by its being cut off from the integral experience of the Church, it does not see, it does not hear, and thus it *does not know*. And it excludes what is precisely the main thing: the eucharistic *knowledge* in the last supper of the ultimate manifestation of the kingdom of God, and thus of the *beginning* of the Church, her beginning as the new life, as the sacrament of the kingdom.

At the same time, it is precisely in Christ's transformation at the last supper of *the end into the beginning*, the Old Testament into the New, that we find the essence of what we denote with the poor and feeble term "institution," a word that by its sound alone draws us downward to a juridical, purely institutionalized reduction. At the last supper Christ did not *institute* any "authority" or "right" to transform bread and wine—he instituted the Church. He instituted his kingdom, appointed for his disciples and all "who believe through their words," as *abiding in his love*. "A new commandment I give to you, that you love one another." This commandment is new, eternally new, because it is Christ himself, the very love of God, who is granted to us in order that we may love one another through it: "even as I have loved you, that you also love one another" (Jn 13:34). And this new covenant in Christ, the love of God, is the Church.

Yes, the institution of the eucharist did occur at the last supper—but not as "another" institution separate from the institution of the Church, for it is the establishment of the eucharist as the sacrament of the Church, of her ascent to heaven, of her self-fulfilment at the table of Christ in his kingdom. The last supper, the Church and the eucharist are "linked" not through an earthly cause-and-effect connection, to which an "institution" is so often lowered, but through their common and single *referral* to the kingdom of God—which is *manifested* at the last supper, *granted* to the Church and *remembered*, in its presence and actuality, in the eucharist.

Therefore, finally, only in relation to this link, to its fulfilment, its actuality, is the genuine meaning of the most profound and joyous mystery of our faith—the transformation in the eucharist of our gifts into the body and blood of Christ—revealed to us. And this mystery we shall be presently speaking of in the following chapter as the *sacrament of the Holy Spirit*.

7

BEFORE THIS, HOWEVER, WE MUST DWELL ON THE ANSWER given by the eucharist itself, by the eucharistic experience of the Church, to the second "reduction": the identification of the commemoration of the last supper with the commemoration of Christ's suffering and death on the cross, and hence, the interpretation of the eucharist as the sacrament above all of the sacrifice on Golgotha.

Let us say immediately that the link between the last supper and Christ's voluntary suffering, which lies at the foundation of this "reduction," was never doubted by the Church and is attested to not only by her entire liturgical tradition but first of all by the gospel itself. According to the gospels, Christ purposefully accomplished the last supper before he suffered (Lk 22:15) and knowing that his hour had come (Jn 13:1). He continued and completed his farewell discourse with his disciples, in which he gave them his new commandment and which began while still at the supper, on the road to the garden of Gethsemane ("Rise, let us go hence," Jn 14:31), so that this very parting, the ascent to the cross, was manifested to us as the completion of the last supper. And the eucharistic prayer itself, I repeat, which invariably links the commemoration of the last supper with the commemoration of the cross, witnesses to this connection.

Thus, we speak not of this link in and of itself but of its theological interpretation. Does all that was said about it justify the approach to the eucharist that sees and interprets the eucharistic remembrance as a *means* to the sacramental actualization of the sacrifice on Golgotha? And is the understanding that ensues from this approach—of the last supper as an act by which Christ, before his passion, in prevision of his sacrifice on Golgotha, made a prototype of it, establishing its sacramental "form," in order that the saving fruits of this sacrifice could always be fed to the faithful in the sacrament—correct?

In the light of all that has been said above about the eucharistic experience and "knowledge" of the last supper, we not only can but must answer "no" to these two questions. This approach is wrong—wrong in that it is determined precisely by the isolation of the eucharistic commemoration and its severance from the wholeness of the liturgical celebration, which as we have seen is entirely oriented to the commemoration, entirely leading to it as its consummation.

Actually, the whole meaning, the entire endless joy of this commemoration is precisely that it remembers the last supper not as a "means" but as a manifestation, and even more than a manifestation, as the presence and gift of the very *goal*: the kingdom for which God created the world, to which he called and foreordained mankind and in which, "in these latter days," he manifested in his only-begotten Son, the kingdom of the Father's love for the Son, the Son's love for the Father and the Holy Spirit's gift of this love to the faithful. "I in them and thou in me, that they may become perfectly one...that the love with which thou hast loved me may be in them, and I in them" (Jn 17:23, 26).

We call the last supper an ultimate event because, being the manifestation of the goal, it is the manifestation of the *end*. This end, the kingdom of God, is "not of this world" and thus is *other-worldly*, although its manifestation is accomplished in "this world." "I am no more in the world," Christ said at the last supper (Jn 17:11). And because he is no longer in the world, the glory he manifested and gave to his disciples on that night, at that table ("the glory which thou hast given me I have given to them," Jn 17:22), is also "not of the world." With the last supper Christ's earthly ministry was completed, and Christ himself witnesses to this in his farewell discourse and high-priestly prayer: "Now is the Son of man glorified and in him God is glorified" (Jn 13:31); "I *glorified* thee on earth, *having accomplished* the work which thou gavest me to do" (Jn 17:4).

But then, everything that Christ accomplished *after* the last supper, and that the eucharistic prayer commemorates after it, is revealed in this prayer and in the faith and experience of the Church as a *consequence* of this manifestation of the kingdom, as its first, decisive and saving *victory* in the world and over the world.

8

CHRIST WAS CRUCIFIED BY "THIS WORLD," BY ITS SIN, ITS EVIL, its struggle against God. In earthly history, in our earthly time, the *initiative* of the cross belongs to sin, just as it belongs to it even today, in each of us, when through our sins we "crucify the Son of God on [our] own account and hold him up to contempt" (Heb 6:6).

If the cross—an instrument of a shameful execution—has become the most holy *symbol* of our faith, hope and love, if the Church never tires of glorifying its unfathomable and unconquerable power, of seeing in it the "beauty of the universe" and the "healing of creation," of witnessing that "through the cross joy has come into all the world," it is because, of course, through that same cross, which incarnated the very essence of sin as *theomachy*, this sin was overcome; because through the death on the cross, death, which had reigned in the world and would appear to have achieved its ultimate victory, was itself destroyed; and finally because from the depths of this victory of the cross radiated the joy of the resurrection.

But what transformed the cross and eternally transforms the cross into victory if not the love of Christ, the same divine love that, as the very essence and glory of the kingdom of God, Christ manifested and granted at the last supper? And where, if not at the last supper, do we find the consummation of the full, complete self-sacrifice of this love, which in "this world" made the cross—betrayal, crucifixion, suffering and death—*unavoidable?*

The gospels and the church services, particularly the wonderfully profound services of passion week, witness precisely to this link between the last supper and the cross, to their connection as the manifestation and victory of the kingdom of God. In these services, the last supper is always *referred* to that night that surrounds it on all sides and in which particularly clearly shines the light of the festival of love that Christ accomplished with his disciples in the "large upper room, furnished," as if prepared in advance from all ages. This was the night of sin, night as the very essence of "this world." And here it thickens to the limit, it prepares to devour the last light shining in it. Already the "princes of the people are assembled together against the Lord and his Christ." Already the thirty silver pieces—the price of betrayal—are paid. Already the crowd, incited by their leaders, armed with swords and spears, are heading out on the road leading to the garden of Gethsemane.

But—and this is infinitely important for the Church's understanding of the cross—the last supper itself took place under the shadow of this darkness. Christ knew "the hand of him who betrays me is with me on the table" (Lk 22:21). And it was precisely from the last supper, from its light, that Judas, *after taking the morsel* (Jn 13:27), went out into that dreadful night, and soon after him, Christ. And if in the services of Holy Thursday, the day of the express commemoration of the last supper, joy is all the time interlaced with sadness, if the Church again and again recalls not only the light but also the darkness overshadowing it, it is because, in the double *exits* of Judas and of Christ from that light into that darkness, she sees and knows the beginning of the cross as the mystery of sin and the mystery of victory over it.

The mystery of sin: Judas' exit is the limit and completion of that sin whose origin is in paradise and whose essence lies in the falling away of human love from God, in choosing, through this love, oneself, and not God. All of the life, all of the history of the world, as the *fallen* world, as "this world," which lies in evil, as the kingdom of "the prince of this world," begins with this falling away and is inwardly determined by it. And now, in the exit of Judas, apostle and betrayer, this history of sin—blind, twisted, devoid of love, which had become *thievery*, for it had stolen life, which was given for communion with God, "for itself"—approaches its end. For the mystically terrible meaning of this exit is that Judas *also left paradise*, he took flight from paradise, he cast himself from it. He was at the last supper, Christ washed his feet, he took into his hands the bread of Christ's love, Christ gave himself to him in this bread. He saw, he heard, he felt the kingdom of God with his own hands. And here, like Adam, fulfilling Adam's primordial sin, taking the entire horrible "logic" of sin to its limit, he *did not want* this kingdom. In Judas the theomachistic desire, the fallen love of "this world," proved the more powerful. And this desire, on the strength of all its horrible logic, could not but be—consequently, inevitably—for the *murder of God*. After the last supper Judas had *nowhere to go* but into the darkness of deicide. When it was done and this desire, and through it his "living" life, was exhausted, Judas would have *nowhere* to go but into self-annihilation and death.

The mystery of victory: In Christ, who through his self-sacrifice manifested his kingdom and its glory at the last supper, *this very kingdom* appeared in the night of "this world." After the last supper Christ also had *nowhere greater to go* than to this encounter, to the deadly duel with sin and death—because these two kingdoms, the kingdom of God and the kingdom of the "prince of this world," could not simply "coexist," because it was in order to destroy the dominion of sin and death, to return his creation, stolen from him by the devil, to himself, to save the world, that God gave his only-begotten Son. Thus, Christ *condemned* himself to the cross with the last supper, with the manifestation in it of the kingdom of love. Through the cross the kingdom of God, which was *secretly* manifested at the supper, *enters* into "this world" and through this entrance becomes struggle and victory.

9

SUCH IS THE KNOWLEDGE, SUCH IS THE ORIGINAL EXPERIENCE of the cross in the Church, as witnessed by her entire liturgical tradition, and above all by the eucharistic *remembrance*. As the prayer of thanksgiving continues:

> Remembering this saving commandment and all those things which have come to pass for us: the Cross, the Tomb, the Resurrection on the third day, the Ascension into heaven, the Sitting at the right hand, and the second and glorious Coming...

This enumeration—in which, let us emphasize, the cross is not isolated from or contraposed to the other events but constitutes together with them as it were one ascending series—is a commemoration of a single victory, gained in Christ by the kingdom of God over "this world." The victory, which is realized, however, in a succession of victories, each finding its fulfilment in the next, is the action of the victorious progress toward that *end*, when Christ "delivers the kingdom to God the Father ...then God shall be all in all" (1 Co 15:24, 28). The sacrificial love of Christ, the single *sacrifice*, integrally offered by Christ through all these victories, unites them together, transforms them into a single victory.

Here, in relation to this single and all-encompassing sacrifice of Christ, is disclosed the "harmfulness" of the identification, inherent in the "dismembering" school theology, of the sacrifice that Christ offers for us *only* with the suffering and death on the cross. This harmfulness is rooted, of course, in the first place in the onesided "juridical" understanding of the very idea of sacrifice as an *atoning* act, correlative to evil and sin as their expiation, and thus an act that according to its very essence "demands" suffering and ultimately death. This understanding, however—and we have already spoken of this in the chapter devoted to the eucharist as the *sacrament of offering*—is precisely onesided and in its onesidedness, false. In its essence sacrifice is linked not with sin and evil but with *love*: it is the self-revelation and self-realization of

love. There is no love without sacrifice, for love, being the giving
of oneself to another, the placing of one's life in another, the perfect obedience to another, is sacrifice. If in "this world" sacrifice
is actually and inevitably linked with suffering, it is not in accordance with its own essence but in accordance with the essence of
"this world," which lies in evil, whose essence lies in the falling
away from love.

We spoke of all this earlier, and there is no need for us to
repeat it here. What is important for us now is that in the eucharistic experience of the Church, in the experience of *the eucharist as
sacrifice*, this sacrifice embraces Christ's entire life, his entire
ministry, or, better still, it *is* Christ himself. For Christ is perfect
love and therefore perfect sacrifice. He is sacrifice not only in his
saving ministry but above all in his eternal *Sonship*, his giving of
himself in love and in perfect obedience to the Father. Indeed we
can, without fear of falling into contradiction with the classic
doctrine of the complete beatitude of God, trace sacrifice to the
very life of the Trinity, and even moreso, we can contemplate the
very beatitude of God in the perfection of the all-holy Trinity as
the perfect self-giving of the Father, Son and Holy Spirit to each
other, as perfect love and, hence, perfect sacrifice.

The Son offers this eternal sacrifice to the Father, transforming it through obedience to the Father into giving himself *for the
life of the world*. He offers it through his being made man, taking
on human nature, and becoming for all eternity the Son of man.
He offers it in receiving baptism from John and in it taking on
himself all the sin of the world. He offers it through his preaching
and miracle-working. And he fulfils this offering by manifesting
and granting to his disciples at the last supper the kingdom of
God, the kingdom of perfect self-renunciation, perfect love, perfect sacrifice.

But because this offering is accomplished in "this world," because it encounters from the very beginning the opposition of *sin*
in all its manifestations—from the blood of the children slaugh-
tered by Herod, from the unbelief and the skepticism of the world
to the frenzied hatred of the scribes and pharisees—this whole offering from the very beginning is the *cross*—the passion and its
acceptance, the moral struggling and overcoming—it is *crucifixion*
in the deepest sense of the word. "And he began to be greatly

distressed and troubled"—this was said about the final struggle, the final exhaustion on the night of betrayal at Gethsemane. But this very distress is the distress over the sin that surrounded Christ, and the troubling is over the loss of faith of "his own," to whom he had come, been present for his entire life and his entire ministry. And it is not for nothing that, on the Feast of the Nativity, while preparing for the joyful celebration of the incarnation, the Church performs a certain prefiguration of passion week, contemplating in this very joy the cross, inevitably inscribed in it from time immemorial.

As the entire earthly ministry of Christ is the offering—in "this world," "for the sake of us men and for our salvation"—of the eternal sacrifice of love, so it is all—in "this world"—the cross. Completed as joy, as the gift of the kingdom of God, at the last supper, his ministry is completed as struggle and victory on the cross. It is the same offering, the same sacrifice, the same victory. And, finally, through the cross and as the cross, this offering, this sacrifice and victory is handed over and granted to us who live in "this world." Because in "this world," and above all in our very selves, it is only through the cross that the ascension into the joy and fulness of the kingdom appointed for us is accomplished.

10

ONLY THROUGH THE CROSS... IN REALITY, EVERYTHING THAT I am endeavoring to say in this chapter—and not in it alone, but throughout this entire work—I deliberately say in feeble and insufficient words: about the essence of the Church as ascension to heaven, into the joy of the kingdom of God, and of the eucharist as the sacrament of this ascension. These very words about joy and fulness would be truly *irresponsible* words were they not referred—through the Church herself, in the eucharist itself—to the *cross*, to the singular path of this ascent, to the means of our participation in it.

"... the cross of our Lord Jesus Christ, by which the world has been crucified to me, and I to the world" (Ga 6:14). Need we point out that in these words the apostle Paul expresses the entire essence of the Christian life as a following after Christ? *The world*

is crucified to me: if following after Christ is the reciprocal love to
his love, the reciprocal sacrifice to his sacrifice, then in "this
world" it cannot but be a spiritual feat of genuine renunciation of
the world in its selfishness and pride, in its "desire" as "the lust of
the flesh and the lust of the eyes and the pride of life" (1 Jn 2:16).
I am crucified to the world: but this sacrifice cannot but be my crucifixion, for "this world" is not only outside of me but above all in
my very self, in the old Adam in me. Its mortal struggle with the
new life granted to us by Christ never ceases in our earthly
sojourn.

"In the world you have tribulation" (Jn 16:33). Anyone who
would in the smallest degree follow the path of Christ, love him
and give himself to him, has this tribulation, recognizes this suffering. The cross is suffering. But through love and self-sacrifice
this same tribulation is transformed into joy. It is experienced as
being crucified with Christ, as accepting his cross and hence taking part in his victory. "Be of good cheer, I have overcome the
world" (Jn 16:33). The cross is joy, "and no one will take your joy
from you" (Jn 16:22).

The eucharistic *remembrance* is the remembrance of the kingdom of God, which was manifested and appointed at the last supper. But the remembrance of the cross, the body of Christ broken
for us, the blood of Christ poured out for us, is inseparable from
it. This is why it is *only through the cross* that the gift of the kingdom of God is transformed into its reception, its manifestation at
the eucharist—in our ascent to heaven, in our partaking at the
table of Christ in his kingdom.

11

THE SACRAMENT OF THE ASSEMBLY, THE SACRAMENT OF
offering, the sacrament of anaphora and thanksgiving and, finally, remembrance, are a single sacrament of the kingdom of God,
of a single sacrifice of Christ's love, and therefore they are the
sacrament of the manifestation, the gift to us of our life as sacrifice. For Christ took our life in himself and gave it to God. Man
was created for the sacrificial life, life as love. He lost it—for there
is no other life—in the falling away of his love from God. And

Christ manifested this sacrifice as life and life as sacrifice in the self-giving of his love; he granted it as ascent to and partaking of the kingdom of God.

We have a witness to and expression of this sacrifice, which in Christ becomes *ours*, and of its all-embracing fulness, in the words that conclude the eucharistic *remembrance*: "Thine own of Thine own we offer unto Thee, on behalf of all and for all." Through these concluding words the *end* is transformed into the *beginning*, into an eternal beginning, for it is the eternal renewal of everything, which the Comforter, the Holy Spirit, manifests and fulfils through his coming.

CHAPTER ELEVEN

The Sacrament of the Holy Spirit

> *"And unite all of us to one another*
> *who become partakers of the one Bread*
> *and Cup in the communion of the*
> *Holy Spirit."*
>
> LITURGY OF ST BASIL THE GREAT

I

WE HAVE NOW REACHED THE SUMMIT OF THE EUCHARISTIC celebration. Everything has been said, everything has been remembered before the altar of God, thanksgiving has been offered for everything, and now the prayer, through which the oblation, this sacrifice of praise, is accomplished, turns to the Father in supplication for the sending down of the Holy Spirit "upon us and upon these Gifts here offered":

Again we offer unto Thee this reasonable and bloodless worship, and ask Thee, and pray Thee, and supplicate Thee: Send down Thy Holy Spirit upon us and upon these Gifts here offered, and make this Bread the precious Body of Thy Christ, and that which is in this Cup, the precious Blood of Thy Christ, making the change by Thy Holy Spirit, that they may be for those who partake for the purification of soul, for the remission of sins, for the communion of the Holy Spirit...and not for judgment or condemnation.

But precisely because we have reached this summit we need to gather together everything that has led us to it, that we spoke of in the preceding chapters. For the very text of the liturgy cited above links the *epiklesis*, the invocation of the Holy Spirit, with the changing of the eucharistic gifts into the body and blood of Christ.

This link, however, as we already know, is variously interpreted: in the western scholastic tradition as the prayer that contains the "consecratory formula," and in the Orthodox East as the prayer that completes the entire eucharistic ceremony—offering, thanksgiving, remembrance—as the fulfilment of the entire divine liturgy in the eucharistic changing of the holy gifts.

The western doctrine gradually crept into the East and was partly accepted by it. I say "partly" because, on the one hand, the Orthodox East as a whole undoubtedly rejects the western teaching on the "words of institution" as the *cause* of the change. On the other hand, it "underrejects" it, and the prayer of the epiklesis has come to be interpreted in the Orthodox East as well as a "consecratory formula."

The centuries-old dispute over the epiklesis and its place in the liturgy was essentially transformed into a dispute over two "moments" of the change, separated from each other in the liturgy not even by minutes but by seconds. In all probability, this explains why, in contrast to the passions and emotions attendant to the great dogmatic disputes of the patristic era, the question of the epiklesis, of the transformation of the holy gifts, and of the theology of the sacraments in general did not arouse particular interest in the East. For, inasmuch as the *reality* of the change of the gifts was never questioned in the East or the West and the western approach to the sacraments inculcated itself into the life of the eastern Church only *gradually*, the people of the Church somehow never took notice of it. Outwardly, both the rites and the prayers remained the same—the usual, *their own*. Thus, when the de facto western perception of the sacraments—and in the first place of the eucharist—became dominant in our textbooks and crept into the "catechism," the overwhelming majority of the faithful, including theologians and hierarchy, simply failed to perceive the change that had occurred.

2

I AM CONVINCED, HOWEVER, THAT THE TIME HAS COME TO *recognize* this change and to understand that we are speaking here not of secondary details but of something infinitely essential for the Church and for our Christian life. For the Orthodox, the basis for the interpretation of the eucharist forever remains the words of St Irenaeus of Lyons: "our teaching is in accordance with the eucharist, and the eucharist, in turn, confirms our teaching."[1] Everything pertaining to the eucharist pertains to the Church, and everything pertaining to the Church pertains to the eucharist and is *tested* by this interdependence.

Meanwhile, precisely this original interdependence proved to be somewhat *ruptured* by the diffusion of the new understanding of the sacraments that came into the Church after the break with the patristic tradition. In this doctrine the eucharist, which had been perceived in the ancient Church as the sacrament of unity, the sacrament of the ascension of the Church and her fulfilment at the table of the Lord in his kingdom, came to be perceived and defined as one of the means for the sanctification of the faithful. This is seen most clearly of all in the transmutation of *partaking of communion* from an act of the Church, of the assembly—from the fulfilment of our membership in the Church, the body of Christ—into a personal act of piety, and for the laity an exceptional act at that, regulated not by the Church but by the personal piety and "option" of the communicant himself.

We continue to pray in the liturgy: "And unite all of us to one another who become partakers of the one Bread and Cup in the communion of the Holy Spirit." But what constitutes this unity in our liturgies without communicants? At both the beginning and the end of the liturgy we pray: "Preserve the fulness of Thy Church"—but what fulness are we talking about? And in this approach, what can be the meaning of the words that the apostle Peter directs to us: "you are a chosen race, a royal priesthood, a holy nation, God's own people, that you may declare the wonderful deeds of him who called you out of darkness into his marvelous light" (1 Pt 2:9)?

[1] *Against Heresies* 4:18:5.

I will not repeat here everything said above about the other consequences for the Church of this metamorphosis in the perception of the eucharist. I think that enough has been said to understand that we are dealing here with great damage to and, hence, distortion of the liturgical tradition of the Church, her *lex orandi*. Consequently, it requires us more than ever to return to this tradition, to restore its genuine perspective and essence.

3

THIS LEADS US YET AGAIN TO THE MULTIFACETED NATURE OF the divine liturgy, for, as we have repeatedly affirmed, it is precisely in it, by and through its having *many parts*, that the eucharist is accomplished.

The liturgy, as a sacrament, begins with the preparation of the holy gifts and the *assembly as the Church*. After the gathering follows the *entrance* and the proclamation of the word of God, and after that the *offering*, the placing of the eucharistic gifts on the altar. After the *kiss of peace* and the confession of faith we begin the *anaphora*: the lifting up of the gifts in the prayer of thanksgiving and remembrance. The anaphora concludes with the *epiklesis*, i.e., the prayer that God will manifest the Holy Spirit, will show the bread and wine of our offering to be the body and blood of Christ and make us worthy to partake of it.

But western scholasticism denies this multifaceted nature of the liturgy, the interdependence of all its elements, of all its rites. It does not enter into the theological interpretation of the eucharist. It is *not needed*, for, in the words of Dom Vonier, which we quoted earlier, the sacraments comprise a sui generis reality, fulfilled only by their institution by Christ and dependent on nothing else in the Church.[2] What is the meaning of this dispute, this divergence? In order to answer this question we must bear in mind that right up to its "western captivity" the Orthodox East never isolated the sacraments as a separate "object" of study and definition, confining them to their own distinct theological treatise. We find such an isolation neither in the early "baptismal" nor in the "mystagogical" works (of pseudo-Dionysius, Maximus

[2]See chapter 2, notes 1 and 4.

the Confessor, etc.) that took their place. The word *sacrament* was never restricted by its identification with our current seven sacraments. This word embraced the entire mystery of the salvation of the world and mankind by Christ and in essence the entire content of the Christian faith. The fathers of the Church perceived the eucharist both as the revelation and the fulfilment of this universal mystery—"hidden from the angels," but to us, the new people of God, manifested in all its abundant fulness. I am not dwelling on the explanations of the great "mystagogues," because they flourished when the order and structure of the liturgical services had already reached their fundamentally finished form. Their influence, or rather the influence of their epigones (Germanus of Constantinople, Symeon the New Theologian)—an influence not always happy or "healthy"—began to run wild into complex allegories, accessory symbolics, etc. Therefore the witness we find in the very piety of the Church, in the perception and experience of the eucharist among the people of the Church, is more important for us. And, according to this witness, each member of the Church knew that from the very beginning, from the deacon's exclamation "καιρός!" ("It is time to begin the service to the Lord") to the concluding "Let us depart in peace," he was taking part in a single *common task*, in one sacred reality, wholly identified with what the Church is revealing, manifesting and granting in the given moment, in her ascent to the heavenly table of the kingdom.

The ceremony itself, I repeat, testifies to this. Thus, while completing the preparation of the gifts, the proskomidē, the priest censes the gifts that have been prepared and bows before them. At the entrance the celebrant *affirms* that God has vouchsafed to us, his humble and unworthy servants, "even in this hour to stand before the glory of Thy holy altar," and then he blesses the *high place*: "Blessed art Thou on the throne of the glory of Thy Kingdom." Finally, during the kiss of peace, before he completes the words "Christ is in our midst... He is and shall be," the priest again bows before the gifts lying on the altar. All this is *really* experienced by all who take part in the liturgy—and precisely as something *real*.

A theological purist might ask: why do people kneel during the Great Entrance? After all, the gifts are still only bread and wine, they have not yet "become" the body and blood of Christ. But the simple worshiper would not be concerned with this question, for he knows, if not by reason then with his whole heart, that at the Great Entrance the offering itself, and not its allegorical representation, is accomplished, and that it is accomplished by Christ, for he is "the Offerer and the Offered, the Receiver and the Received." One can say that the liturgy is entirely in Christ; throughout the liturgy Christ is with us and we are in Christ.

4

BUT ONE MAY ASK: DOES WHAT WAS SAID ABOUT THE MULTI-faceted nature of the liturgy not mean that the change of the gifts into the body and blood of Christ happens *gradually*, step by step, so that it is ultimately unclear precisely when it is accomplished? This question itself, consciously or unconsciously, determines the doctrine of *consecration*, i.e., of a consecratory formula, of how and when the bread and wine become the body and blood of Christ. But this question could arise only in an era of the expiration in scholastic theology of its eschatological dimension and the essence of the Christian faith. And this places us before the *question of time.*

The liturgy is served on earth, and this means in the time and space of "this world." But if it is served on earth, *it is accomplished in heaven, in the new time of the new creation*, in the time of the Holy Spirit. The question of time has immense significance for the Church. For, in constrast to the *spiritualism* widespread throughout the world, which is founded on the rejection of time, on the striving to *leave* it, on its identification with evil, for Christians time, like everything in creation, is of God and belongs to God. From the first words of the book of Genesis, "In the beginning God created the heavens and the earth," to the words of the apostle Paul, "when the fulness of time had come," and, finally, the affirmation of St John the Theologian, "the hour is coming, and now is" (Jn 5:25), it is not *outside* of time, but in it and in relation to it that the divine certification "and God saw that it was *good*" resounded and eternally resounds.

The "spiritualists" are opposed in our "religious world" by the "activists," whose spiritual horizon is limited to time, history, the solution of social problems. If the "spiritualists" reject time, then the "activists" seemingly fail to sense its ontological fallenness. They do not sense that it not only reflects the fall of the world but is itself the "reality" of this fall, the triumph of "death and time," which reign on earth. "The image of this world is passing away," and the "old time" is precisely an image of the passing of everything earthly down the road to an inevitable death. Meanwhile, it is precisely into this fallen time—and here both spiritualists and activists become bankrupt—into this fallen world that Christ condescended in his becoming man. In it he proclaimed that the kingdom of God which is to come, salvation from sin and death, "the beginning of another life, new and eternal," had drawn near. And he not only proclaimed it, but through his voluntary suffering, crucifixion and resurrection he realized this victory in himself and granted it to us.

On the day of Pentecost the Holy Spirit—and with him and in him the *new time*—descended onto the Church. The old time did not disappear, and outside in the world nothing changed. But to the Church of Christ, which lives in the Spirit and by the Spirit, the commandment and the power to convert it into the *new time* was given. "Behold, I make all things new" (Rv 21:5). This is not the *replacement* of the old with the new, not an exit into some "other" world. It is the same world, created through the love of God, which in the Holy Spirit we see and receive as God created it: heaven and earth, full of the glory of God.

To abide in the new time means to abide in the Holy Spirit. "I was in the Spirit on the Lord's day" (Rv 1:10). These words of John the Theologian apply, of course, to all believers who live even to a small degree for the acquisition of the Holy Spirit, of which St Serafim of Sarov spoke as the essence and goal of life. But in the first place they apply to the source of this acquisition—to the liturgical life of the Church, and in it to the divine liturgy. For the essence of the liturgy consists in raising us up in the Holy Spirit and in him transfiguring the old time into the new time.

It is wrong to interpret Christian worship and particularly its summit, the sacrament of the eucharist, in categories of the *cult*. For the cult is constructed not on the distinction of *old* and *new*, but "sacred" and "profane." The cult "sacralizes" and is itself the fruit of sacralization. It distinguishes "sacred days" and "periods" in time, "sacred places" in space, "sacred pieces" in matter, but it does all this in the "old" time, for the cult is *static*, not *dynamic*, and does not know the other, new time.

A striking example of this is the first Christians' opposition to the *temple*. From time immemorial the temple was the "focus" of sacralization. And thus one of the chief accusations against Christians in the era of persecution was the accusation of *atheism*, of the absence of a *sacred center*. In the Acts of the Apostles the first martyr, St Stephen, answers this accusation. To the infuriated crowd that was stoning him he declared, "the Most High does not dwell in houses made with hands; as the prophet says, 'Heaven is my throne, and earth my footstool. What house will you build for me, says the Lord, or what is the place of my rest? Did not my hand make all these things?'" At the moment of his death Stephen cried out, "Behold, I see the heavens opened, and the Son of man standing at the right hand of God" (Ac 7:48-50, 56). St John Chrysostom, in turn, in his second homily on *The Cross and the Thief*, says: "when Christ came and suffered outside the city, he cleansed the entire earth, he made every place suitable for prayer... Would you want to know how the entire earth, finally, *was made a temple* and how every place became suitable for prayer?"[3]

Not a temple made by hands, but the opening of the heavens, the world transfigured into a temple, all life into the liturgy—such is the foundation of the Christian *lex orandi*. And if to this day we call a temple a *church*, i.e., an assembly or gathering, it is because it arose not from a thirst for "sacralization" but from the eucharistic experience of the Church, the experience of *heaven on earth*.

5

IF IN THE LIGHT OF ALL THAT HAS BEEN SAID WE TRY TO understand the meaning and "liturgical necessity" of the multifaceted nature of the liturgy, we must bear in mind that it is rooted in the eucharist as the sacrament of *remembrance*: "do this in remembrance of me." Tradition rightly sees the establishment of the eucharist at the last supper in these words. But the error, the

---

[3]*Second Homily on the Cross and the Thief*, PG 49:409.

harmfulness of scholastic interpretations is that they relate the word *this* exclusively and only to the changing of the eucharistic gifts into the body and blood of Christ, and by the same token isolate this establishment from the liturgy as a whole. Meanwhile, the essence of the liturgy and its multifaceted nature consists in the fact that it is all, from beginning to end, a *remembrance*, manifestation, "epiphany," the salvation of the world accomplished by Christ.

In the eucharist, the *commemoration* is the gathering together of the entire experience of salvation, the entire fulness of that *reality* that is given us in the Church and that constitutes our life. It is the reality of the world as God's creation, the reality of the world as saved by Christ, the reality of the new heaven and the new earth, to which we ascend in the sacrament of the ascension to the kingdom of God. To commemorate means to *remember* and to live in what is *commemorated*, to receive and to preserve it. But how can one remember if it is "not done"? How can one live by what is unseen, how can one perceive it, preserve it and, above all, preserve this experience in its fulness? Christianity is always *confession, acceptance, experience*. But in the fallen and shattered time of "this world" this integral remembrance is impossible other than in the succession of the parts that comprise it. For this old time is horizontal, not vertical. And thus each liturgy is a *gathering*, a restoration and an "identification" of the fulness of our remembrance. I have just said that while the liturgy is served on earth, it is accomplished in heaven. But most important is the fact that what is accomplished in heaven is already accomplished, already *is*, already *has been accomplished*, already *given*. Christ has become man, died on the cross, descended into hades, arisen from the dead, ascended into heaven, sent down the Holy Spirit. In the liturgy, which we have been commanded to celebrate "until he comes," we do not *repeat* and we do not *represent*—we *ascend* into the mystery of salvation and new life, which has been accomplished once, but is granted to us "always, now and forever and unto ages of ages." And in this heavenly, eternal and otherworldly eucharist Christ does not come down to us, rather we ascend to him.

The liturgy can be likened to a man going through a building—which, though familiar and beautiful, is hid in darkness—

with a flashlight, part by part, and in these parts identifying the entire building in its wholeness, unity and beauty. So it is with our liturgy, which, while being accomplished on earth is accomplished in heaven. In it the mystery of the salvation of the world by Christ is revealed and granted to us, in it the Church fulfils herself, in it the "beginning of another life, new and eternal" triumphs.

6

AND SO, THE LITURGY IS ACCOMPLISHED IN THE *NEW TIME* through the Holy Spirit. It is entirely, from beginning to end, an *epiklesis*, an invocation of the Holy Spirit, who transfigures everything done in it, each solemn rite, into that which it manifests and reveals to us. In other words, in its outward appearance, in the time of "this world," the liturgy is a *symbol* and is expressed in *symbols*—but "symbol" in the meaning of which we spoke in the beginning of this book, where we termed a symbol a reality that cannot be expressed or manifested in the categories of "this world," i.e., to the senses, empirically, visibly. It is the reality that elsewhere we termed the *sacramentality* inherent in everything created by God, but which man has ceased to sense and recognize in "this" fallen world.

Thus it is impossible to explain and define the symbol. It is realized or "actualized" in its *own* reality through its transformation into that to which it points and witnesses, of which it is a *symbol*. But this conversion remains invisible, for it is accomplished by the Holy Spirit, in the new time, and is certified only by *faith*. So also the conversion of the bread and wine into the holy body and blood of Christ is accomplished invisibly. Nothing perceptible *happens*—the bread remains bread, and the wine remains wine. For if it occurred "palpably," then Christianity would be a magical cult and not a religion of faith, hope and love.

Thus, any attempt to *explain* the conversion, to locate it in formulas and causes, is not only unnecessary but truly harmful. "I believe that this is truly Thine own most pure Body, and that this is truly Thine own precious Blood..." It is as if the original faith and experience of the Church, expressed in the words of this prayer, are insufficient. I believe, but do not know, for in "this world" no knowledge, other than that disclosed in faith, and no "science" can explain what is accomplished in the new time, in the coming of the Holy Spirit, in the conversion of life into the new life of the kingdom of God, which is "in our midst."

In like manner, when I say that the entire liturgy is a *transformation*, I have in mind something very simple: that in the liturgy each of its parts, each solemn ceremony, each rite is transformed by the Holy Spirit into *that which it is*, a "real symbol" of what it manifests. So, for example, the repeated veneration of the *altar*—the censing, the kissing, the prostrations, etc.—are a confession of our presence around the throne of God's glory, in the heavenly sanctuary. Thus, in the liturgy the "assembly as the Church" is transformed into the fulness of the Church of Christ, while the entrance with the gifts is transformed into the Church's offering of the saving sacrifice, "on behalf of all and for all."

And so, everything in the liturgy is *real*, but it is a reality not of "this world" and not in its fallen and splintered time, but in the assembled new time. When attempts at a "rational" explanation of the eucharist arose in the West in the beginning of the eleventh century, Berengar of Tours proposed a distinction of what is "mystical," i.e., symbolic, on the one hand, and what is "real," on the other. In his teaching the sacrament is *mystice non realiter*. The council that condemned this doctrine (Lateran 1059) answered that it is *realiter non mystice*, i.e., real and therefore not mystical, not symbolic. This is the dead end into which scholasticism inevitably falls. Its essence lies in the gradual departure from the original understanding and perception of *time*, and together with that the gradual "expiration" of the eschatological essence of the Church and the sacraments. Beginning with the thirteenth century, writes Louis Bouyer, the eucharist in the West came to be "buried under untraditional formularies and interpretations."[4] As far as the Orthodox are concerned, although they never accepted all of the western explanations and formulas, for want of their own doctrine on the sacraments they made the western problematics, the western questions, "their own," which in turn affected their own interpretations and definitions of the eucharist.

[4]*The Eucharist* (South Bend, Ind.: Notre Dame, 1968) 381.

7

NOW WE CAN ASK, WHAT IS THE SPECIFIC FUNCTION OF THE epiklesis, the prayer for the sending down of the Holy Spirit, which we find to be the concluding part of the anamnesis in the Orthodox liturgy?

Above all it is what the very text of the epiklesis, which begins in both the liturgies of St John Chrysostom and St Basil the Great with the words "remembering therefore," testifies to: the organic connection of this prayer with the remembrance.

I cited Chrysostom's text in the very beginning of this chapter, and therefore I will limit myself here to citing the parallel prayer, the epiklesis in the liturgy of St Basil the Great:

> Therefore, we also, O Master, remembering His [i.e., Christ's] saving Passion and life-creating Cross, His three-day Burial and Resurrection from the dead, His Ascension into heaven and Sitting at Thy right hand of the God and Father, and His Glorious and awesome Second Coming, Thine own of Thine own we offer to Thee, in behalf of all, and for all. . . . we now dare to approach Thy holy altar and, offering to Thee the antitypes [ἀντίτυπα] of the holy Body and Blood of Thy Christ, we pray Thee and call upon Thee, O Holy of Holies, that by the favor of Thy goodness Thy Holy Spirit may come upon us and upon the gifts now offered. . .

As we see, the prayer of the epiklesis constitutes the conclusion of the *remembrance*. In the categories of the *new time* in which the eucharist is accomplished, it unites "all those things which have come to pass for us," the entire mystery of salvation accomplished by Christ, the mystery of Christ's love, which embraces the whole world and has been granted to us. The remembrance is the confession of the *knowledge* of this mystery, its reality, and likewise faith in it as the salvation of the world and man. Like the entire eucharist, the remembrance is not a *repetition*. It is the manifestation, gift and experience, in "this world" and therefore again and again, of the eucharist offered by Christ once and for all, and of our ascension to it.

The eucharist is accomplished from beginning to end over the bread and wine. Bread and wine are the *food* that God created from the beginning as *life*: "you shall have them for food" (Gn 1:29). But the meaning, essence and joy of life is not in food, but in God, in communion with him. Man, and in him "this world," fell away from this food, "in paradise the food of immortality" (Liturgy of St Basil the Great). Food came to reign in him, but this reign is not unto life, but unto death, disintegration and separation. And that is why Christ, when he had come into the world, called himself "the bread of God... which comes down from heaven, and gives life to the world" (Jn 6:33). "I am the bread of life; he who comes to me shall not hunger, and he who believes in me shall never thirst" (Jn 6:35).

Christ is the "bread of heaven," for this definition contains the entire content, the entire reality of our faith in him as Savior and Lord. He is life, and therefore food. He offered this life in sacrifice "on behalf of all and for all," in order that we might become communicants of his own life, the new life of the new creation, and that we might manifest him as his body.

To all this the Church answers *amen*, she receives all this through faith, she fulfils all this in the eucharist through the Holy Spirit. All the *rites* of the liturgy are a manifestation, one after the other, of the *realities* of which the saving work of Christ is comprised. But, I shall repeat once more, the *progression* here is not in the accomplishment but in the manifestation. For what is manifested is not something *new*, that did not exist before the manifestation. No—in Christ all is already *accomplished*, all is *real*, all is granted. In him we have obtained access to the Father and communion in the Holy Spirit and anticipation of the new life in his kingdom.

And here the epiklesis, which we find at the end of the eucharistic prayer, is also this manifestation and this gift, and likewise the *Church's acceptance of them*. "Send down Thy Holy Spirit upon us and upon these Gifts here offered." For the invocation of the Holy Spirit is not a separate act whose one and only object is the bread and wine. Immediately after the invocation of the Holy Spirit the celebrant prays: "And unite all of us to one another who become partakers of the one Bread and Cup in the communion of the Holy Spirit" (St Basil the Great). "That they may be to those who partake for the purification of soul, for the remission of sins, for the communion of Thy Holy Spirit, for the fulfillment of the Kingdom of Heaven..." Furthermore, again without interruption, the prayer goes on to the *intercession*, of which we shall speak later. The purpose of the eucharist lies not in the change of the bread and wine, but in our partaking of Christ, who has become our food, our life, the manifestation of the Church as the body of Christ.

This is why the holy gifts themselves never became in the Orthodox East an object of special reverence, contemplation and adoration, and likewise an object of special theological "problematics": how, when, in what manner their change is accomplished. The eucharist—and this means the changing of the holy gifts—is a mystery that cannot be revealed and explained in the categories of "this world"—time, essence, causality, etc. It is revealed only to faith: "I believe also that this is truly Thine own most pure Body, and that this is truly Thine own precious Blood." Nothing is explained, nothing is defined, nothing has changed in "this world." But then whence comes this light, this joy that overflows the heart, this feeling of fulness and of touching the "other world"?

We find the answer to these questions in the epiklesis. But the answer is not "rational," built upon the laws of our "one-storied" logic; it is disclosed to us by the Holy Spirit. In almost every ordo of the eucharist that has reached us, the Church prays in the text of the epiklesis that the eucharist will be for those who partake *"for the communion of the Holy Spirit"*: "And unite all of us to one another who become partakers of the one Bread and Cup in the communion of the Holy Spirit" (εἰς κοινωνίαν τοῦ ἁγίου Σου Πνεύματος), and, further, "for the fulfillment of the Kingdom of Heaven" (εἰς βασιλείαν οὐρανῶν πλήρωμα). These two definitions of the purpose of the eucharist are in essence synonyms, for both manifest the eschatological essence of the sacrament, its orientation to the kingdom of God, which is to come but in the Church is already manifested and granted.

Thus the epiklesis concludes the *anaphora*, the part of the liturgy that encompasses the "assembly as the Church," the entrance, the proclamation of the good news of the word of God, the offering, the oblation, the thanksgiving and the remembrance.

But with the epiklesis begins the consummation of the liturgy, whose essence lies in *communion*, in the distribution to the faithful of the holy gifts, the body and blood of Christ.

CHAPTER TWELVE

The Sacrament of Communion

> *"The mystery of Thy dispensation, O Christ our God, has been accomplished and perfected as far as it was in our power; for we have had the memorial of Thy death; we have seen the type of Thy Resurrection; we have been filled with Thine unending life; we have enjoyed Thine inexhaustible food; which in the world to come be well-pleased to vouchsafe to us all, through the grace of Thine eternal Father, and Thine holy and good and life-creating Spirit..."*
>
> LITURGY OF ST BASIL THE GREAT

I

THE LITURGY UNDERWENT MANY CHANGES OVER THE centuries of its prolonged development, but no change was more profound and more significant than that registered in the last part of the eucharistic ceremony—the order of partaking of the holy gifts of the body and blood of Christ. Inasmuch as this part truly concludes and fulfils the most holy sacrament of the eucharist, and thus the entire liturgy, we must dwell on it, or rather on the changes that distorted it, in the beginning of this last chapter.

From the very beginning the Church perceived the partaking of all the faithful at the liturgy as the obvious goal of the eucharist and as the realization of the words of the Savior: "that you may eat and drink at my table in my kingdom" (Lk 22:30). Therefore the table was the "form" of the eucharist and common partaking its fulfilment. All this is self-evident and requires no demonstration in the Orthodox perspective.

What does demand explanation is the fact of the gradual falling away over history of great numbers of members of the Church from this perception of the eucharist, its reduction to an *individualistic* perception. The contemporary faithful, churchly person sees no necessity of approaching communion at every liturgy. He has learned from the catechism that "with a maternal voice, the Church commands us to confess before a spiritual father, and to partake of the body and blood of Christ, with most ardent reverence, four times a year, or once a month, but without fail once a year."[1] One who desires to receive communion is obliged to go to the sacrament of confession. And, finally, we need to emphasize, if anyone among the laity wishes to partake "beyond the usual norm," then this desire, for want of and in the full absence of references to the assembly, to the ecclesial perception of the sacrament, is usually characterized as a quest for "more frequent communion" and not as a church member's fulfilment of his Christian vocation, the fulfilment of his membership in the body of Christ. All of this became so firmly entrenched in church life that the *Catechism* contains special questions on "how can those who only hear the divine liturgy, but do not approach for holy communion, participate in it?" The answer is: "they can and must take part through prayer, through faith and through unceasing remembrance of our Lord Jesus Christ, who precisely commanded us to do this in remembrance of him." Let us note that Christ commanded us *precisely* to taste the gifts: "take, eat...drink of it all of you...." And let us also note that both these questions and answers concerning noncommunicants relate in fact to the huge majority of the Church, and not to certain exceptional cases. Alas, in this doctrine the exceptions are the communicants.

What has happened? How was this metamorphosis in the per-

---

[1]Filaret (Drozdov), Metropolitan of Moscow, *Longer Catechism* (Paris, 1926; rep. Jordanville, N.Y., 1961), "Confession," part 1, question 90.

ception—not only on the part of the people of the Church but also on the part of the episcopate, the clergy and, finally, the theologians—of the very essence of the eucharist, its reduction to "one of the sacraments," one "means of sanctification," accomplished, and why has it been maintained for centuries? Strange as it may seem, we find almost no attempt to answer these questions in our official academic theology. Meanwhile, as I noted above, we are dealing here not simply with the evolution of church discipline, a decline in piety, western influences, etc., but with a spiritual turning point in the self-consciousness and self-perception of the Church as a whole. We are dealing, in other words, with an *ecclesiological crisis*, on which we shall focus our attention.

2

THE MOST PREVALENT, CUSTOMARY EXPLANATION FOR THE gradual disappearance of *communion* as participation in the fulfilment of the Church consists of references to the *unworthiness* of the overwhelming majority of the laity to approach the cup frequently and therefore their need, as it were, to bear supplementary requirements and guarantees. The laity live in the world, in continual contact with its impurity, untruth, sinfulness, lies, and thus they need special cleansing, special preparation—a special effort of repentance.

I will call this explanation pious, for in fact, in its best expressions and explanations it stems from a consciousness of sinfulness, from "respect" for the holy, from fear of one's own unworthiness. In one form or another, fear is inherent to all religions. In medieval Christianity it permeated all of life: "We have sinned, we have transgressed and done wrongly before Thee..." (Canon of St Andrew of Crete, ode 7, heirmos). Asceticism, often in its extreme form, constituted the moral ideal of Christian society, and while not always observed, it proved to have an enormous influence. And the decline of the secular or "white" clergy—as witnessed, for example, in the canons of the Council *in Trullo* (691)— led to the leadership of church life passing over to monasticism. It is impossible for us to dwell here on the causes and forms of this many-sided process. What is important is that it gradually led to the *clericalization* of the Church, to a great distancing of clergy and laity from each other. The whole "atmosphere" of the Church changed. At the end of the fourth century St John Chrysostom wrote: "but there are cases where the priest does not differ from those under him, for instance, *when he must partake of the Holy Mysteries.* We are all equally honored with them, not as in the Old Testament, when one food was for the priests and another for the people and when it was not permitted to the people to partake of that which was for the priests. Now it is not so, for the same body and the same cup is offered to all...and all of us equally embrace each other..."[2]

But in the end "sacralization" and "clericalization" triumphed. This is also seen in the development of the temple and its structure, which more and more emphasized the separation of the laity from the clergy. Again Chrysostom wrote: "when Christ came and suffered outside the city, he cleansed the entire earth, he made every place suitable for prayer...Would you want to know how the entire earth, finally, was made a temple and how every place became suitable for prayer?"[3] But the interpretation of both the temple and the liturgy in this "key" disappeared early enough from the Church. Entry to the altar, approach to the sanctuary came to be forbidden to the laity, and their presence at the eucharist became *passive.* It is accomplished on behalf of them, for them, but they do not take part in its accomplishment. If earlier the line separating the Church from "this world" embraced the laity, it now excluded them, a perfect witness to this being their very definition as *miriane* or "worldly ones" (κοσμικοί), instead of the former *laikós*, members of the people of God (λαός), "God's own people" (1 Pt 2:9).

3

IN OUR DAY PREPARATION FOR COMMUNION—AND THIS IS CLEAR in the light of what was said above about the perception of communion as a private, personal act—has likewise become a *private* preparation. Our prayerbooks contain prayers before communion,

[2]*Homily on II Corinthians* 18, PG 61:527.
[3]*Second Homily on the Cross and the Thief,* PG 49:409.

but, with the exception of two or three read before the communion itself, they are not a part of the actual text and rite of the liturgy. The prayerbooks also include prayers of thanksgiving after communion, also private and not included in the liturgy itself. This is understandable inasmuch as far from everyone present at the liturgy comes to the chalice and, consequently, for them these prayers would be "nominal." The composition, practice and time of the reading of these prayers vary from book to book, as do their instructions on fasting. Taken by themselves, the majority of these prayers are beautiful, inspiring and very beneficial. Hence we are speaking not about them, but about their place in the liturgy, in the sacrament.

The point is that nowhere in the liturgy, from the beginning of the anaphora, the liturgy of the faithful, to its very end, do we find a single reference to the roles of two "categories" of worshipers: the communicants of the holy mysteries and the noncommunicants. On the contrary, even the most vaguely attentive reading of the preanaphora, anaphora, and postanaphora prayers cannot but convince us that after the dismissal of the catechumens (and, in the early Church, the "penitents"), "the doors being shut," we all celebrate the eucharist, which is simultaneously the offering of the bloodless sacrifice and the preparation of the faithful for partaking of the holy body and blood of the Lord:

> Again and oftentimes we fall down before Thee, O God who lovest mankind, that looking down upon our petition Thou wouldst cleanse our souls and bodies from all defilement of flesh and spirit; and grant us to stand blameless and without condemnation before Thy holy altar. Grant also to those who pray with us, O God, growth in life and faith and spiritual understanding. Grant them to worship Thee blamelessly with fear and love, and to partake without condemnation of Thy Holy Mysteries, and to be accounted worthy of Thy heavenly Kingdom.
>
> [Second Prayer of the Faithful,
> Liturgy of St John Chrysostom]

> Unto Thee we commend our whole life and our hope, O Master who lovest mankind. We ask Thee, and pray

Thee, and supplicate Thee: Make us worthy to partake of
the heavenly and awesome mysteries of this sacred and
spiritual table with a pure conscience: for remission of
sins, for forgiveness of transgressions, for the communion
of the Holy Spirit, for the inheritance of the Kingdom of
Heaven, for boldness towards Thee, but not for judgment
or condemnation.

> [Prayer before "Our Father,"
> Liturgy of St John Chrysostom]

O Lord, our God, who hast created us and brought us into
this life; who hast shown us the ways to salvation, and
bestowed on us the revelation of heavenly mysteries: Thou
art the One who hast appointed us to this service in the
power of Thy Holy Spirit. Therefore, O Lord, enable us to
be ministers of Thy new Testament and servants of Thy
holy Mysteries. Through the greatness of Thy mercy, accept us as we draw near to Thy holy altar, so that we may
be worthy to offer to Thee this reasonable and bloodless
sacrifice for our sins and for the errors of Thy people. Having received it upon Thy holy, heavenly and ideal altar as
a sweet spiritual fragrance, send down upon us in return
the grace of Thy Holy Spirit.

> [Prayer of the Offering, on the Placing of the Divine Gifts
> on the Holy Altar, Liturgy of St Basil the Great]

And finally,

And unite all of us to one another who become partakers
of the one Bread and Cup in the communion of the Holy
Spirit.

> [Anaphora, Liturgy of St Basil the Great]

It is hardly possible to reveal more clearly the organic link of
the anaphora—the offering of the gifts, the bloodless sacrifice of
praise—with preparation and communion. In the holy gifts we
recognize the holy body and blood of Christ, the sacrifice offered
by Christ "on behalf of all and for all"; in communion we receive
it with faith, hope and love in unity with Christ, with his life,

with his kingdom. And, however frightening this is to say, in their separation the genuine meaning of the eucharistic sacrament is damaged. It begins to be perceived no longer as the fulfilment of the Church, the manifestation of the kingdom of God and the new life, but as the tasting of "sacred matter," which converts the sacrament, in the words of Khomiakov, into a certain "anatomical miracle." It is precisely here that all the dead ends of the explanation of the eucharist come to light. "What both sides [i.e., Protestant and Catholic] only do," Khomiakov continues, "is either deny or affirm the miraculous change of known earthly elements, without understanding at all that the essential element of each sacrament *is the Church*, and that properly it is for her alone that the sacraments are accomplished, without any relation to the laws of earthly nature. He who has disdained the duty of love also loses the memory of its power, loses together with it the memory of what reality is in the world of faith."[4]

4

LET US RECALL, ABOVE ALL, THE ORDER OR SEQUENCE OF THE *preparation*, as it has come down to us in the Byzantine liturgical tradition. I do not mean the proskomidē, of which we already spoke. We shall restrict ourselves to the liturgy of the faithful.

Immediately after the epiklesis the celebrant begins the reading of the *prayer of intercession*. It would be more precise to define this prayer as the prayer of *the gathering of the Church, the body of Christ*, her manifestation in all fulness:

> And unite all of us to one another who become partakers of the one Bread and Cup in the communion of the Holy Spirit. Grant that none of us may partake of the holy Body and Blood of Thy Christ for judgment or condemnation.

> Instead, may we find mercy and grace with all the saints who through the ages have been well-pleasing to Thee:

[4]*O Tserkvi* (On the Church), in *Complete Works* II (Moscow, 1900) 129, or in the edition of L. Karsavin (Berlin, 1926) 75.

ancestors, fathers, patriarchs, prophets, apostles, preach-
ers, evangelists, martyrs, confessors, teachers, and every
righteous spirit made perfect in faith.

Especially with our most holy, most pure, most blessed
and glorious Lady Theotokos and ever-virgin Mary. With
the holy Prophet, Forerunner, and Baptist John; the holy,
glorious, and all-laudable apostles; and with all Thy
saints. By their prayers, visit us, O God. Remember all
those who have fallen asleep before us in hope of resurrection to eternal life, grant them rest in forgiveness of soul,
O our God, where the light of Thy countenence shines on
them.

Again we entreat Thee: Remember, O Lord, Thy Holy,
Catholic, and Apostolic Church, which is from end to end
of the universe; give peace to Her whom Thou hast obtained with the precious Blood of Thy Christ; also preserve this holy house until the end of the world.

Remember, O Lord, those who offered Thee these gifts,
and those for whom and through whom they offered
them. Remember, O Lord, those who bring offerings and
do good in Thy holy churches, and those who remember
the poor; reward them with Thy rich and heavenly gifts;
for their earthly, temporal, and corruptible gifts, do
Thou grant them Thy heavenly ones, eternal and in-
corruptible.

Remember, O Lord, those who are in the deserts, mountains, caverns and pits of the earth.

Remember, O Lord, those who live in chastity and godli-
ness, in austerity and holiness of life.

[Prayer for the civil authorities]

Remember, O Lord, the people here present and also
those who are absent for honorable reasons. Have mercy

on them and on us according to the multitude of Thy mercies. Fill their treasuries with every good thing; preserve their marriages in peace and harmony; raise the infants; guide the young; support the aged; encourage the faint-hearted; lead back those who are in error and join them to Thy Holy, Catholic, and Apostolic Church; free those who are held captive by unclean spirits; sail with those who sail, travel with those who travel; defend the widows; protect the orphans; free the captives; heal the sick. Remember, O Lord, those who are in courts, in mines, in exile, in harsh labor, and those in any kind of affliction, necessity, or distress.

Remember, O Lord our God, all those who entreat Thy great loving-kindness; those who love us and those who hate us; those who have asked us to pray for them, unworthy though we be; and remember all Thy people O Lord, our God. Pour out Thy rich mercy upon all of them, granting them all the petitions which are for their salvation.

And remember, Thyself, O God, all those whom we have not remembered, through ignorance, forgetfulness or the multitude of names; since Thou knowest the name and age of each, even from his mother's womb. For Thou, O Lord, art the Helper of the helpless, the Hope of the hopeless, the Savior of the bestormed, the Haven of the voyager, the Physician of the sick. Be all things to all men, O Thou who knowest each man and his request, his home and his need.

Deliver this city, O Lord, and every city and country, from famine, plague, earthquake, flood, fire, sword, invasion by enemies, and civil war.

[For the episcopate:]
Among the first, remember, O Lord, [names]. Grant them for Thy holy churches in peace, safety, honor,

health and length of days, to rightly define the word of Thy truth.

Remember, O Lord, my unworthiness also, by the multitude of Thy compassions; forgive my every transgression, both voluntary and involuntary. Because of my sins, do not withhold the grace of Thy Holy Spirit from these Gifts here set forth.

Remember, O Lord, the priesthood, the diaconate in Christ, and every order of the clergy. Let none of us who stand about Thy holy altar be put to confusion. Visit us with Thy loving-kindness, O Lord; manifest Thyself to us through Thy rich compassions. Grant us seasonable and healthful weather; send gentle showers upon the earth so that it may bear fruit; bless the crown of the year with Thy goodness.

Prevent schisms among the churches; pacify the ragings of the pagans; quickly destroy the uprisings of heresies by the power of Thy Holy Spirit.

Receive us all into Thy Kingdom, showing us to be sons of the light and sons of the day. Grant us Thy peace and Thy love, O Lord our God, for Thou hast given all things to us.

And grant that with one mouth and one heart we may praise Thine all-honorable and majestic name: of the Father, and of the Son, and of the Holy Spirit, now and ever and unto ages of ages.

Amen. And the mercies of our great God and Savior Jesus Christ shall be with you all.

And with your spirit.

[Liturgy of St Basil the Great]

5

I HAVE QUOTED THE TEXT OF THIS PRAYER IN FULL BECAUSE IT most clearly and best of all reveals the meaning of the "preparation for communion," with which it begins in the structure of the eucharistic rite. As I have already said above, this prayer gathers and unites the entire cosmic, ecclesiological and eschatological content of the eucharist, and thus also manifests and grants to us the very essence of communion, the essence of the body of Christ and the new life in Christ. Yet it is not accidental, not from a love of repetition, that we are not immediately summoned to approach the chalice, that we delay it by this wonderful prayer, which seemingly slows down the rhythm of the eucharist. The reason for this delay is not that we once again confess our sins and prepare ourselves for receiving the holy things, but rather that the Church may fulfil herself in all fulness as the sacrament of the kingdom, as the *reality* of the new time and the new life.

I have called the prayer of intercession *cosmic*: "Visit us with Thy loving-kindness, O Lord; manifest Thyself to us through Thy rich compassions. Grant us seasonable and healthful weather; send gentle showers upon the earth so that it may bear fruit; bless the crown of the year with Thy goodness." I have called it *ecclesiological*: "Prevent schisms among the churches; pacify the ragings of the pagans; quickly destroy the uprisings of heresies by the power of Thy Holy Spirit." And, finally, I have called it *eschatological*: "Receive us all into Thy Kingdom, showing us to be sons of the light and sons of the day. Grant us Thy peace and Thy love, O Lord our God, for Thou hast given all things to us."

And thus: *the world, the Church, the kingdom.* All of God's creation, all salvation, all fulfilment. Heaven on earth. One voice and one heart, one glorification and singing of the all-honorable name: of the Father, and of the Son, and of the Holy Spirit, now and ever and unto ages of ages. Amen. Here is the essence of this great, crowning prayer; here is the ultimate supplication of the eucharist, united around the Lamb of God, in Christ—the entire spiritual world, beginning with the Theotokos and the saints and ending with *all—be all things to all men.*

This is what we are summoned to behold, to recognize, to

perceive each time the eucharist is celebrated. In this we must immerse our whole consciousness, all our love, all our *desire*, before approaching "our immortal King and God."

6

IT IS INDEED ONLY AFTER CONCLUDING THE PRAYER OF INTER-cession that we enter into what we earlier termed the *private* preparation for communion, i.e., preparation not by the whole gathering, not by the whole Church, but our individual prayer for personal cleansing:

> ...so that receiving a portion of Thy holy things with a pure conscience we may be united with the holy Body and Blood of Thy Christ. Having received them worthily, may we have Christ dwelling in our hearts, and may we become the Temple of the Holy Spirit. Yes, O our God, let none of us be guilty of these, Thy awesome and heavenly Mysteries, nor be infirm in soul and body by partaking of them unworthily. But, enable us, even to our last breath, to receive a portion of Thy holy things worthily, as a support on the road to eternal life and an acceptable defense at the dread judgment seat of Thy Christ. That we also, together with all the saints who through the ages have been well-pleasing to Thee, may become partakers of Thy eternal good things, which Thou hast prepared for those who love Thee, O Lord.

As we see, the emphasis here shifts from the general and as it were exultant self-preparation of the entire Church to the personal preparation of each member of the Church. As St Paul writes to the Corinthians:

> ...as often as you eat this bread and drink the cup, you proclaim the Lord's death until he comes. Whoever, therefore, eats the bread or drinks the cup of the Lord in an unworthy manner will be guilty of profaning the body and blood of the Lord. Let a man examine himself, and so

eat of the bread and drink of the cup. For any one who eats and drinks without discerning the body eats and drinks judgment upon himself. That is why many of you are weak and ill, and some have died. But if we judged ourselves truly, we should not be judged. But when we are judged by the Lord, we are chastened so that we may not be condemned along with the world. (1 Co 11:26-32)

There can be no doubt that in the "spirituality" of early Christianity the "communal" reinforced the "personal," and the "personal" was impossible without the "communal." There is, however, a big difference between that perception of both personal and communal and our own. The apostle Paul convicted the believers who partook unworthily; he threatened them with condemnation by it. He summoned them to examine themselves. But never at any time did he present them with a *choice*: "you, the worthy, partake; and you, the unworthy, abstain." It is this choice that little by little led to the abstention of roughly the majority of the members of the Church and to the loss of the feeling and perception of the eucharist as a "common task," as a *liturgy*. And this very feeling of abstention, as it were, lost its power, expired and turned into a form of disciplinary prescription ("four times a year"!), with confession obligatory as almost a ticket to communion.

The early Church knew that, in all creation, there is no one who is *worthy* through his own spiritual effort, through his own "worthiness," to partake of the body and blood of Christ, and that therefore preparation consists not in a calculation and analysis of one's "preparedness" or "unpreparedness," but in the answer of love to love: "That we also, together with all the saints who through the ages have been well-pleasing to Thee, may become partakers of Thy eternal good things, which Thou hast prepared for those who love Thee, O Lord." When the celebrant proclaims the words "Holy things are for the holy," the Church responds, "One is Holy. One is the Lord Jesus Christ, to the glory of God the Father. Amen." But in affirming and declaring this confession, she knows that the doors to the "homeland of the heart's desire" are open to all, and that "there will be no separation from each other, O friends."

Thus, this preparation is concluded in the unity of the common and the private: the *Lord's Prayer*, which was given to us by Christ himself. For, in the last analysis, everything depends on one thing: can we, do we "earnestly desire," with our whole being and in spite of all our insufficiency, fallenness, betrayal and laziness, to receive the words of this prayer as our own, desire them as *our own*? "Hallowed be Thy name. Thy kingdom come, Thy will be done, on earth as it is in heaven."

7

IN RECENT TIMES THE ORTHODOX CHURCH HAS WITNESSED A eucharistic revival of sorts, which has been expressed first of all in a desire on the part of a great number of the laity for more *frequent communion*. This revival occurs differently in different places and "cultures." But however joyful this revival is, I believe that a great number of dangers threaten it, chief of which consists in the deeper "sacralization" of the Church. Over the centuries of her coexistence with the government and the empire, the Church became transformed into an organization, into an institution for attending to the "spiritual needs" of the faithful, into an organization on the one hand subordinated to these "needs" and on the other defining them and governing them. The boundary separating the world from the Church but also joining the world to the Church—which was so obvious for the early Church—became simply a boundary separating the world from the Church.

I am convinced that the genuine revival of the Church begins with *eucharistic revival*, but in the fulness of this word. The tragic flaw in the history of Orthodoxy has proven to be not only the incompleteness but, I daresay, the absence of a theology of the sacraments, its reduction into western schemes and categories of thought. The Church is not an organization but the new people of God. The Church is not a religious cult but a *liturgy*, embracing the entire creation of God. The Church is not a doctrine about the world to come but the joyous encounter of the kingdom of God. It is the sacrament of peace, the sacrament of salvation and the sacrament of the reign of Christ.

It remains for us to conclude these far from complete thoughts with a few brief remarks about the order of receiving communion itself. These remarks are of a primarily "technical" order, "cultic" in the most obvious sense of the word. Their content has been sufficiently expounded by Archimandrite Kiprian Kern. Inasmuch as they reflect the defects that we were compelled to speak of above, I would like to summarize their main points.

The first defect, in my opinion, is the profusion of *symbolism*—not the symbolism that we spoke of above as the sacramentality of all God's creation, but that *allegorical* symbolism that confers on each part of the sacred rite a special meaning, making it a representation of something that it is not. For example, regarding the prayer at the "fractioning of the lamb," Fr Kiprian concludes: "while the choir sings 'amen' [and they have to sing it slowly—why?] the priest reads that secret prayer before the fractioning of the Lamb... While this prayer is read the deacon, standing before the royal doors, binds the orarion about himself crosswise. Usually he does this during the singing of 'Our Father' [who does what and when?]."[5] But it turns out that, "according to Symeon the New Theologian, the deacon is adorned with the orarion as if it were a certain set of wings, and he covers himself with reverence and humility when he partakes of communion, thus imitating the seraphim, who, as it is said, have six wings, two of which cover the feet, two the face, and two flutter with the singing of 'holy, holy, holy.'"[6]

The second defect consists of the *secret prayers*, as a result of which the overwhelming majority of the laity do not know and never even hear the text of the eucharist itself and are thus deprived of this priceless treasure. No one has ever explained why the "chosen race, a royal priesthood, holy nation, God's own people, that they may declare the wonderful deeds of him who called them out of darkness" cannot listen to the prayers that they offer to God.

The third defect is the distinction between the clergy and the laity during communion, a distinction with tragic consequences for church consciousness, but of which we have already spoken repeatedly.

[5]*Evkharistia*, 301-2.
[6]*Ibid.*

Defects of this sort can add up to a great multitude, but this
subject remains a kind of incomprehensible *taboo*, and neither the
hierarchy nor the theologians seem to take notice of it. This needs
to be done, but no one is permitted to discuss the matter. Yet I
repeat what I have repeated many times already in this book: what
concerns the eucharist concerns the Church, and what concerns
the Church concerns the eucharist, so that any ailment in the liturgy reflects on our faith and on the whole life of the Church. "Ibi
ecclesia, ubi Spiritus Sanctus et omnis gratia,"[7] and we, "who
stand about Thy holy altar" (Liturgy of St Basil the Great), need
to pray zealously to God that he will enlighten our inner vision
with the illuminating simplicity of the most holy of the holy
sacraments.

8

THE DIVINE LITURGY IS COMPLETED. BLESSING THE ALTAR WITH
with the chalice, the priest exclaims, "O God, save Thy people,
and bless Thine inheritance." Then he censes the holy altar three
times, saying, "Be Thou exalted, O God, above the heavens, and
Thy glory over all the earth." Then the people answer:

> We have seen the true light! We have received the heav-
> enly Spirit! We have found the true faith! Worshipping
> the undivided Trinity, who has saved us.

And he takes the chalice away from the altar.
Then comes the little litany, the short thanksgiving that:

> Thou hast made us worthy this day of Thy heavenly mys-
> teries. Make straight our path; strengthen us all in Thy
> fear; guard our life; make firm our steps...

And after that, "Let us depart in peace!"

---

[7]"Where the Church is, there is the Spirit and all grace." St Irenaeus of Lyons, *Against Heresies* 3:24:1.

All is clear. All is simple and bright. Such fulness fills everything. Such joy permeates everything. Such love radiates through everything. We are again in the *beginning*, where our ascent to the table of Christ, in his kingdom, began.

We depart into life, in order to witness and to fulfil our calling. Each has his own, but it is also our common ministry, common liturgy—"in the communion of the Holy Spirit."

"Lord, it is good that we are here!"